CHAOS, CORRUPTION, COURAGE AND GLORY

A YEAR IN BOXING

BOOKS BY THOMAS HAUSER

General Non-Fiction
Missing
The Trial of Patrolman Thomas Shea
For Our Children (with Frank Macchiarola)
The Family Legal Companion
Final Warning: The Legacy of Chernobyl (with Dr. Robert Gale)
Arnold Palmer: A Personal Journey
Confronting America's Moral Crisis (with Frank Macchiarola)
Healing: A Journal of Tolerance and Understanding
Miscellaneous
With This Ring (with Frank Macchiarola)
A God To Hope For

About Boxing
The Black Lights: Inside the World of Professional Boxing
Muhammad Ali: His Life and Times
Muhammad Ali: Memories
Muhammad Ali: In Perspective
Muhammad Ali & Company
A Beautiful Sickness
A Year At The Fights
Brutal Artistry
The View From Ringside
Chaos, Corruption, Courage and Glory

Fiction
Ashworth & Palmer
Agatha's Friends
The Beethoven Conspiracy
Hanneman's War
The Fantasy
Dear Hannah
The Hawthorne Group
Martin Bear & Friends
Mark Twain Remembers
Finding The Princess

CHAOS, CORRUPTION, COURAGE AND GLORY

A YEAR IN BOXING

BY THOMAS HAUSER

SPORT CLASSIC BOOKS

www.sportclassicbooks.com

Published in the United States of America by Sport Media
Publishing Inc., Wilmington, Delaware, and simultaneously in
Canada.

For information about permission to reproduce selections from this
book, please write to:
Permissions
Sport Media Publishing, Inc.,
21 Carlaw Ave.,
Toronto, Ontario, Canada, M4M 2R6
www.sportclassicbooks.com

Cover design: Paul Hodgson
Cover photo: Bernard Hopkins, by Holger Keifel
Author photo: Holger Keifel
Interior design: Greg Oliver

ISBN: 1-894963-38-5

Library of Congress Cataloging-in-Publication Data

Hauser, Thomas.
  Chaos, corruption, courage and glory : a year in boxing / by
Thomas Hauser.
      p. cm.
ISBN 1-894963-38-5 (pbk.)
1. Boxing. I. Title.

GV1133.H344 2005
796.83—dc22

                                          2004027004

Printed in Canada

*For Jerry Izenberg
and other good writers*

AUTHOR'S NOTE

Chaos, Corruption, Courage and Glory contains the articles about professional boxing that I authored from August 2003 through September 2004. The articles I wrote about the sweet science prior to that date have been published in *Muhammad Ali & Company, A Beautiful Sickness, A Year at the Fights,* and *The View From Ringside.*

Special thanks are due to Secondsout.com, under whose aegis most of the articles in this book first appeared.

TABLE OF CONTENTS

ROUND 1

FIGHTS AND FIGHTERS

On November 4, 2003, I spent the hours before and after the first Jones-Tarver fight in the dressing room with Roy Jones. It was a night when he proved his mettle.

ROY JONES AND RJ

Roy Jones Jr. is the most gifted fighter of his time. For almost a decade, the pound-for-pound rankings have been divided into Jones and everybody else.

But Roy Jones has not been without critics. The entertainment value of boxing comes from risk. There is a dramatic ebb and flow to great fights. Yet, in the ring, Jones has been so dominant that there has been little drama in many of his fights. One reason for this has been his choice of opponents. Over the years, Jones has beaten Bernard Hopkins, James Toney, and quite a few other quality boxers. But he hasn't always sought out the most dangerous inquisitors. Some say that Jones will never put himself in a situation where he thinks he might lose a fight; that he won't ever take a fight that he's not certain he'll win.

Then there's the matter of how Jones fights. There's always an element of danger when a boxer steps into the ring. But Jones has improvised a style that, given his extraordinary talents, is as close to risk free as possible.

"Roy Jones," says Lou DiBella, "is the most careful great fighter I've ever seen."

And Larry Merchant recently opined, "I don't get a feeling of magic from Roy Jones any more. Early in his career, I felt there was a certain magic; that he was a like a brilliant jazz musician running off riffs of punches that nobody had ever seen before. But as Roy moved up in weight, you didn't see that as often. His fights took on a pattern of opponents trying to pressure him, and Roy using his intelligence and very fast hands to discourage them. And what upsets a lot of boxing people is he won't even try to close the show. That is, we're into the tenth round of a championship fight; Roy is ahead nine rounds to one; and he's content to play it out and walk away with a decision. In Roy's mind, it's, 'Why should I give the other guy a chance? If I try to knock him out, he might hit me with a big punch.' But it isn't very entertaining. Roy sucks the drama out of his fights by dominating his opponents in the first six rounds and coasting in the last six. From an entertainment point of view, instead of building to a climax, Roy builds to an anti-climax. Is it because he's so good? Yes. Is it because he's so smart? Yes. But it turns a lot of people off."

Jones's defenders counter that, over the years, he has fought every challenger of note. They also question the mindset of those who wax nostalgically about Willie Pep winning a round without throwing a punch yet criticize Jones for fighting defensively.

Still, the bottom line has long been that Roy Jones's detractors would never concede his greatness until he proved to their satisfaction that he had a fighting heart. The ultimate question they asked was, "On a night when Jones is brutally tested, when he's hurt, when his body aches, when he feels like he has nothing left; on that night, will Roy Jones just try to survive or will he walk through fire to win?"

Enter Antonio Tarver.

Tarver is a former U.S. amateur champion, world amateur champion, and Olympic bronze medalist. In April of this year, he captured the WBC and IBF light-heavyweight titles by winning all twelve rounds against Montell Griffin. The sole blot on his record was a decision loss to Eric Harding avenged by knockout two years later. And Tarver is used to going in tough. His six previous opponents before his November 8th fight against Roy Jones had compiled a record of 173 wins against 12 losses and 4 draws.

Tarver is a talker. That much was clear as he set his sights directly on Jones:

- "Bring on the man; the guy with all of the accolades; the guy that's supposed to be unbeatable and invincible and unstoppable. I know what a victory over Roy Jones will give me, and that's what I want."
- "People continue to consider Roy Jones the light-heavyweight champion, and I feel disrespected. There's a new king in town. It's my time; it's my season. I'm anxious to prove myself once and for all as the best light-heavyweight in the world, bar none, including Roy Jones."
- "The majority of Roy Jones's opponents came for the payday. I'm coming to make Roy Jones pay. He knows my ability. I'm a slick confident southpaw with power in both hands; a defensive wizard and a guy that knows his way around that ring. This time, for the first time in Roy Jones's career, the risk outweighs the reward. Deep down in his heart, Roy Jones knows that. He sees me as a major threat, and that's a fact. I'm focused, hungry, and determined to close the show on Roy Jones."

● "I'm going to destroy him. Instead of Roy Jones's corner people giving him a shower after every round like they do, they'll have to give him an IV drip so he doesn't go into shock as I beat his ass."

For good measure, Tarver also called Jones a "country bumpkin." But the 7-to-1 odds in Jones's favor reflected people's skepticism. The general view was that Tarver was the second-best light-heavyweight in the world. But he was about to face a man who might be the best light-heavyweight in history. Jones had won 23 world championship fights. Tarver had fought a total of 22 bouts in his entire professional career.

Also, despite the tough talk, several days before the fight, Tarver relinquished his IBF championship belt. He claimed it was because he wouldn't be able to make a mandatory title defense for at least a year and a wait of that duration would be unfair to Clinton Woods and Glencoffe Johnson, who would be fighting on the eve of Jones-Tarver in a "mandatory elimination" bout. But there was more to this gesture of noblesse oblige than met the eye. By giving up the belt, Tarver paved the way for Woods versus Johnson to become a world championship bout. And more than coincidentally, the winner of Woods-Johnson was committed to making his first title defense against Tarver. In other words, if Tarver lost to Roy Jones, he wanted a chance to get at least one of the belts back.

Meanwhile, if Tarver was talking big, Jones wasn't exactly quiet.

"Can he beat me?" Roy asked rhetorically. "Hell no. Do I think he can beat me? Hell no. Do I take his trash-talking as real disrespect? Nah, that's cowardice. Where I come from, if I got something to say to you, I say it to your face as soon as I see you. Tarver only does it in front of cameras. This guy, outside the ring, he's boring to me. But when I get in there, I'm going to be excited because I get to tear his ass up. I always, always, keep my damn word. And I'm telling you; I'll whip his ass. His ass is toast. I'm going to utilize his big mouth for a target all night."

Then, in the days just before the fight, Jones began talking about the difference between the good "Roy Jones" and the bad "RJ". The latter, he claimed, hadn't appeared in the ring since his one-round demolition of Montell Griffin in 1997, but was bubbling to the surface for Tarver.

"I'm bad, but it's just how I get," Jones explained. "It just happens sometimes. It kind of scares me. I don't really want it to happen, but it almost seems like it's inevitable. You know what I mean? I don't ever want to see that because I don't like to be like that. RJ is a bad dude. I don't like to mess with him too much. But my subconscious, which is where he usually dwells, seems to be jacked up. Tarver has the type of disposition that will make me be the me that I don't like to be. It ain't going to be nothing nice. You don't get to see me like that often."

One man who had an up-close view of Jones's personality transformation was Alton Merkerson. "Coach Merk" was in the Army from late 1959 through early 1990. He and Jones bonded at the 1988 Olympics in South Korea, when Roy fought at 156 pounds and Merkerson guided Ray Mercer, Andrew Maynard, and Kennedy McKinney through the Games. Merkerson has been Jones's most constant ally throughout the fighter's ring career. He considers himself a teacher rather than a trainer.

"It's now personal for Roy," Merkerson said shortly before the fight. "But I wouldn't necessarily say that it motivates him. Being motivated and being pissed off are two entirely different things."

As for Jones's well-known aversion to taking instruction from others, Merkerson acknowledged, "It was difficult for me at first. In the military, everything was regimented. People did what I told them to do when I told them to do it. But Roy is a control person. He likes being in full control. It comes from his upbringing. There were times when his father made things pretty hard on him. When you're told what to do your whole life and finally you get to draw your own picture, you don't want to give that freedom up. But I know my troops; I trust Roy's judgment. And I understand that, if Roy loses, he wants it to be because he was doing things the way he thought they should be done; not because someone else told him to do it a certain way and he did what they told him. So Roy listens to me. What he does after that is his choice, but I know he considers what I tell him."

Well and good. But as Jones-Tarver approached, Jones found himself in a situation that he couldn't fully control. Six months earlier, he'd gone up in weight to fight John Ruiz for the WBA heavyweight crown. That night, he had tipped the scales at 197 pounds. Now, for the first time in history, a heavyweight beltholder was going down in weight to fight for the light-heavyweight title. That meant, thirty hours before Jones-Tarver, Roy had to weigh in at 175 pounds.

Not even Roy Jones can defy the laws of nature.

When Jones fought John Ruiz, his body fat had been a remarkably low six percent. Mackie Shilstone, who supervised Roy's conditioning for that fight, explains, "Body fat is something you carry around. Muscle is something that carries you around."

For Jones-Tarver, Roy opted to do without Shilstone's services. But he wasn't just shedding fat. He had to lose muscle.

Jones called making weight for Jones-Tarver the hardest thing he'd ever done in his life. By his own admission, he'd underestimated how difficult it wouild be to get down to 175 pounds. "It's one of the worst times I ever had," he acknowledged. "You sacrifice so much, you want to kill somebody. I had to run more, diet more. You're hungry and thirsty half the time. You're mad. You start taking out your frustrations on everybody you come across."

Roy's weight loss added drama to the fight. There were times when he seemed more concerned with making weight than preparing for Tarver. But in truth, the weight problem was his own doing. Over the years, Jones has been great in the ring because his preparation and decision-making outside the ring have been superb. There was a time when Roy was so dedicated to boxing that, every New Year's Eve at the stroke of midnight, he was in the gym at Square Ring. And he always seemed to find the right weight division in which to compete. Thus, just as James Toney bore responsibility for being drained from the loss of weight prior to fighting Roy in 1994, so too, Jones had no one to blame for his weight debacle but himself.

But there was another problem that wasn't of Jones's making. In mid-October, he had gone to the dentist to have a cavity filled and another tooth capped. That had occasioned a certain amount of comment within the Jones camp.

"Roy doesn't like needles; they frighten him," says Jones's longtime friend Derrick Gainer. "When he was in the hospital for arthroscopic knee surgery and they told him he had to have a shot, Roy told everyone to leave the room. I was going too but he said to me, 'No; you got to stay.' He made me hold his hand while he got the shot. He's gonna kill me for telling you that."

"Needles aren't my favorite thing," Jones admits. "It used to be, when I went to the dentist, I'd ask for gas so I wouldn't have to get a needle. But I'm better about that now."

On his October trip to the dentist, Roy opted for a needle. But less humorously, the filling and cap had bothered him ever since. He hadn't returned for corrective dentistry out of fear of making the situation worse. But for the three weeks leading up to Jones-Tarver, the pain had interfered with his sleep.

On Friday, November 7th, at 2:00 p.m., Jones weighed in at precisely 175 pounds. Then he went upstairs to his suite and began sipping from a bottle of fruit juice. At first, his thoughts centered on the fight ahead.

Tarver was the WBC light-heavyweight champion. Technically, Jones was the challenger. For weeks, they had battled over who would enter the ring and be announced first. Finally, it was agreed that the matter would be settled by a coin toss officiated over by Nevada State Athletic Commission executive director Marc Ratner. Then, moments before the toss was to occur, Jones deferred to Tarver.

Now, in his suite, Roy acknowledged, "I never ever planned on a coin toss. Ninety percent of what goes on before a big fight is mind games. I never cared about who went in the ring first. Against Ruiz, I went in first. But Tarver was counting on the coin toss. He figured that was where he had a fifty-fifty chance. If he won the toss, he'd be saying, 'Okay; things are going my way.' So I took that away from him and now he's shook."

Then the conversation turned to a law banning the possession of fighting animals that had been passed recently by the Florida legislature. Jones owns seven hundred fighting cocks that he breeds, trains, and takes to fights in neighboring Louisiana, where cock-fighting is legal.

"I'm not giving up my birds," Jones said. "I wake up in the morning hearing them. If I have to, I'll move to Louisiana." His anger began to build. "They're killing twenty million chickens a day to eat, and not one of those birds has a fighting chance. You put me on earth and ask me what kind of bird I want to be; a fighting bird or one they eat. That's an easy choice. We got kids dying in a war in Iraq, and the politicians are worrying about game roosters. People don't understand. They just don't understand."

A pensive look crossed Roy's face, and one couldn't help but think of some thoughts shared by Stanley Levin. Levin is a Pensacola attorney who, with his brother Fred, guided Jones for much of the fighter's amateur run and professional career. During a period when young Roy and his father were fully estranged, Roy lived in Stanley's house for a year.

"Roy was thirteen when I met him," Levin reminisced recently. "On the surface, he seemed happy enough. But there was something in his eyes that made him different from anybody I'd ever seen. There was a determination there and also a way of looking at you that made me feel as though he was probing into my mind; as though he wanted to know what I was about before he let me in. And there was a sadness in his eyes, a loneliness that pulled me to him. It was as though he was in need, and I wanted to help him. Roy has the world at his feet now. But I still see that sadness, that loneliness, when I look at him. Not in the days leading up to a fight or when he's on the basketball court or playing with children. But when he's in an alone space, that sadness is still there. And a lot of me hurts for Roy because, deep down inside, I don't think he's happy. Inside of Roy Jones, there's the most beautiful young man I've ever known. But I think now he's trapped into playing the roll of rap impressario, movie star, superstar this and superstar that. He's young, good-looking, wealthy, a great athlete; but there's still a sadness there."

● ● ●

On Saturday, November 8th, Roy Jones arrived at the Mandalay Bay Arena at 6:40 p.m. He was wearing a white warm-up suit, red jersey, white socks, and sandals. A headband with an Air Jordan logo graced his brow. At his request, he had been assigned to a dressing room with Gabe Brown, Vernie Torres, Julian Townsend, and Lemuel Nelson; four fighters from Pensacola who were slated for undercard bouts. The room was large with three straight-backed chairs and wall-to-wall wood benches.

Upon his arrival, Jones circled the room, shaking hands with close to two dozen friends. Then he hugged Alton Merkerson, who had been at the arena with the undercard fighters since four o'clock. Take away Merkerson and a few others with gray hair and the room had the feel of Peter Pan surrounded by the lost boys as he readied to do battle against Captain Hook.

The contemporary rock music that had been playing changed to rap. Roy sat down on a bench, took a pair of blue-and-white high-topped boxing shoes from a Kronk Gym bag, and set them down on the bench. Larry Merchant entered the dressing room with HBO production coordinator Tami Cotel for a brief pre-fight interview. Ken Bayless, who would be refereeing Jones-Tarver, followed with pre-fight instructions. Roy put on his shoes. Mario Francis rubbed vaseline on his arms and legs. Then Jones took two bands of silver tassels from a clear plastic bag, tied them around his shoetops, and walked the length of the room to see how they felt.

Merkerson began taping Roy's hands. When that was done, Jones laced up his protective cup and donned a pair of cobalt-blue boxing trunks with white trim. At 7:40 p.m., Cotel returned and announced, "Seventeen minutes." Everyone in the room joined hands. Al Cole led them in prayer. Then Roy gloved up.

It all seemed low-key and routine; like another day at the gym in Pensacola. But boxing isn't pre-scripted. It's not a computer game. When two fighters enter the ring, regardless of what they might have done before, they start even at the opening bell every time.

Also, Jones had a problem, After the weigh-in on Friday, despite being famished, he had eaten lightly. He didn't want the type of stomach cramps that Roberto Duran is believed to have suffered from in his "no mas" fight against Sugar Ray Leonard. Nor did he want to come in bloated as James Toney had done in their 1994 encounter. "It's been so long since I ate a lot," Roy explained. "I didn't want to take a chance and eat too much and have a problem."

But on Saturday, there was a problem anyway. Merkerson had speculated that Roy would enter the ring just shy of 190 pounds. However, an hour before the fight when Jones stepped on the HBO scale, it registered 186. That included five pounds of clothes and personal accessories. In other words, Roy weighed 181 pounds. His stomach had been queasy all day. He had barely eaten. He would be entering the ring in a depleted physical state.

Every great fighter has a night when he engages in battle and just doesn't have it. November 8th was that kind of night for Roy Jones.

In the early rounds, both men fought cautiously, feeling each other out and showing respect. But unlike previous fights, Jones was unable to dictate the pace and do what he wanted to do. And unlike some of Roy's previous opponents, Tarver belonged in the ring with him.

Jones looked sluggish from the start. At the halfway mark, he was ahead four rounds to two but tiring badly. Then, in round seven, the unthinkable happened. For the first time in his career, Roy Jones lost form. He lost control of what was going on in a boxing ring.

Rounds seven and eight were probably the most difficult rounds of Jones's life. Tarver began pressing the action and landed legitimate power punches. In the past, the ropes have been a sanctuary for Roy. Boxing fans have grown accustomed to seeing him retreat and then strike back hard when an opening presented itself. Now, when Jones went to the ropes, he got pounded.

Jones's only defeat as a professional was a disqualification loss against Montell Griffin. In that bout, he lost rounds but wasn't getting beaten up. He simply had to change tactics and become more aggressive to alter the flow of the action and prevail. He was disqualified as he stood on the verge of knocking Griffin out.

This was different. Tarver was strong and began stepping things up. By the end of round eight, Roy's left eye was closing and he was exhausted.

"When a rooster's got one eye," Roy Jones once said, "he becomes dangerous because he knows every lick could be his last; so he puts everything he's got into that lick. Same with boxing. Every punch from a man with one eye is going to have kill in it." Then Jones had added, "I don't go anywhere to lose. Remember that."

So in round nine, Jones dug deep and unveiled a new weapon in his arsenal; his heart. And in rounds nine through twelve, he showed the world that "RJ" isn't a front-runner who blows out opponents. RJ is a fighter who summons up strength where there appears to be none, sucks up his guts, and does what has to be done on a bad night to win against a strong, skilled opponent.

Jerry Roth scored the fight even. Glen Hamada and Dave Harris gave the nod to Jones by margins of 117-111 and 116-112. This writer had it 115-114 for Jones.

After the fight, Roy returned to his dressing room and sat down heavily on the same bench he'd been on a little more than an hour earlier. "That was tough," he said wearily. "I had to bite down hard tonight."

The skin around his left eye was discolored and swollen. Alton Merkerson began pressing an Enswell against the wounded area.

"That was tough," Jones said again. "I'm through with 175. It's too hard to get down. The only thing I want to do next is fight Tyson. Then it's over." A satisfied look crossed his face. "People thought, if the going got tough, I'd quit. But I dug deep tonight. All you can do is all you can do, and that's what I did. You tell the world, the Roy Jones show ain't over yet."

So what comes next?

Jones has been fighting as a professional for fifteen years. That's a long journey and the end is in sight. It wasn't just the weight that handicapped him against Tarver, although certainly weight was a factor. Roy is getting older. He'll be 35 in January. More than anything else, his quickness and speed are the assets that have separated him from other fighters. He says that he was in his prime when he fought at 168 pounds. Now his speed and quickness are starting to diminish.

A look at history's other great light-heavyweights puts things in perspective. Billy Conn's last victory came at age 31. Ezzard Charles lost 17 of 27 fights after the age of 32. Bob Foster never won a title fight after the age of 34. Only Archie Moore flourished in the light-heavyweight division at an age older than Jones is now.

A Jones-Tarver rematch at 185 pounds would be interesting. And then there's Mike Tyson. "Fighters want to fight for titles," Roy said earlier this year, "but not as much as we want to fight for money."

There is, of course, considerable skepticism that Jones will actually get in the ring with Tyson. "Roy started talking about fighting heavyweights in 1996," notes Larry Merchant. "And it took him seven years to find John Ruiz, who was a safe heavyweight to fight."

Also, Tyson hits exponentially harder than anyone Jones has fought. "If Mike hits Roy right," says Mark Breland, "they can cancel Christmas in Pensacola."

Still, as Jim Lampley observes, "The way Roy Jones conducts his career continually confounds people because you expect the behavior of a normal athlete and there is absolutely nothing about this guy that's normal or predictable."

So if Jones is offered, say, thirty million dollars and Tyson starts salivating at the thought of Roy going to the ropes . . . Who knows?

Meanwhile, it should be said in closing that Jones-Tarver was something new for Roy Jones. In all of his previous fights, he entered the ring with physical gifts that were superior to those of his opponent. But on November 8th, the superior physical arsenal belonged to Antonio Tarver. Roy Jones won the fight, not because of his physical gifts, but because he did what great fighters are supposed to do. He was courageous and brave. And his will was stronger than Tarver's.

Some fighters grow larger through the prism of history. Roy Jones will be one of them.❏

Lennox Lewis can be hard to get a handle on, but getting to know him is worth the effort. The following article evolved from a conversation we had in August 2003, shortly after his TKO victory over Vitali Klitschko.

LENNOX LEWIS: NOTHING LEFT TO PROVE

One year ago, like Shakespeare's Caesar, Lennox Lewis bestrode the world of heavyweight boxing like a colossus.

Size, strength, good reflexes, and power don't necessarily make a fighter. More is required. Lennox matured late as a boxer. But as his career progressed, it became clear that he had the required intangibles. Now he's an aging athlete. He knows it, and he's coming to grips with it well.

Lewis today is relaxed and confident. "People are different from one another," he says. "You have to be comfortable with who you are. I can trash-talk like Mike Tyson. I can rap like Roy Jones." A smile lights up his face and he intones:

Lennox Lewis is the best
I'll lay them all to rest
I'll put Chris Byrd back in his nest
Cut off his dreadlocks and stuff them in a chest

The lyrics continue, ending with:

One Klitschko for breakfast; one Klitschko for brunch
Tyson and Roy Jones for lunch

Lewis laughs. "See; I can do it. But that's not me."

History's most popular heavyweight champions have reflected the eras in which they reigned. Jack Dempsey personified the Roaring '20s. Joe Louis was perfectly juxtaposed with the trials of The Great Depression and World War II. Rocky Marciano mirrored the simple optimism of the 1950s. Muhammad Ali was inextricably intertwined with the turmoil of the '60s. Mike Tyson embodied the excess and wanton greed of the late 1980s and '90s.

Lennox Lewis is different. He has always marched to his own drummer. At times, that has frustrated the media and, as a result, the pundits haven't always been kind. "The media can build you up and they can knock you down," Lewis notes. "They can create rumors that make people think a certain way. On a personal level, you read these things and you have to be strong to not let it effect you."

Lennox has been strong. The pay-off came in Memphis on June 8, 2002. "It was always important to me to prove that I'm the best," he acknowledges. "But from the start of my career, there was always Mike Tyson. Whatever else happened, people always said, 'Lennox beat this guy, and Lennox beat that guy, but what about Tyson?' I had to fight Tyson. Otherwise, the history books would have read, 'Yeah, Lennox was good but he never beat Tyson.'"

The fight almost didn't happen. First, HBO and Showtime had to iron out their differences. Then the fighters had to come to terms with their respective networks. And once that was done, Tyson came close to sabotaging the entire event at the January 22, 2002, kick-off press conference in New York.

"I didn't know if Mike would show or not," Lennox reminisces. "But I got dressed up and went to the press conference. Once I was there, I asked about security and was told it was all taken care of, but I had a funny feeling. We were supposed to be announced separately, walk out on stage, get on separate platforms, and face the audience. Mike was announced first. Right away, I could see that he was like a pot steaming. Then I was announced. As soon as I walked onstage, Mike came toward me. One of my security people stepped in front of him. Mike took a swing at him. And my security is an extension of me, so it was like he took a swing at me."

Chaos followed. Lewis whacked Tyson with an overhand right. Both fighters were pushed to the floor. Mike then bit through Lennox's pants and took a chunk out of his thigh. Tyson subsequently denied the bite, but as Lennox observes, "When someone is biting you, you tend to look down to see who it is that's doing the biting." The press conference concluded with an obscenity-laced tirade that was vintage Tyson.

"I wondered afterward, 'What the hell is wrong with this guy?'" Lennox says. "Either he didn't want to fight or he was mad or both. I decided it was both. None of his ranting bothered me. I'm into reality, and that was cartoon talk. But the bite motivated me. When I went into training, it was in my mind that Tyson had drawn first blood."

When all the hoopla was done, it came down to the fight. It always does. Eventually, the moment arrived when Lewis and Tyson left their respective dressing rooms and walked down the aisle to the ring in Memphis. Lightning bolts of excitement flashed through the arena. "It's happening! They're really here."

Lewis remembers his ring-walk well. "I was totally focussed on what I wanted to do in the fight," he says. "Nothing else around me mattered. I was already fighting as I walked to the ring. And from the moment I stepped into the ring until the end of the first round, my eyes never left Tyson. When I got in the ring, Mike tried to appear menacing but he wasn't. During the referee's instructions, I heard what the ref was saying but I wasn't listening. I was focussing completely on Mike."

The bell for round one sounded, and it quickly became clear that Lennox had more of an attitude than Tyson. He had come to Memphis to whack Mike out; he thought he would; and he did.

"The first round of a fight is like the first move in chess," Lewis explains. "It's about who has control of the board. The bell rings and it's a struggle until you know what you can and can't do and everything comes into place. In Memphis, right away, I knew that mentally Tyson wasn't there. But you have to remember, you're out there all alone and you have to know when to take chances and when not to. One punch can change everything. One punch and you're hanging on to survive and no one else can save you."

The only weapon the lion has to fight with is the lion. Over eight brutal rounds, Lewis did his job and Tyson didn't.

"The biggest problem I had was the referee," Lennox remembers. "I had to be careful because it was obvious that the referee was against me. I'm not a dirty fighter but he was acting like I was, so there was pressure on me the whole fight. If Tyson had hit me with one good shot and wobbled me for an instant, that ref would have stopped the fight."

It ended in round eight with Tyson stretched out on the canvas; blood streaming from his mouth, nose, and cuts above both eyes. Then, in the post-fight interview, Iron Mike all but genuflected before his conqueror.

"Some people say he punked out when he reached over and wiped the blood off my cheek," Lennox acknowledges. "But I didn't see it that way. I saw it as a sign of respect from one gladiator to another once the fight was over. In that moment, Mike was saying, 'You're going on TV so get the blood off your face.' But to be honest, when he did it, I had no trust for him at all. I could see him giving me a hug in the ring and then biting off my ear. Even now, if Tyson came over to shake hands with me, I'd keep my eyes on him. I don't have any hate toward Mike Tyson, but I still want to make sure that any situation we're in together is secure."

Lewis-Tyson was the high point of Lennox's career. "That was my ultimate fight," he states. "After Memphis, it was, 'Thank you; mission accomplished.'"

The next ten months were, in Lewis's words, devoted to "family time, social time, and girlfriend time." Then he readied to fight Kirk Johnson. But two weeks before their scheduled June 21st bout, the challenger pulled out with an injury.

"And all of a sudden," Lennox remembers, "the Klitschko fight was there. Manny [Emanuel Steward] was saying I should go for it. Adrian [business manager Adrian Ogun] was saying go for it. HBO told me it was Klitschko or nobody. And looking at the whole spectrum, the business as well as the boxing aspects of it, I decided to take the fight. I'd been preparing for Kirk Johnson. All of my sparring had been with short guys, the boxing type. I thought I'd be able to adjust to Klitschko's style as the fight went on. But in retrospect, the change of opponents threw me off."

Lewis versus Vitali Klitschko was an exciting inartistic brawl that ended after six rounds when the ring doctor ruled that a jagged cut on the challenger's left eyelid mandated stopping the fight. Klitschko objected vehemently. The crowd also voiced its discontent.

"The booing bothered me," Lennox admits. "We'd both fought as hard as we could. We'd fought and fought, giving it everything we had." As for the fight itself, Lewis posits, "Klitschko got off to a good start, but he was fighting off emotion and that lasts just so long. Also, I'm a slow starter. As a fight goes on, I get stronger. I could have been in better shape. If I'd been in Tyson shape or Rahman-rematch shape, I would have looked better. But I'm satisfied with the Klitschko fight. Not happy about it, but satisfied. I brought Klitschko into the deep water. And if the ring doctor hadn't stopped it, he would have drowned."

That view is seconded by Lewis's longtime adversary, Evander Holyfield, who says, "Lennox doesn't give Klitschko enough credit because Lennox doesn't give anybody credit. Lennox is arrogant. But it doesn't matter who was winning the fight. What matters is who won. Lennox busted him up. They had to stop it. Lennox won the fight."

Klitschko was the mandatory challenger for Lewis's WBC title. That means, under WBC rules, Lennox has until June 21, 2004, before he must defend or relinquish his crown. Recently, he announced that he won't fight again this year. Meanwhile, the WBC has been sending out signals that it will authorize a fight between Vitali Klitschko and Hasim Rahman for an "interim" heavyweight belt.

Once, boxing had "world champions." Now, the desire for multiple sanctioning fees has given us "world" champions, "super" champions, and "interim" champions. But there's only one heavyweight champion of the world at present, and everyone knows who it is. Lewis would still be favored in a bout against any other fighter. He has no fear of a Klitschko rematch and means it when he says, "I've already proven that I can beat Vitali Klitschko on my worst day."

As for Roy Jones, Lennox says flatly, "When fighting Roy was brought to my attention, I could see that it was a big-money fight but I wasn't serious about it. It wouldn't be good for either one of us, given where we are and what we've accomplished in boxing. If Roy runs away from me all night, it's a boring fight. If he doesn't, he gets hurt. The only way either of us would win is economically, and neither of us needs the money."

That, of course, leads to the question of retirement. A year ago, after beating Mike Tyson, Lennox acknowledged, "There's always someone to fight. That's the drug of the sport." Then he added, "What else is there for me to prove? That I can be Evander Holyfield and not know when to quit? Or prove that I'm stuck in the sport and won't get out until I'm speaking so people don't understand me?"

Now Lewis is even closer to calling it a day. He's talking about that time in the future "when I see myself taking my children out, doing whatever my kids want me to do with them." As for the role that boxing might play in his future, he says, "Having been in the business for so long, I think it's time for me to share my knowledge with some of the young fighters coming up. Boxing needs people with good ethics and good knowledge to step up and help the fighters. I'm not sure how I'll do that, but it's something I want to do."

Then Lennox raises his right hand to eye level, holding his index finger and thumb three inches apart, and declares, "I couldn't retire without fighting Tyson because that argument had to end. After Tyson, I was this close to retiring, but I decided to give it one more year. Now . . ."

The heavyweight champion adjusts his index finger and thumb so there's only a hair's width between them.

"Now I'm this close."

HBO will wave a lot of money in Lewis's face to encourage him to fight again. That means the temptation will be there. But Lennox's present plan is to retire. He knows that only two heavyweight champions (Rocky Marciano and Gene Tunney) retired with their titles in tact. All the others—Muhammad Ali, Joe Louis, Jack Dempsey, and Jack Johnson among them—left on a loss. Also, Lennox is a student of history. It's not lost on him that Marciano and Tunney were both white.

Now is the time to go. Lennox seems to acknowledge as much when he says, "Someone will emerge after I'm gone. A new star will be born and the cycle will continue. All I ask is that you write the truth; about me, about boxing, about the world. The truth is fine. What I've accomplished will speak for itself."

Lennox Lewis is a man of dignity and grace who has been the best heavyweight in the world during his reign. Boxing will miss him more than it knows.❑

Lennox Lewis and I talked again to revisit a little-known facet of his rivalry with Mike Tyson.

LEWIS-TYSON: 1984

When Mike Tyson steps into the ring to face Danny Williams, once again he'll be fighting a British citizen. Williams follows in the wake of Frank Bruno, Julius Francis, and Lennox Lewis. Boxing fans know that Tyson fought Bruno twice. It's a lesser known fact that he and Lennox met in the ring several times.

Lewis's road to boxing was a circuitous one. After moving to Canada from London, he was subjected to frequent taunts in school because of his size and accent. Fights with disciplinary consequences often followed. At age twelve, to avoid a row that would have brought further punishment, he suggested that the would-be combatants settle their differences at a local gym—the Waterloo Regional Police Boxing Association facility. Lennox showed up for the confrontation; the other side didn't. And out of curiosity, Lennox went inside on his own.

The gym was run by a police sergeant named Jerome "Hook" McComb. He introduced Lennox to a coach named Arnie Boehm. In his first amateur fight, Lennox knocked out his opponent in two rounds. By age fifteen, after three years of boxing, he was undefeated and the Ontario Golden Gloves 165-pound champion. At age eighteen, he won a gold medal at the World Junior Championships. Then, in the spring of 1984, Boehm brought him to Catskill, New York, to spar for a week with a young man named Mike Tyson, who was training under the tutelage of Cus D'Amato. Lennox was eighteen; one year older than Tyson.

"Arnie and I got to Catskill and met Cus," Lennox recalls. "He told us that Mike would be home later in the day, but he wasn't there before I went to bed that night. The first time I saw him was the next day at the gym. I was tall and lanky back then. Mike was stocky, very muscular, a real powerhouse. He looked a lot older than seventeen."

"We put the gloves on," Lennox remembers. "The bell rang. And Mike ran across the ring trying to hurt me. He wasn't sparring. It wasn't about the two of us learning and working out together. He was trying to knock me out. I threw a jab. He ducked under it and came back with a hook that sent me back against the ropes. Later in the round, he

17

knocked me down and bloodied my nose. And I realized then, 'Okay, this is how it goes. It's not a sport. This is life and death.' You need certain dramas to wake you up to certain realities in life. That round introduced me to the reality of boxing."

Arnie Boehm later recalled that, on the first day, Lennox "dodged and ran to get away from Mike because he wasn't accustomed to meeting a guy that ferocious."

Lennox says simply, "The whole first day in the ring, I was adjusting. And each day after that, I got better. I guess you could say that I was doing my Muhammad Ali impersonation and Mike was doing his Joe Frazier impersonation. By the third day, I was holding my own. And I gave him a busted lip, which made me feel good because I felt that then we were even."

"Outside the ring," Lennox remembers, "even though Mike and I were staying in the same house, there was very little interaction betweeen us. One evening, we looked at footage of old fight films together. One of the films was of Jersey Joe Walcott. I could see how Walcott would step back to lure his opponent in and then—BAM—come back with a quick right hand. And one afternoon, I went with Mike to some girl's house to pick up a package she had for him. But overall, he was cold to me."

Lennox captured a gold medal in the super-heavyweight division at the 1988 Olympics in Seoul. Then he turned pro, won the WBC title in 1993, and became undisputed heavyweight champion of the world in 1999. But Mike Tyson was always lurking in the background. And as time went on, things got ugly between them.

"The ugliness was a surprise," Lennox acknowledges. "After our sparring sessions in Catskill, Mike was always pleasant to me. Then, all of a sudden, I saw him on television threatening to eat my children. And after that, there was the press conference, when he attacked me and bit my thigh. Once that happened, people kept asking me, 'Aren't you afraid of Tyson.' And I'd tell them, 'No; not at all. I don't want to be one of his statistics outside the ring. But inside the ring, Tyson should be afraid of me.'"

"Manny [Emanuel Steward] told me for years that Tyson would be an easy fight for me," Lennox continues. "Mike's strengths are his left hook, the uppercut, and his body attack. But I knew that, if I kept him away with my jab, he wouldn't be able to get inside to go to my body or throw the uppercut. And if I kept my right hand glued to my cheek, I'd be protected against the hook. Buster Douglas showed how to beat Tyson before I did. Box him and push him back; that's all. And those sparring sessions in Catskill helped me when Mike and I fought in

Memphis. Every experience in life helps. And because of those sessions, on a very primitive level, I knew what to expect from Mike."

Lennox now has a scar the size of a quarter on his left thigh. Like Evander Holyfield's ear, it's a permanent reminder of Tyson's savagery. But the retired champion prefers to dwell on a fonder memory of his Tyson experience.

"Right before I left Catskill," Lennox recalls, "Cus D'Amato told me, 'You're good and you'll get better. Someday, you and Mike will meet in the pros.'" A pensive look crosses Lennox's face. "I wish Cus were still alive," he says. "I wish he could see what Mike and I reached and what we achieved in boxing."❏

Evander Holyfield versus James Toney was a great "writer's fight" because of the character of the participants. This was my opening salvo.

JAMES TONEY REACHES FOR GLORY

On October 4, 2003, James Toney will step into the ring with Evander Holyfield. Holyfield is a fighter of legendary proportions now past his prime. Toney is a very good fighter who wants to be recognized as a great one.

Toney was born on August 24, 1968. At age fourteen, he began fighting as an amateur. "One year later," he remembers, "I was sparring with pros. They'd beat my ass, drop me with body shots, because I had too much mouth. That's the way I was. I wasn't into being close. I did everything on my own, alone. I'm more of a people person now. I'll give you the shirt off my back if I like you, but I'll still show my bad side if I'm provoked. And just so you know, when those pros were beating my ass, I never gave in."

Fighting at 156 pounds, Toney won his first seventeen amateur bouts. Then he turned to another sport. "Football was my first love," he says. "In high school, I played quarterback and free safety. Jack Tatum was my favorite player because he was a vicious hitter. I got a scholarship offer to play quarterback at Western Michigan, and the University of Michigan wanted me as a defensive back. But I wasn't a team player and I wasn't good at taking orders, so I went back to boxing. I still love football," Toney adds wistfully. "I play the John Madden video game. No one can beat me at it. I haven't lost in three years."

Toney graduated from high school in 1987 and turned pro a year later. His gridiron weight had been 205 pounds, but he slimmed down to 160 for the start of his professional ring career. In his first twenty-six fights, the only blemish on his record was a draw against Sanderline Williams. Then, on May 10, 1991, he journeyed to Davenport, Iowa, the hometown of IBF middleweight champion Michael Nunn, and stopped the previously-undefeated Nunn in eleven rounds.

Toney successfully defended the IBF title six times. After that, he moved up in weight and KO'd Iran Barkley for the IBF super-middleweight crown. By late 1994, he was undefeated in forty-six fights and near the top of most "pound-for-pound" lists. That bubble burst when he fought Roy Jones and lost in a bout that Jones dominated from beginning to end. Toney attributes the defeat to his having to make weight and losing forty-four pounds in the two months preceding the fight. But ballooning past two hundred pounds was his own fault. And in his next outing, he was outquicked and outworked by Montell Griffin in a battle for the IBF light-heavyweight title. In 1996, he lost to Griffin again. Six months later, he came out on the short end of a decision against Drake Thadzi. Overall, his record is a laudable 66 wins, 4 losses, and 2 draws with 42 knockouts. In seventy pro fights, he has been beaten convincingly only once. And he has never been beaten up. But in recent years, he has fought mostly mediocre opposition, winning but often coming in out of shape and appearing to be just going through the motions.

"Lack of motivation hurt me," Toney admits. "I didn't train right. I didn't run for eight years. After the Barkley fight, I was never really in shape."

Enter Dan Goossen.

Goossen made quite a splash in boxing as the driving force behind America Presents. But while he often guided fighters to big fights, they rarely won them. Lest one forget; if you're a boxing promoter, the name of the game is to show a profit; and Goossen didn't. To use his analogy, he got as far as the Super Bowl when David Tua fought Lennox Lewis. But his fighters seemed to always come up short when it mattered most. Now Goossen has resurrected Toney, and Toney has been part of the resurrection of Dan Goossen.

Toney's first fight for Goossen's newly-formed Goossen-Tutor Promotions was a seventh-round knockout of Jason Robinson in August 2002. Then, on April 26, 2003, he won a hard-fought decision over Vassiliy Jirov for the IBF cruiserweight crown. Goossen has been beating the drums loudly for Toney ever since. "I've been zero for seven years," the promoter chortled after James's victory over Jirov. "It's nice to finally win a big one."

That brings us to Holyfield versus Toney. In truth, both fighters wanted other opponents. Toney was hoping for a bout against Bernard Hopkins, and Evander had his sights set on Roy Jones. But there was an obstacle named Don King, who has options on Jones's first WBA title defense and is Hopkins's exclusive promoter.

Toney thought he had a deal to fight Hopkins, but it fell apart because King and Hopkins couldn't agree on numbers. Then negotiations for Jones-Holyfield went down the drain because King demanded options on all of Holyfield's championship fights should he beat Jones and presented Evander with a dollar amount that the Holyfield camp considered insulting.

More specifically, Jim Thomas (Holyfield's attorney), says, "Under the final offer that Don gave us, Evander would have made $8,000,000, and $36,000,000 would have been divided between Roy Jones and Don King."

Holyfield elaborates, saying, "I want to fight for the title, but I don't want anyone to abuse me. I shouldn't have to sign a long-term contract with Don King just to fight for the title. I went through that one time, and I don't want to put myself in that situation again. I don't want to deal with Don King anymore. I don't want anything to do with him. I won't give options to Don King."

Holyfield will turn forty-one on October 19th. During the course of his career, he has defeated Mike Tyson, Riddick Bowe, George Foreman, Larry Holmes, Buster Douglas, Michael Moorer, Pinklon Thomas, Michael Dokes, John Ruiz, and Hasim Rahman. That's ten men who have worn a major heavyweight championship belt. But in the past five years, Evander has won only twice in seven bouts.

Still, Toney knows he has a hard night ahead. "Only a fool would take Evander lightly," he acknowledges. "People say that he's old and washed up, but let's see those people beat him. Everyone knows how Evander fights; the way he uses his head and all that. We won't be holding and hugging in there. Things get ugly in the ring. It's life and death; it's not a game. This fight will be blood and guts, but I can break Evander down. It won't be easy, but I can do it. I hurt people for a living. That's my job."

Age is Toney's edge. Size and strength are Evander's. Toney says he'll come in for the fight at a muscled 205 pounds. The fear among his backers is that, without James being required to make weight, the number could be closer to a soft 210. Some people see this fight as similar to Holyfield's brutal fifteen-round conquest of Dwight Muhammad Qawi for the WBA cruiserweight crown in 1986. But James has more skills than Qawi; and Evander is seventeen years older than he was then.

Meanwhile, Toney has a lot riding on this fight. His hope is that a win over Holyfield will put him in the midst of the big-money heavyweight mix. As far as many pundits are concerned, there's a split in the heavyweight ranks. The "super-heavyweight" division is populated by big men like Lennox Lewis and the Klitschkos. The "small" heavyweights are fighters like Roy Jones and Chris Byrd. But when Mike Tyson rampaged through the heavyweight division, he was well under 220 pounds. Holyfield at his best fought in the neighborhood 215. The biggest guy doesn't necessarily win, and that leaves Toney dreaming of glory.

"I'm not jealous of the guys who are making big money," Toney says. "Oscar De La Hoya, Lennox Lewis, Floyd Mayweather, all those guys; they deserve it, they earned it. But now it's my turn, and not just with the money. My legacy is important to me. I never ducked anyone. I went in with the best. For a long time, it was a big thing for me to fight Roy Jones again. Now I understand that I don't need Roy to do my thing. This is my opportunity to show the world how good I am. My skills are the best. My willpower is strong. Anyone who says I don't fight three minutes of every round; let them get in the ring with me and see how active I am. I want people to know that I'm a great fighter. I deserve to be called great."

And then, true to form, Toney adds, "I've got more discipline now. I've learned to slow down. I still get mad when things don't get done right, and there's that road rage if someone cuts me off when I'm driving. But I'm holding my temper; staying out of trouble. I've softened up some, but I'm still not kissing ass."❏

In the end, Holyfield-Toney was a sad night for people who cared about Evander.

THE WARRIOR

Fighters do things that most of us can only fantasize about, endure pain that most of us can't imagine, and go places that most of us will never go. Evander Holyfield is as pure a fighter as there is in boxing. He enobles the sport.

Everyone acknowledges that Holyfield is a warrior. What is overlooked sometimes is that he has been to war on a scale that is matched by only a few ring greats in boxing history.

There have been twenty-three claimants to the heavyweight title since Holyfield turned pro in 1984; thirty-two if one considers the WBO. Evander has fought twenty bouts against these men, compiling a record of 12 wins, 6 losses and 2 draws. Including his most recent bout against James Toney, Holyfield has fought twenty-two times since winning the heavyweight championship from Buster Douglas in 1990. At the time of these twenty-two fights, his opponents had a cumulative record of 857 wins, 52 losses, and 4 draws,

"It's not winning," Evander says, "if you haven't fought the best."

Warriors can be brutal. They don't just absorb punishment; they impose it too. The great ones can be mean, and Holyfield has inflicted his share of pain. But he embodies the best of the reasons why people are drawn to boxing. "Everything else about Evander is too little," says Earnie Shavers. "But his heart is the right size."

Holyfield has confidence in himself and also that the Lord is on his side. His goal is to reclaim the heavyweight crown and, in his mind, it won't be enough to simply win a title. He wants to consolidate all of the belts and retire as undisputed heavyweight champion of the world. That leads to analogies between Evander and Captain Ahab's self-destructive obsession with the White Whale. After all, Holyfield hasn't scored a knockout since 1997. He has won just two of his last eight fights. His greatest glory, the first Holyfield-Tyson fight, took place seven years ago. He's forty-one years old with a body that carries the wear and tear of a man about to enter his twentieth year as a professional fighter.

"People say they don't want to see me hurt," Holyfield acknowledged recently. "I don't want to see me hurt either. But they've tried to bury me two or three times before and found out that I wasn't dead. For the last ten years, people been popping the same question at me: 'When you gonna quit?' They started asking after I fought Riddick Bowe the first time. So I went out and beat Bowe in the rematch, and they still said I should retire. They've been singing the same song ever since. And when they're not singing, they've been threatening that I'm gonna get carried out on my back. But I'm still standing. I'm still here."

"People keep telling me that boxing is a brutal business," Holyfield continued. "Do they think I don't know that? I've been in the ring three times with Bowe; twice with Lennox Lewis. I beat Larry Holmes and George Foreman. I whupped Mike Tyson twice; had my ear chewed off and spat on the ground in front of me. I know this business better than anyone. When I was young, I woke up sore but I still had to do what I had to do. Now I'm older and I wake up sore, but I still gotta do what I gotta do. Ain't nothing changed. I've set a goal to retire as undisputed heavyweight champion of the world. I'm not in a hurry. I'm picking my fights carefully. The goal is still there. The question is, how do I exit as champion?"

Holyfield versus James Toney was part of the plan. But looking realistically at the situation, Evander went into the fight as a gatekeeper for the heavyweight division. If he won, he would reemerge as a contender. If he lost, Toney would become the contender and Evander would be relegated to "opponent" status.

Toney is a world-class fighter who has squandered much of his potential. After losing to Roy Jones in 1994, he went into a funk and stopped training seriously. His bout with Evander was the first time in nine years that he'd been in the ring for a fight that the public cared about.

Toney has been accused of having an attitude problem. James says that it's a case of other people having a perception problem and that he has simply been in a bad mood for thirty-five years. Either way, a little bit of James Toney goes a long way. And in the days leading up to the fight, he was exceedingly vocal.

"This will be Holyfield's last fight," Toney promised. "I'm retiring him. He's past his prime; he's had his time. He can grab his Bible, bring his choir, do whatever; it don't matter. He's in trouble. It's going to be a bloody night. I'm gonna give this old southern boy an ass-whupping; bust him up good, put him to sleep. I'm the hardest-punching boxer out there. I can't wait to prove to the world that I'm the future of the heavyweight division. Any man, except for me, can be beat. I'm the greatest fighter of the millennium."

But talking doesn't win fights, and the Holyfield camp was equally confident. To a man, they believed that Evander was the better fighter, punched harder and, given his reach advantage, would be able to control Toney with his jab. Moreover, Holyfield had been hit lots of times by people who punched harder than Toney, but James had never been hit by anyone who punched as hard as Evander. Sparring with heavyweights is different from fighting one.

Thus, in the days leading up to the fight, Holyfield said of Toney's trash-talking, "Everyone has the freedom to say what they want. Some can back it up and some can't. The question is, can he take what I give him? Toney says he's going to stand in front of me and fight me. I look forward to that. That's great. That means I won't miss. If he doesn't move, they're gonna wind up moving him. He may stand there, but it won't be for long."

Meanwhile, Atlanta attorney Jim Thomas, who has done exemplary work for Evander since 1991, said simply, "The best way to deal with guys who are disrespectful is to knock them out."

The day of the fight was typical for Evander. Mandalay Bay had provided him with a palatial three-bedroom suite featuring a huge living room and kitchen area. At 10:30 a.m., wearing blue workout shorts and a gray T-shirt, he sat with Jim Thomas, conditioning coach Tim Hallmark, and several friends from Atlanta over a plate of steak and eggs and a stack of pancakes that conjured up the image of a tall office building.

There was no sign of nerves. Everyone seemed relaxed and confident as they awaited the battle. One reason for the confidence was that, ever since his second fight against Lennox Lewis, Evander had been plagued by an ailing left shoulder that left him unable to throw effective lefthand leads or hook off his jab. But after being outpointed by Chris Byrd last December, he'd undergone surgery to repair a torn rotator cuff. Now the shoulder was fully healed.

Both Holyfield and Toney had looked good at their final pre-fight physicals. Evander weighed 219 pounds and seemed to be in the best shape possible for a fighter two weeks shy of forty-one. Toney had come in a bit heavy at 217. But he'd worked hard during the preceding months, cleaned up his eating habits, and been off red meat for eight weeks.

"It don't matter what Toney weighs," Holyfield said when the subject arose. "If I start paying attention to what he weighs, it means I'm not paying enough attention to what I'm gonna do." Then Evander stood up from the table in his suite and demonstrated how, when Toney turns his head and shoulders on the inside to avoid a punch, he exposes his ribs. "You break something if you hit a man there," Evander said.

At noon, Holyfield went out for a walk. A half-hour later, he returned and sat down on the sofa to watch the playoff game between the New

York Yankees and Minnesota Twins.

One of the noteworthy things about Evander is how much more verbal he has become over the years. "Coming out of the Olympics," he acknowledged, "I wasn't comfortable communicating with people. I was concerned with my articulation and how I sounded. I thought people were laughing at me when I expressed myself. I worried about things like whether or not I was right in putting an 's' at the end of a verb."

Those days are past. Evander now understands that he's as smart as the next person and, as the afternoon progressed, he talked freely. "This isn't a championship fight," he noted. "But it's getting a lot of attention and that's a good feeling. Obviously, the fight is significant for me, but it's nice to know that it's significant for other people too."

Then the conversation turned to an overview of his career. "I've been boxing for thirty-two years," Evander reminisced. "I've had my ups and I've had my downs, but it's been good. The fight that meant the most to me was the first fight against Tyson. I knew I could beat him, but the public didn't. The fight I learned the most from was my first fight against Qawi. Before that fight, I wasn't sure if I belonged in the ring with him. Then he burned a shirt that had my picture on it. That was disrespectful. It made me mad."

The Qawi fight marked the emergence of the public perception of Evander Holyfield as a warrior. He entered the ring at 190 pounds and left it weighing 175. But he survived fifteen of the most brutal rounds in boxing history and captured the cruiserweight crown. Then, bruised, battered, and badly dehydrated, he was taken to the hospital for overnight observation.

"I lay in that bed," Evander remembered, "and even though I won, I said out loud, 'Oh, Lord; I don't know if I want to do this anymore.' But to be a true success, you have to endure hardship. Being a warrior isn't just being destructive. A warrior is a man who takes it to the end and doesn't quit. If you quit every time you have a setback, you'll be starting over your whole life."

Then came the familiar refrain: "When I become undisputed heavyweight champion of the world again is when I close the book on being a fighter. I might not get it when I want it, but I'll get it. The only way I won't reach my goal of becoming heavyweight champion of the world again is if I quit. And I won't quit."

Evander stayed in his suite for the rest of the afternoon. Then, after the Atlanta Braves secured game four of their playoff series against the Chicago Cubs, he journeyed down a service elevator and through back passageways to the Mandalay Bay Events Center. At 5:25 p.m., he arrived in a room with plush ivory carpeting, a large-screen television, a sofa, and club chairs. It looked like the dressing room for a concert performer.

Evander sat on the sofa, directly opposite the television. "Braves won," he said. "Got one thing straight. Now it's time for the other."

The first pay-per-view fight of the evening, Cruz Carbajal versus Gerardo Espinoza, was underway. Evander turned his attention to the television and watched impassively. The atmosphere in the room was like a handful of fans sitting at home in someone's living room watching a fight. Except soon, one of the group would get up off the sofa to be in the main event.

Long stretches of time went by without anyone saying a word. Evander watched silently, and everyone else followed his lead. Espinoza got beaten up. The fight ended with a left hook to the body that left him writhing on the canvas in pain. Evander stood up from the sofa, walked over to a six-foot mirror, and threw a handful of punches in exaggerated slow-motion.

At 5:50 pm, Marc Ratner (executive director of the Nevada State Athletic Commission) entered the room with Jay Nady, who would be refereeing the main event. Nady gave Evander his preliminary instructions, closing with, "Good luck. It's an honor to be in the ring with you."

Nady and Ratner left. Evander went into the adjacent bathroom to provide a urine sample for the Nevada commission. Then he returned; turned off the sound on the television, and inserted a tape of gospel music into a cassette player.

"All praise to the King . . . Praise to Jesus . . . Nothing compares to His love."

Evander put on his high-top fight shoes and began lacing them up, singing along with the music.

"My Jesus, my Saviour . . . Glory to His name."

A look of rapture came over Evander's face and his body began to sway. The mundane work of lacing shoes took on the aura of a devotional act.

On the television screen, Joel Casamayor versus Diego Corrales began.

"Lift up your hearts to Jesus . . . Glory unto His name."

At 6:05 p.m., trainer Donald Turner began taping Evander's hands. The two men had been together for each of Evander's fights since 1994.

Still, no one spoke. Evander's eyes were closed and his head swayed to the music as he sang, "We lift up our hands and bless Your Holy Name . . . Blessed be the name of The Lord."

All the while, Turner worked efficiently, mechanically, taping Evander's hands. When the taping was done, Tim Hallmark stood opposite Evander and led him through a series of stretching exercises, Meanwhile, Joel Casamayor versus Diego Corrales unfolded silently on the screen.

"Blessed be the name of the Lord . . . Because He is worthy to be praised and adored . . . Hallelujah."

The stretching exercises ended. Evander pulled his protective cup up over his gym shorts. Blood was gushing from gashes on Diego Corrales's cheek and inside his mouth. After the sixth round, ring doctor Margaret Goodman stopped the fight.

"Good stoppage," declared Donald Turner.

"Twenty minutes," Jim Thomas said.

Everyone in the room joined hands in prayer.

"We lift up our hands and bless Your Holy Name. Blessed be the name of The Lord for He is worthy to be praised."

Then came the carnage.

"If a fight can be made," Evander once said, "I can win it." But as Larry Holmes has observed, "Sometimes the mind makes a date that the body can't keep."

Holyfield-Toney was a reality check for Evander and the check bounced.

Evander came out hard and looked pretty good at the start, but Toney was difficult to hit flush. Finally, in round three, he whacked James with his best right hand and nothing happened. Then, in round four, James hit him back solidly and Evander wobbled.

Thereafter, Toney beat Holyfield up. By round seven, he was hitting him at will with right hands. In the past, Evander had been on the opposite side of the same equation. Once, he had been the young fighter facing aging lions like George Foreman and Larry Holmes. And of course, Evander had taken beatings before and, inspired by a deep belief in God, had come back to prevail. But in boxing, belief alone isn't enough.

By round eight, Evander's face was swollen and blood was streaming from his mouth. In round nine, a barrage of blows punctuated by a brutal body shot put him on the canvas. Most likely, Nady would have allowed the fight to continue. After all, Evander is boxing's consummate warrior. But as Evander rose, Donald Turner stepped into the ring and halted the punishment. Whatever else Turner might have done in boxing, that was his finest moment.

All three judges had Toney comfortably ahead at the time of the stoppage.

Back in his dressing room, Evander glanced at his image in the mirror, opened a bottle of water, and took several gulps. Then he slumped in a chair. "I got beat up," he said to no one in particular. "The body shots got me. Toney got off before me. He outhustled me; he beat me to position. I found myself thinking, not reacting. I was a step behind all night."

Evander bowed his head in disappointment, not prayer. For the moment, the emotional pain seemed worse than the physical. "I don't have no excuses," he continued. "My shoulder didn't bother me. I fought like I had a hurt shoulder, but the left arm was fine. The shoulder wasn't hurt at all. But I'm not ready to retire. I'll go home, rest a while, and look for a signal from the Lord."

There was a post-fight press conference marked by a standing ovation from the boxing media. Then Evander journeyed through a maze of corridors and back upstairs on a service elevator. At 9:30 p.m., he was in his suite. "I feel good," he told the friends gathered around him. "I got beat; that's all. I got my head up, so don't you all be sad."

So what comes next for Evander Holyfield?

Athletes get old in a cruel way; and for fighters, the aging process is particularly cruel. Many people who care about Evander hope he retires. He, in turn, observes, "The Bible teaches that a man's end is more important than his beginning. That's why I want to retire as undisputed heavyweight champion of the world."

But there are few happy endings in boxing. And in broader terms, at age forty-one, Evander is merely at the mid-point of what one hopes will be a long happy life.

Several hours before he fought James Toney, Evander spoke of maturing and how he had learned to be less selfish over the years and put larger interests ahead of his own personal goals. Then he'd added, "I understand now that happiness is a journey; not a destination. You don't work for twenty years, make a lot of money, retire, and be happy forever. The journey goes on."

One might add that a fighter doesn't fight for twenty years, retire as undisputed heavyweight champion of the world, and be happy forever. The journey goes on.

Regardless of what happens next in the ring, the second half of Evander's life is about to begin. Thus, one might draw a parallel between his life and the Bible, which is divided into the Old and New Testaments.

The God of the Old Testament is commonly thought of as a God of Wrath. The God of the New Testament is a God of Love. Evander grew up in harsh surroundings and has spent the past twenty-five years in the brutal confines of a boxing ring. Perhaps the time has come for Book Two of his life to begin.

Evander Holyfield believes in service. He must now decide how best to serve.❏

As Evander Holyfield's career soured, Mike Tyson was also in extremis.

HELPING MIKE TYSON

There was a time when Mike Tyson was known for his awesome ring talent. Now he's more like Michael Jackson. Jackson can still dance and sing a bit, but that's not why people turn on their television sets to watch him. Likewise, the heart of Tyson's appeal is no longer his ability as a fighter but rather his potential for deviant behavior.

"The Tyson of before was the best heavyweight in the world," Oscar De La Hoya said earlier this year. "Now it's different for him, and he knows it. People don't want to watch him for his boxing skills. They just want to know what he'll do next."

At the final prefight press conference for his July 30th fight against Danny Williams, Tyson sounded an optimistic note. "My future seems so much brighter than my past," he said. Then he got knocked out. But worse, he quit. "This is a guy he should beat, and he didn't," Tyson's trainer Freddie Roach told the media afterward. "I give Danny Williams some credit; I'm not going to tarnish his win. But you can't be a contender if you can't beat Danny Williams."

The end game wasn't supposed to be this way. The young Mike Tyson entering a boxing ring resembled a carnivore ready to devour its kill. He came forward as inexorably as the ocean tide, throwing punches that crashed down upon hapless foes like ten-foot waves. When he hit opponents, their ribs caved in and they went down like they were wearing roller-skates.

Eddie Futch, the legendary trainer who spent seven decades in boxing, observed, "The root of Tyson's effectiveness was his quickness. What made him so effective was the speed with which he delivered his power. He had the quickest delivery of any hard puncher since Joe Louis."

Tyson was groomed, not merely to be heavyweight champion of the world, but to be one of the greatest fighters of all time. The message he transmitted was, "I hit harder than you can take; and at some point in the fight, I will destroy you." He won the World Boxing Council title with a second-round knockout of Trevor Berbick at age twenty after

boxing for only twenty months as a pro. Next, he consolidated and suc-
cessfully defended the crown with victories over Pinklon Thomas, Tony
Tucker, Tyrell Biggs, Larry Holmes, Tony Tubbs, Michael Spinks, Frank
Bruno, and Carl Willams.

But there came a time when the fists of opponents began to talk back
in myriad ways. From the hands of Buster Douglas: "Does that hurt,
Mike?" From Evander Holyfield: "Mike, I did it to you once, and I'm
doing it again." From Lennox Lewis: "You're not bobbing and weaving
away from punches the way Cus D'Amato taught you." And from Danny
Williams: "You're a three-round fighter now, Mike."

Tyson was 23 years old when he lost to Douglas in 1990. Since then,
he has wasted more talent than any heavyweight in history. Most boxers
get by for a while on technique when their physical skills start to
decline. But with Tyson, it was the other way around. His technique
declined years ago, and he survived by virtue of his physical skills. Now,
those assets too are diminishing, and the glory years have become the
gory years.

Tyson's fall from grace has been without grace. He seems to enjoy
beating people up, but is less enamoured of competitive fights. The man
who once demanded of opponents, "How dare they challenge me with
their primitive skills?" has won only five fights in the past eight years.
During that time, his record has been 5 wins, 4 losses, and 2 no contests.
Given the multiplicity of titles and the mediocre state of the heavyweight division, he could conceivably win a belt again someday. But he
is now 38 years old, and "Iron Mike" Tyson is no more.

There's considerable debate as to how great Tyson was in his prime.
His uninterrupted reign as undisputed heavyweight champion lasted for
thirty-eight months. That's pretty good. Over the past seventy-six years,
only Joe Louis, Rocky Marciano, Muhammad Ali, and Larry Holmes
exceeded that standard.

Still, even when he was at his peak in the ring, Tyson was beset by
demons. He was a man who, worse than actually being ugly, believed
that he was ugly. And he seemed to think that he should be allowed to
do whatever he wanted to do when he wanted to do it. But life doesn't
work that way.

"There are no baby pictures of Mike Tyson," Tom Junod wrote in
defense of his subject. "Nobody cared enough either to keep them or
take them in the first place. There are no pictures of Mike Tyson
smiling without teeth or sleeping in a crib or being held aloft in the arms
of his father. He is around twelve years old by the time of his first extant
photograph. And because no pictures of him exist before that one, it's
almost as though he didn't either, until the first click of the shutter

nudged him into being and he was born on film, fully formed, already finished, already stocky, already strong, already scared, already heart-broken, already truant, already violent, already in trouble, and already captured thirty-eight times between the ages of ten and thirteen and delivered into the hands of the law."

Hence, the Mike Tyson reality show. Tyson was charged with assault and battery after striking a parking-lot attendant and settled the case for $105,000. A street fight with boxer Mitch Green resulted in a $45,000 jury award in Green's favor. An incident in which Tyson was knocked unconscious after driving his BMW into a tree led to press reports of a suicide attempt. Myriad lawsuits filed by various women alleged sexual misconduct. A disastrous marriage to actress Robin Givens ended in a much-publicized divorce. Finally, on February 10, 1992, Tyson was con-victed of rape. "I'm not sure if he's a psycho or if he's just no damn good," prosecutor Greg Garrison said.

Tyson was released from custody after serving three years in prison. In his first fight back, he knocked out Peter McNeeley in 89 seconds. The bout did nothing to bolster his ring credentials, but spoke volumes regarding his earning power. Victories over Buster Mathis Jr., Frank Bruno, and Bruce Seldon followed. Next on the list of intended victims was Evander Holyfield.

Holyfield was presumed to be a shot fighter. But in an upset of mon-umental proportions, he knocked Tyson out in the eleventh round. Then came the fight that has come to define Mike Tyson's career. On June 28, 1997, he met Holyfield in a rematch and was disqualified for biting off part of Evander's ear.

"At first, when the pain came and I saw him spit the ear out of his mouth, it was a shocking thing," Holyfield said later. "Shocking things are supposed to happen to other people. But when I came back straight at him, it was his turn to be shocked. I broke Tyson's heart that night."

Thus, the demons raged on. Tyson married Monica Turner, but that marriage too ended in divorce. He broke a rib and punctured a lung when a motorcycle he was riding skidded off the highway after hitting a patch of sand. He filed a lawsuit against Don King, accusing the pro-moter of cheating him out of tens of millions of dollars. And he wound up in jail again; this time for three months, after assaulting two motorists in the wake of a traffic accident.

Meanwhile, Tyson's mental state had becoming an issue in Nevada, where his most lucrative bouts were held. After biting Holyfield, he had been fined $3,000,000 and his license was revoked by the Nevada State Athletic Commission. Now he wanted to fight again in Las Vegas. But the commission insisted that, before being relicensed, he undergo a psychiatric evaluation at Massachusetts General Hospital. Thus, in September 1998, Tyson was examined for five days by a team of physicians in Massachusetts.

"Mr. Tyson did agree to proceed with the evaluation and cooperated with the process," the subsequent medical report stated. But the report added the caveat, "There were times when his anger over the process made it difficult for him to continue. Appropriate breaks were taken and Mr. Tyson was able to continue."

In other words, Tyson was difficult to handle. Stopping for "appropriate breaks" is psychiatric shorthand for "we had to manage him through the evaluation." The physicians couldn't just do their job; but when Tyson was reminded of the consequences of acting out, he calmed down.

"Mr. Tyson was open and direct throughout the evaluation," the report continued. "Part of his openness and honesty, however, was to express clearly to us his sense of humiliation at being asked to undergo an evaluation by mental health professionals."

To translate: If a fighter bites off a piece of someone's ear in a boxing ring, there are repercussions. But Tyson didn't fully accept that, so he was humiliated by, and indignant at, the evaluation process.

Much of the evaluation focussed on Tyson's "anger management" or lack thereof. And regrettably, much of it was reminiscent of the 1980 Mayo Clinic report that found Muhammad Ali physically fit to challenge Larry Holmes.

For example, the road rage incident that led to Tyson's imprisonment for three months was dismissed with the notation that it "was explained by Mr. Tyson in a manner consistent with his representations to others [i.e. Tyson lied]. No further details of that incident are outlined here," the report continued, "in light of the fact that the alleged incident [which involved uncontrolled rage under stress] is potentially the subject of an ongoing criminal hearing."

Ultimately, the report found Tyson's neurological condition to be normal. But a neuro-psychological evaluation designed to detect possible brain damage by observing how the brain functions found problems with attention and weaknesses in both short-term working memory and fine motor coordination. The physicians also found dysthymia (chronic mild depression), hyper-vigilance (a condition similar to, but less severe than, paranoia), and "issues related to his personality (i.e. psychiatric jargon for a borderline personality)."

The report closed with the conclusion that Tyson was mentally fit to return to boxing and, most likely, wouldn't "snap" again as he'd done when he bit Evander Holyfield. In that regard, the physicians wrote,

"Boxing provides a different set of stresses, in many ways less troubling for Mr. Tyson, than the process he underwent in our offices."

One wonders whether these health care professionals understood the stress associated with being in a boxing ring.

The Massachusetts General Hospital psychiatric report was forwarded to the Nevada State Athletic Commission in early October 1998. On October 13th, the commission voted 4-to-1 to restore Tyson's boxing license.

On January 16, 1999, Tyson fought in Las Vegas and knocked out Frans Botha after trying to snap Botha's arm off at the elbow in a clinch. Nine months later, his bout against Orlin Norris was declared "no contest" after he knocked Norris down with a punch thrown after the bell ending round one. At that point, the Nevada commission told Tyson to take his act on the road, and he fought in the United Kingdom against Julius Francis and Lou Savarese. The latter bout was noteworthy for Iron Mike striking Savarese and referee John Coyle after Coyle stopped the fight—an act that led the British Boxing Board of Control to levy a $187,500 fine against him. On October 20, 2000, Tyson added another "no contest" to his record when he tested positive for illegal drugs after a fight in Michigan against Andrew Golota. That promotion was noteworthy for a Tyson tirade at the kick-off press conference.

"I don't care about living or dying," Tyson told the assembled media. "I'm a dysfunctional motherfucker. Bring on Golota; bring on Lewis. They can keep their titles. I don't want to strip them of their titles, I want to strip them of their fucking health. I'm in pain, so I want them to be in pain. I want their kids to see pain. You don't know me; you can't define me. I'm a convicted rapist, a hell-raiser, a father, a semi-good husband. I raise hell. I know it's going to get me in trouble or killed one day, but that's just who I am. I can't help it. Listen, I'm a nigger. No, really, really, listen to me. I'm a street person. I don't even want to be a street person; I don't like typical street people. But your grandchildren will know about me. They'll be like, 'Wow, wasn't that a bizarre individual?'"

The Golota debacle was followed by a seventh-round knockout of Brian Nielsen in Denmark. Then Tyson signed to fight Lennox Lewis. But at a January 22, 2002, press conference to announce the bout, there was a meltdown of historic proportions. Tyson assaulted Lewis; bit him on the thigh, let loose with an obscenity-laden rant, and masturbated on stage as television cameras recorded every moment. The self-proclaimed "baddest man on the planet" had become the maddest man on the planet.

Tyson's conduct at the press conference was the conduct of a man who wanted trouble. In some ways, it seemed deliberate; like a premeditated loss of control, if there is such a thing. After the initial assault on

Lewis, he prowled the stage looking for more trouble. Metaphorically speaking, and with a bit of the physical thrown in, he hadn't been fully satisfied yet. That didn't happen until he unleashed his verbal tirade and masturbated.

What would happen if an anonymous person with a history of violence (including convictions for rape and assault) assaulted someone, bit him, engaged in an obscene threatening rant, and masturbated in public?

In all likelihood, there would be a telephone call to 911 (the police emergency number). A police officer would be dispatched to the scene to arrest the perpetrator. If necessary, an emergency medical technician would physically restrain him with a pharmacological restraint. The perpetrator would then be brought to the local police station or a hospital emergency room. None of that happened with Tyson on January 22nd, but the incident did shed further light on his psyche.

Here a disclaimer is necessary. I'm not a psychiatrist, nor have I conducted a psychiatric examination of Mike Tyson. But I have talked extensively with psychiatrists who say that Tyson exhibits the characteristics of what is known as a "Cluster-B personality disorder."

People who fit into this category move back and forth between neurotic and psychotic behavior. Many were hyperactive and difficult to control as children and had difficulty focussing for sustained periods of time. They were neglected, beaten, sexually molested, or otherwise abused. From an early age, their basic needs were unmet. They threw things and had temper tantrums. Frequently, they suffered from learning disabilities. And they evolved into adults with little sense of morality, few boundaries, and limited impulse control. As adults, they suffer from feelings of persecution. There's no core; no organizing self or ego for another person to have a mature adult relationship with. Everything gets distorted. There's very little reality testing. And they don't understand that it's bad to be the way they are. The problem, as they see it, is all the awful things that other people do to them. Their self-esteem is terrible. They suffer from chronic humiliation. The only way they can excel is with their genitals and their fists. Aggression and sex become intertwined, and often they can't tell the difference. There's horrible rage. They're turned on by violence. They have obsessive thoughts about hurting other people. As they get older, they get even more depressed and deteriorate further. Some of them start hearing voices. And what you end up with is a person who is like a caged animal in pain.

People with a Cluster-B personality disorder function well in some situations. But they can, suddenly and without warning, collapse under stress. After the January 22nd incident, Tyson should have been put in a closely-monitored treatment program. After all, how many high-profile public figures masturbate in public? The world was witnessing the conduct of a man who was out of control and, in some ways, screaming for help. But if the criminal authorities don't force the issue (and in this instance, they didn't) it's very difficult to get someone into the mental-health-care system against his will. The people around him have to be willing to take him on. Someone who cares about the patient has to initiate an involuntary proceeding.

That, of course, didn't happen. Instead, plans for Lewis-Tyson proceeded apace. But first there was the matter of Tyson being relicensed to box by the Nevada State Athletic Commission. On January 29th, he appeared before the commission, stated that he was not on medication, hadn't been for six months, and that his psychiatric therapy had ended the previous spring. "I'm no longer in need of treatment," Tyson said in response to one of the questions put to him. The commission then voted 4-to-1 against granting him a license. Two of the four commissioners (John Bailey and Flip Homansky) stated that they viewed the situation as a medical issue, not a disciplinary one. They believed that Tyson was suffering from an inadequately-treated mental illness and represented a danger both to himself and others.

If there were uniform medical standards for boxers in the United States, Tyson would have been forced at that point to sit down with the medical professionals at the Nevada State Athletic Commission and deal directly with his emotional problems. But unfortunately, no such standards exist. If a state such as Nevada takes a stand on principle and loses a lucrative prizefight, another jurisdiction is always willing to step into the breach.

Thus, on June 8, 2002, Mike Tyson entered the ring in Memphis, Tennessee, and was annihilated by Lennox Lewis over eight brutal rounds. Afterward, Tyson acknowledged, "During the fight, I said, 'This is not a good night.' I could beat him if I was well, but I'm sick right now. I don't mean sick physically. I mean emotionally." Later, that admission gave way to the declaration, "I might have kissed him after our first fight, but I'll crush his head when we're next in the ring."

The following months were marked by further outbursts of rage and self-pity from a man who sounded very much like he hated himself and blamed everyone but himself for it. Perhaps the most telling of these outbursts came in a documentary taped by Fox Sports Net in late 2002.

"I'm a real angry and bitter man," Tyson said. "When I went to prison, it changed my whole outlook on life. It really screwed me up. My attitude became really ugly and nasty. I fell in love with hate in prison. It made pretty much an animal out of me. White society thinks

I'm an animal; wild beast out of control, ready to rape their daughters or hurt them or do something drastic to them. I don't got a chance in this society. I understand this society that I live in hates me."

Then Tyson likened his heart to "ground beef," acknowledged, "when I'm unhappy, I'm very self-destructive," and declared, "I got some serious serious demons I'm fighting. I hate my life now. I've been abused and used any way a person can be abused and used. I've lost my soul as a human being. I've lost my self-respect. None of my friends have any respect for me. A lot of times, I hate myself. Maybe in my next life, I'll have a better life. That's why I'm just looking forward to going to the other world."

But there was no acceptance of responsibility; no recognition that, somewhere along the line, a person must learn that he's accountable for his own conduct no matter how disadvantaged he might have been; no acceptance of the truth that everyone has a right to be angry but not to be brutal or cruel; no understanding that it's wrong to bite people, that either you control your demons or they control you.

Instead, Tyson posed the query, "Why can't I have what I want? Why shouldn't I have it all?"

Then Tyson signed to fight Clifford Etienne on February 22, 2003, and the circus was on display again. On February 10th and 11th, he failed to go to the gym to train after rumored all-night parties. On February 12th, he arrived late, sporting a large tattoo—what trainer Freddie Roach called "an African tribal thing"—on the side of his face.

In the past, there had been times when people were able to forget the nature of Tyson's psyche. Now the tattoo was there to remind them. Its application was an act of self-mutilation. And its timing was a clear indication that Tyson didn't want to fight.

As Anne Laumann (a dermatologist and assistant professor of clinical medicine at the University of Chicago) explained, "When the tattooing instrument pricks the skin, blood is released. The area gets swollen and it gets crusty. You should leave it alone, except for washing it or putting on ointment, for a two-week period. During that healing period, there can be oozing and scabbing. I would put new tattooing in the same category as an open wound."

The following day (February 13th), bout promoter Gary Shaw claimed that Tyson was suffering from "vomiting and other flu-like symptoms." Advisor Shelly Finkel added, "Mike's not feeling well. He's had some bronchitis, some temperature stuff." Meanwhile, Roach told the media that a dramatic change in Tyson's demeanor the previous week had led him to wonder whether something had changed with regard to medication that Tyson was taking to control his behavior.

On February 14th, 15th, and 16th, Tyson's condition allegedly worsened. On February 17th, Tyson-Etienne was formally postponed. "I can understand if there's anger," Finkel said in reference to Showtime, which had invested millions of dollars in promoting and readying to televise the fight. "But I would hope we could mend it. In the crazy world of Mike Tyson, he'll always be in demand. He's a star. There's always going to be someone eager to have him, but I hope we can work things out with Showtime."

Finkel was right. There was a lot of anger. A lot of people, including Tyson, stood to lose a lot of money. There was screaming and yelling followed by threats of lawsuits. Then—lo and behold—on the morning of February 18th, Tyson woke up feeling fine.

The fight took place as planned. Etienne went down in the first round. And at the post-fight press conference, Tyson repeated the mantra that had become familiar to friend and foe alike. "I've been doing this for twenty-five years of my life," he said. "I haven't received any dignity from it. I've received a lot of pain from it. I'm in pain. It's made me not like Mike Tyson no more. I don't know if I'm ever going to love anybody. I definitely don't think anybody's going to love me."

"Mike Tyson doesn't need anyone to feel sorry for him," Ron Borges of the *Boston Globe* wrote afterward. "He's doing enough of that himself."

The next year brought more of the same. In May 2003, Tyson granted a television interview to Greta Van Susteren of Fox News. When asked about Desiree Washington, who he'd been convicted of raping a decade earlier, he declared, "I didn't rape that slimy bitch. She's a lying monstrous lady. I just hate her guts. She put me in that state where, I don't know; I really wish I did now. I really do want to rape her and fuck her mama."

One month later, on June 21, 2003, Tyson was arrested and charged with assault in conjunction with a brawl in the lobby of the Marriott Hotel in Brooklyn. Subsequently, he pled guilty to disorderly conduct. Then he stepped out of the spotlight before returning to public view to fight Danny Williams.

It was a "new mellower Mike Tyson" who spoke with the media during the build-up to Tyson-Williams. "When I want to make a fool out of myself, there's no changing my mind," he joked. Then he turned serious, saying, "I've come to the conclusion that I've had a bad psychological opinion of myself. I'm a maniac, but I'm a good guy. I'm just trying to manage my life properly. That's something I've never done before. I feel good when I'm training. I feel like I'm doing something with my life."

Then Mike Tyson got knocked out in four rounds. Great fighters don't get knocked out by Danny Williams.

What comes next?

Tyson's immediate future will unfold within the framework of his ongoing bankruptcy proceeding. Last year, he filed for protection from his creditors, listing $38,400,000 in debts. Among the sums owed were $13,400,000 to American tax authorities; $4,000,000 to their British counterparts; and $9,000,000 to his second wife, Monica Turner.

The bankruptcy proceeding offered insight into Tyson's profligate ways. Documents filed with the court revealed that, during the 33 months immediately following his 1995 release from prison, Tyson spent $4,477,498 on automobiles and motorcycles; $1,712,727 on their insurance and repair; $748,369 on lawn care; $411,777 on pigeons and a tiger; and $239,552 on pagers and mobile phones. His total expenditures for those 33 months were in excess of $37,000,000. Roughly six-tenths of one percent of that amount went to child support.

In June 2004, Tyson settled his lawsuit against Don King for $14,000,000 and announced a plan to pay the bulk of the $38,400,000 owed to creditors over a three-year period. A central component of that plan was a projected $19,500,000 contribution from seven fights to be held over the next three years. In other words, the people who are advising and "helping" Mike Tyson mapped out a plan that envisions his fighting until he's 41 years old.

Tyson is still capable of earning large amounts of money in the ring. His left knee, which was operated on for a ligament tear after the Williams fight, is healing well. Richard Emerson (the orthopedic surgeon who performed the surgery) estimates that Tyson will be able to resume training in eight weeks.

There's an insatiable public curiosity regarding Tyson, and he can be repackaged to take advantage of that phenomenon. Many countries would host a Tyson fight against a "grade D" opponent simply to have him within their borders. Las Vegas casinos, most notably the MGM Grand, would pay a substantial site fee for a Tyson bout should he be relicensed by the Nevada State Athletic Commission.

Then there's the possibility of a Tyson fight on "free" television in the United States for the first time since 1986. The story-line here would be, "Mike wants this bout on free TV. Mike wants the public to become acquainted with the new Mike Tyson. Mike wants to show his fans how much he appreciates their support."

A Tyson fight on free television, no matter how inept the opponent, could generate the largest domestic audience for any boxing match in history. It would create "Tysonmania" and pave the way for a stream of even more lucrative future contests.

But there's a larger question: "Should Mike Tyson fight again?"

Tracking Tyson's statements over the past twenty months makes it clear that his life remains unsettled. At the November 26, 2002, press conference announcing Tyson-Etienne, he told the media, "I feel good; I'm very happy. Things basically have come together as far as my personal life. I just feel so much good about my transformation and just forming to be a decent human being."

But then, two weeks before the fight, Tyson talked with Tim Smith of the *New York Daily News* about his ex-wife Monica Turner. "I have three kids with her," Tyson confided. "I believe she's a little bitter because she doesn't allow me to see my children. I have to come and have a supervised visit like I'm a child molester. She makes me feel less than a man a lot." And with regard to his 13-year-old daughter, Mikel (one of five children he has fathered), who was living with him at the time in Las Vegas, Tyson declared, "If I don't get my butt together as far as introspection as a father, I'm going to kill my daughter. She doesn't respect me. I'm being real honest. I don't let no one talk to me the way she talks to me. I want her to stay with me forever, but this is looking very difficult."

Finally, earlier this summer, Tyson acknowledged, "My life has been a total waste. My personal life stinks. I don't have anyone; I'm alone. I don't think I'll ever be able to trust again. In order to trust someone else, you have to trust yourself. I just wish that I was more of a loyal person with my girlfriend, my wife. I was never loyal. My infidelity got me in more trouble, because not having a strong relationship and partner environment allows other people to get involved in your life and poison your influence. I broke up with my girlfriend. It just devastated me. I don't even know why; it's just a woman. I'm so accustomed to being with her and talking with her. She was my friend as well as my girlfriend. She's pretty finished with me now because I'm a pig."

There is no "quick fix" for these problems. Doctors can medicate the depression that comes with them. Drugs like Zoloft and Neurontin might sedate Tyson a bit, but they won't change the overall way in which he relates to the people around him.

Tyson is a man who often deals with personal relationships and life in general in a dysfunctional manner. His judgment is impaired as a consequence of things that have been building and crystalizing in him since early childhood. Can he be successfully treated? The key is whether or not he suffers from misgivings and depression after his episodes. Once the high has faded away, does he feel bad about what happened? If so, that can be an entry-way for treatment. But unfortunately, Tyson is surrounded by enablers who tell him that everything he does is fine. He has fallen into a system run by people who use his illness to their advantage and cling to him with the loyalty and steadfastness of a leech. Whatever he does, no matter how bad it is, there are people who tell him that his conduct is acceptable. And even when he pays a price, like going to jail, the enablers tell him that it wasn't really his fault.

Still, many people (and many fighters) have social pathologies, and these difficulties can be overcome. Tyson doesn't have to enter a psychiatric facility; nor would prison and prison treatment solve the problem. But one thing is certain. In the field of mental health, a patient can't go to a different treating physician at every turn. Doing so deprives the care-giver of the overall view necessary for success and also precludes the development of trust between patient and doctor. There must be a long-term professional psychiatric relationship. Tyson has to talk, and someone has to listen, for a long time.

Also, it will be particularly difficult for Tyson to improve his life in a meaningful way as long as he's boxing. A fighter must be able to redirect, switch on and off, channel, and control normal human emotions. Tyson has enough trouble dealing with these emotions on an everyday basis without the added pressures that come with being in the ring.

And one must question the long-term effects of whatever medication Tyson has been taking to prolong his ring career. For example, it's known that, in the past, he was dependent upon Zoloft; an inhibitor that increases the availability of serotonin in the brain. Serontonin transmits impulses and regulates mood. Zoloft blocks the re-uptake of serotonin so more is available in the brain.

How important is Zoloft to Tyson? On February 5, 1999, when he was sentenced for assaulting two motorists following their traffic accident, Tyson's lawyers told the court that he needed Zoloft as part of his therapy. Then, during his October 1999 hearing before the Nevada State Athletic Commission, doctors testifying on Tyson's behalf stated that he suffered from "deficits in executive function that make him prone to impulsive behavior." However, they voiced the view that his condition could be controlled through psychotherapy and medication.

For a while, Tyson was taken off Zoloft each time he fought. That led to demands that the people who were supposed to be looking out for his best interests reconsider their actions. "I think it's crazy," said Dr. William Hoffmann, a psychiatrist with experience in the athletic arena. "If you go on and off Zoloft, you're messing around with a patient's neuro-transmitters. To get the maximum benefit from Zoloft, you have go on it and stay on it long term. To put a patient on Zoloft and take him off Zoloft and put him on and take him off is abusive."

The status of Tyson's current medication is not publicly known. But

Dr. Margaret Goodman (medical director of the Nevada State Athletic Commission) declares, "A 'don't ask, don't tell policy' is unacceptable. Safety must come first when it relates to a boxer's emotional well being. State athletic commissions must determine if a particular treatment is conducive to a boxer continuing in the sport."

And Goodman's predecessor, Dr. Flip Homansky, adds, "This is an ongoing issue for boxing, not just because of Mike Tyson but also because of a number of other fighters. My view is that, if someone needs a drug like Zoloft, then he shouldn't be taken off it to get him into the ring or make him better in the ring or make him more aggressive in the ring. That's simply not the right thing to do in terms of the welfare of the individual."

At the final press conference for Tyson-Williams, Tyson spoke of his problems and acknowledged, "I got addicted to the chaos."

So remove the chaos. Get him out of boxing. It's quite possible that, in his heart, Tyson himself doesn't even want to fight anymore.

HBO boxing commentator Jim Lampley was in Tyson's dressing room shortly after Tyson was knocked out by Lennox Lewis. "It was the happiest I'd seen Mike in twelve years," Lampley recalls. "And I honestly believe that's because he felt that it was finally over; that at last, he could walk away from it all."

"I just box to box," Tyson said last month. "I'm fighting basically for my respect, self-esteem; and of course, I have my situation with my creditors."

But as middleweight champion Bernard Hopkins observed recently, "It's a lonely feeling when a guy's confidence is built on guys who are hollering and shouting how great he is and then the bell rings and they're not there with him anymore."

One is hard-pressed to avoid the conclusion that boxing has become Mike Tyson's prison cell. Also, there's added urgency to the situation now because Tyson is at a point in his life where the neurological damage he sustains while fighting will add to his other problems.

Early in Tyson's career, he fought a journeyman named Jesse Ferguson. "Jesse takes a good beating," Tyson's co-manager Jim Jacobs said. "He'll last a few rounds."

Now it's Tyson who's taking the beatings. He has done it four times. And, quite possibly, it would have been five but for the fact that he bit off part of Evander Holyfield's ear.

Here, the thoughts of Dr. Margaret Goodman are instructive. In a recent article, she listed some of the psychiatric disorders that can be caused or aggravated by head injuries sustained in boxing. In Goodman's words, they are:

● "Psychosis—When it occurs, individuals tend to be paranoid. An example would be feeling persecuted and believing that everyone is against you."

● "Mood disorders—Frontal lobe damage is often associated with depression, while temporal lobe injury can produce periods of mania or hyper-activity. Drugs and alcohol can accentuate these symptoms."

● "Anxiety—Characterized by excessive worry and phobic avoidance of the event, restlessness, fatigue, and irritability. Perhaps a boxer who cannot get back into the ring to resume his career."

● "Sexual disorders—Changes in sexual interest/performance or the development of inappropriate/unusual sexual behaviors. Frontal lobe damage is often believed to be associated with inappropriate sexual behavior."

● "Personality Disorders—Personality changes due to head trauma include symptoms of belligerence, anger, episodic violent behavior, impulsivity, loss of drive, loss of spontaneity, childishness, helplessness, lack of awareness, or need for active supervision."

Sound familiar?

When Mike Tyson was at his peak, what he did in the ring defined the sport of boxing. Now that his skills have eroded, his presence defines the sordid business end of the sport.

One can argue that Tyson doesn't have any identity other than boxing and that he needs to fight in order to pay his bills. But Tyson is capable of gathering acclaim and making $100,000 any weekend he chooses by signing autographs at a sports memorabilia show. That might not enable him to live in a mansion with life-sized statues of Alexander the Great, Genghis Khan, and other conquerors as he once did. But as Freddy Roach asked rhetorically after Tyson was knocked out by Danny Williams, "What good is all the money in the world if you can't count it?"

"I'm stupid, foolish; that's one thing I am," Tyson told an interviewer last year. "I've always been foolish my whole life."

It's now time for Mike Tyson to wise up. There's life after boxing. And the further Tyson gets from the sport, the better able he'll be to evolve into a new persona.

Meanwhile, let it be said that some of what Tyson has done in boxing has been magnificent and some has been horrific. There was a time when he appeared to be headed for true greatness. What happened to him shows how thin the line is between ring immortality of legendary proportions and something less.❏

Most women fighters are curiosities. But Christy Martin and Laila Ali deserve credit for being honest fighters, as I noted in this lead-in to their August 23, 2003, encounter.

CHRISTY AND LAILA

There's a time-honored rite of passage in boxing. And it can be ugly. A great fighter gets old. A young fighter has the look of greatness. They meet in the ring . . . Muhammad Ali versus Larry Holmes . . . Joe Louis against Rocky Marciano.

There are no great fighters in women's boxing. But for the past seven years, the standard-bearer has been Christy Martin. On August 23rd, Martin will step into the ring against Laila Ali. From a marketing standpoint, this will be the most significant matchup ever in women's boxing.

The contract weight is 162 pounds. Laila is five-feet-ten-inches tall and a well-sculpted 162-plus. Christy is six inches shorter and has never weighed more than 145 pounds for a fight. She fought at 138 in her prime. Laila is a 3 to 1 favorite. For the first time, Christy will enter the ring as an underdog.

Laila Ali versus Jacqui Frazier was about Muhammad and Joe. This one is about Christy and Laila.

Martin's father was a coal miner who retired last year after three decades on the job. "I'm very down-to-earth, easy-going, laid-back," Christy says. "Every day that I wake up makes me happy, but I have that other side. I can flip the switch pretty quickly if someone is disrespectful or gives me attitude."

Martin graduated from Concord College in West Virginia, with a degree in education in 1990. She got into boxing on a dare. "I'd just started college," she remembers. "Some friends and I went to a tough-woman contest in Beckley, West Virginia. My friends started saying, 'Come on, Christy. Do it! You play basketball. You're in good shape.' I didn't know anything about boxing. I'd never hit a heavy-bag or done anything like that in my life. But I was an athlete. Athletes are cocky. I liked the challenge. And the winner was supposed to get a thousand dollars. That's what decided it for me. I thought I could win a thousand dollars, so I entered the contest. I was pretty nervous when I got in the ring for the first fight. I remember asking myself, 'What am I doing here? Why did I let these people talk me into this?' But I won three fights. There were some hard moments but no real problems. And when it was over, they gave me five hundred dollars instead of a thousand."

Martin fought seven toughwoman bouts between 1986 and 1989, winning six and losing one. Then she turned pro. After four fights, her record stood at 2-1-1. Now it's 45-2-2 with thirty KOs. There was a time when she scored eight consecutive first-round knockouts. But her opponents in those bouts had a grand total of three professional fights with zero wins among them.

Christy exploded on the national scene on March 16, 1996, when she fought in the pay-per-view opener for Mike Tyson versus Frank Bruno at the MGM Grand. Her opponent was Deidre Gogarty. Christy and Iron Mike were paired again on September 7, 1996, when she fought Melinda Robinson on the undercard of Tyson-Seldon; on November 9, 1996, when she took on Bethany Payne prior to Tyson-Holyfield I; and on June 28, 1997, when she met Andrea DeShong on the undercard of Holyfield-Tyson II. Martin battered Gogarty for six rounds en route to a unanimous-decision win and stopped her other three foes. The DeShong victory was particularly satisfying, since Andrea had handed Christy her only defeat in the toughwomen ranks and her first defeat as a pro.

What captured the public's imagination about Martin was that, unlike most woman fighters, she could PUNCH. Meanwhile, Christy reminisces, "It was unbelievable to fight on the Tyson cards. The hype, the intensity. I still don't believe I was on the cover of *Sports Illustrated*. Sometimes I think it's like one of those deals where you go to an arcade and they take your photo and put it on the cover of a magazine."

But that was then, and now is now. Martin's last knockout was three years ago. She has had only one fight since November 2001. In that bout, she was taken the distance by Mia St. John.

"Against Mia, my timing was terrible," Christy acknowledges. "I hadn't fought in a year. I wasn't in shape. I sparred less than ten rounds. And the fight itself was a huge letdown. The building was empty; it was cold inside. I knew going in that I wasn't going to get paid, and that didn't make me happy. So the fight was like a bad sparring session; that's all."

Still, if Martin has fallen so far that she couldn't hurt Mia St. John (who was knocked woozy by Rolanda Andrews, a 3 and 5 opponent with only one prior knockout), how can she hurt Laila Ali? Shot fighters don't improve with the passage of time.

"The truth is," Christy says, "I've been up there a long time. I've had a pretty good run for my fifteen minutes of fame. I don't have kids yet.

My biological clock is ticking but, so far, I've put my career first. I always tell myself, 'This will be it.' And then another fight comes along. Maybe it's getting near that time."

Meanwhile, if Christy Martin's father is a retired coal miner, Laila Ali's father is the most famous man in the world and arguably the greatest fighter of all time.

Laila is straightfoward and honest. "I don't know why I chose to express myself through boxing," she admits. "Fighting is crazy; I know that. If everything was completely my way, I probably would have chosen something else. But boxing is my calling. And what I feel is, we're all gonna die some day, so I might as well do what I want to do while I'm here. People talk about the advantages I've had in boxing because I'm Muhammad Ali's daughter. Obviously, in a lot of ways, my name helps, but there are disadvantages too. It was hard starting out with so much attention on me. When I first got in the ring, a lot people took it as a joke. Most fighters get to learn with no one watching. If you'd seen my father in the ring when he was twelve, he wouldn't have looked like much either."

"I don't like the celebrity side of it," Laila continues. "Being famous isn't all it's cracked up to be. Everyone wants something from you. You don't know who to trust. But I've never ever wished that I wasn't Muhammad Ali's daughter. Knowing that his blood runs through my veins is very special to me."

Laila's record shows fifteen wins, no losses, and twelve knockouts. Her most hyped fight to date was an eight-round decision victory against Jacqui Frazier two years ago. Her toughest fight was a six-round decision over Kendra Lenhardt in October 2000. "Kendra hit me with a punch that dazed me," Laila remembers. "I thought, 'Oh God, am I going to be knocked out?' But I've been hit hard enough times now in the gym and in fights that I know how to deal with it."

Laila is quick to draw a distinction between her own ring career and that of Jacqui Frazier. "Jacqui was never in the sport to be the best that she can be," she says. "Jacqui was in it to fight me. My goal is to be a well-rounded fighter. I want to continue fighting and keep getting better. I can't say that I'm a great fighter, but I'm a good fighter and I want to be respected as a fighter by people who know boxing. Being the greatest female fighter in the world doesn't mean that much to me because of the level of the sport. It's not like the men. There's not much out there now in women's boxing. There are very few talented women fighters, especially in my weight class, so I can go only so far in my time. The public doesn't really understand boxing, so what the public thinks about my boxing skills isn't that important to me. I want to be respected by people in the boxing game."

"I've worked very hard at this," Laila continues. "Boxing is hard. It's not something you play with. People see my picture in a magazine and say, 'Oh, she's pretty.' They don't realize what it means to be a fighter. You brutalize your body. When I'm training for a fight, I do everything in the gym that the men do, including sparring with men. There's weight-training. I run four to six miles several times a week. I do mountain runs and windsprints simulating two-minute rounds. Before every fight, I ask myself, 'Why am I doing this?' But during the fight, I love it. It's a real rush for me during the fight. And when the fight is over, I can't wait to do it again."

Ironically, the first women's fight that Laila ever saw was Christy Martin versus Deidre Gogarty. And that brings us to Christy versus Laila. Both women say that there's bad blood between them. Each one attributes the hard feelings to the other being disrespectful and having an attitude.

"Laila," says Martin, "is a spoiled stuck-up brat who thinks and acts like she's better than anyone else. She wears a tiara, not a title belt. She was born with a silver spoon in her mouth, and it's time someone like me knocked it out. She ain't her daddy."

Christy's game plan will be based on Jacqui Frazier's fight against Laila. Jacqui was crude, but she kept coming forward and throwing punches. Laila won the first three rounds. Then she got tired and her form began to break down.

"Laila showed heart in that fight," Christy acknowledges. "She took some shots and didn't quit, but that fight should have been scored a draw. I've watched tapes of Laila. She's improved since then, but I still see things I can take advantage of. And Laila is underestimating me. When we're in the ring, she'll see a level of fighter that she's never seen before."

"This is totally a different position for me," Martin concedes. "I've always been the favorite. Now I'm a heavy underdog, but I'm okay with that. Laila will come in confident. She'll try to use her size to push me around and take it to me, and that will suit me fine. Some people say I have no chance. Laila says she'll knock me out in less than five rounds. I'm keeping quiet except to say that I think it will go the distance and I'm going to win."

Laila says considerably more. "I'm not worried about Christy," she declares. "I'm training hard; but to be honest, I don't see the challenge. I couldn't care less if I fought her. But she called me out; the public wants to see it; and we can make money."

"Christy is a brawler," Laila continues. "She's strong and tough, but I don't care much for Christy as a fighter. I don't think she has a lot of skills. She says she'll be aggressive and put pressure on me. But it's hard to be aggressive when you're getting busted up every time you come forward, and she'll have to deal with my movement too. I'm bigger; I'm faster; I'm stronger; I'm more skilled as a boxer. I have a good jab and throw every punch in the book. Christy is slow and short, and any weight she puts on will be fat. It's going to seem silly after the fight. She's too little. She doesn't belong in the ring with me. And I have a mean streak. I'm not a nice fighter. When I'm fighting, I'm not there to be friends; I want to hurt someone. I have killer instincts. I'm there to take you out. I see me knocking Christy out before the end of the fifth round. And to the mainstream public, it will be, 'Wow! Look at that!" But it won't be a big deal to me. I'm supposed to knock her out. I'd beat her even if we were the same size."

That's tough talk. After all, Martin will come to fight, even if she's outsized. And with her experience and heart, Christy might take Laila into waters deeper than any she has been in before. We already know about Christy Martin as a fighter. August 23rd will tell us about Laila. The issue to be resolved isn't, "How much does Martin have left?" It's, "How much does Laila have?" But keep in mind; just winning won't be enough to satisfy Laila Ali. How she wins will be more important in measuring her as a fighter.❏

Joe Mesi was the story at the start of the evening on December 6, 2003. But that changed as the night wore on.

VITALI KLITSCHKO CRASHES JOE MESI'S GARDEN PARTY

December 6th was supposed to be Joe Mesi's night. The regional phenomenon from Buffalo with a 27-0 record and eighteen knockouts in his last eighteen fights was going national.

Boxing needs a feel-good story. HBO needs a new marketable heavyweight. Put the two together and you've got Joe Mesi. One could even imagine an HBO mini-series entitled *Joe Mesi and Boxing: A Love Story.*

Any television drama starts with character development. The 30-year-old Mesi is articulate and outgoing; a perfectionist with a good work ethic. The available evidence points to his being a genuinely nice guy; friendly with an aura that conjures up images of Jay Leno. He engages in extensive community service and actively works to raise public awareness with regard to the need for organ donations. The latter endeavor is in memory of his cousin, Genelle Shanor, who died at age 32 while awaiting a kidney transplant. Several years ago, Mesi took and passed the preliminary examination to become a New York State trooper. For good measure, in 2001, he graduated from Erie Community College. In terms of boxing economics, it doesn't hurt that he's white.

The words that come out of Mesi's mouth sound like a Hollywood screenplay written in a more innocent era . . . "My faith, my family, and my community are the things that are most important to me . . . I love where I was born and raised and plan on living here for my entire life . . . I'm a people person. I like people; I care about people . . . My parents are my biggest heroes. My father is more than my father; he's my best friend. I look forward to having children someday, and my father is the kind of parent I hope to be."

Meanwhile, boxing fans have become familiar with the details of the Joe Mesi story. He was a multi-sport athlete in high school, and the sport he loved most changed with the seasons. He played nose tackle and guard in football. In baseball, he was a catcher. He also wrestled. But there came a time when he was out of school and out of sports, working as a bartender. He ate a lot of chicken wings and his weight ballooned to 290 pounds. Disgusted with his condition, he went to a

PAL gym to hit the heavy-bag and work out a bit. After a few months, he decided to give boxing a try. That's a tough way to lose weight. Most people would opt for aerobics.

Mesi was 21 when he took up boxing. Two years later, in the penultimate bout at the 1996 Olympic Trials, he decisioned Lawrence Clay-Bey. Then came one last fight against Clay-Bey, with the winner going to Atlanta. "I got stopped in the first round," Mesi recalls. "I was on my feet at five, but it was a good stoppage. That's the most hurt I've been so far as an amateur or a pro. I look back on that now and the truth is, I was in way over my head. I'd only been boxing for two years. But I was there."

Mesi settled for being the U.S. super-heavyweight alternate in Atlanta. A year later, he made his pro debut with a second-round knockout of Dwayne Cason at the Apollo Theatre in Harlem. He's now ranked No. 4 amongst the heavyweights by the WBC and No. 9 by the WBA.

"I think I'm good for boxing," Mesi said earlier this month. "And I'm happy to help a sport that has a bad name right now. I know that some people question my chin and heart because I haven't been tested yet in the pros. But look at what I accomplished as an amateur. Most of the guys I faced as I moved ahead in big tournaments had been boxing since they were twelve years old. I'd been boxing for less than two years. My skills weren't nearly as good as theirs. I got as far as I did because of my toughness and heart. And I'm still learning. I'm moving slowly as a professional because I don't have as much experience as a lot of the other guys have. If the critics don't want to believe in me, that's fine; they don't have to. I believe in myself. I'm not trying to be the best fighter ever; just the best that I can be. And I'm a fighter; don't get that wrong. I'm a good fighter; I'm a tough fighter. I can punch and I can take a punch. Don't take me lightly."

Still, as Mesi suggests, there are critics who note that the few recognizable names on his ledger were long past their prime when he fought them. "Joe Mesi," they say, "isn't a serious contender. And he isn't in boxing to win the heavyweight title; only to make as much money as he can without ever being seriously tested. We're always told that the next fight will be the big one, but it never happens. Every fight is against a guy who could never fight or is washed up or is coming up in weight and can't take a punch. That might play in Buffalo, but it wouldn't play in a real fight town where they know boxing like Detroit or Chicago or New York."

Much of this criticism has been aimed at Joe's father. Jack Mesi worked in law enforcement for 37 years; thirty of them as a cop in Buffalo. Jack is Joe's manager and has been accused of being the ultimate stage father, living through and over-protecting his son. Often, he hangs on Joe's shoulder during interviews, occasionally interrupting to add a thought or finish a sentence for him.

"Yes, my dream is unfolding before my eyes," Jack acknowledges. But then he adds, "This is about Joe, not me."

Mesi's December 6th coming-out party in New York was held at Madison Square Garden as the first half of an HBO doubleheader. His opponent was 32-year-old Monte Barrett, who sported a record of 29 wins, 2 losses, and 16 knockouts with decision victories over faded lions like Greg Page, Phil Jackson, and Tim Witherspoon.

"Don't count me out," Barrett warned before the fight. "People say that I'm Joe's biggest test, but I look at Joe as my biggest opportunity."

Mesi said simply, "Monte is the next logical step in my career."

It was the first fight card in the big Garden arena in 26 months and the first of any kind at the Garden since April 2002. Duva Boxing was the lead promoter, and ticket sales were humming until a late-autumn blizzard dumped 12-to-18 inches of snow on the New York metropolitan area. That limited sales to a shade over 12,000 with 10,823 fans actually coming through the turnstiles.

It was an interesting night. In the early rounds, Mesi was the aggressor and consistently beat Barrett to the punch. But by round four, he was frustrated by his opponent's elusiveness and began over-reaching with his blows. Then Barrett made some adjustments, started landing the more telling punches, and became the aggressor. Rounds nine and ten were gut-check time for Mesi, who was visibly tired and had never gone ten rounds before.

There were two knockdowns. In round five, Mesi caught Barrett at the end of a long right hand. In round seven, Barrett returned the favor with a left hook. Neither man was noticeably hurt by the knockdown blows; although it was the first time in Mesi's pro career that he tasted the canvas and, after the fight, his left eye was badly swollen.

Most observers thought that Mesi won rounds one, two, five, and six, while Barrett took the final four stanzas. The swing rounds were three and four. Tom Schreck scored the fight even at 94-94. Arthur Mercante Sr. and Joe Dwyer had it 95-93 and 94-93 in favor of Mesi. This writer scored it 95-93 for Barrett.

"I learned a lot from this," Mesi said afterward. "I could have been better."

But the real learning experience was still to come. Mesi is a huge ticker-seller in Buffalo, and it was assumed that he was the fighter that the Garden crowd most wanted to see.

Not so.

After the conclusion of Mesi-Barrett, Vitali Klitschko and Kirk Johnson made their way to the ring. And suddenly, the upper reaches of Madison Square Garden were awash in a sea of blue-and-yellow Ukrainian flags. Klitschko's fans had braved blizzard conditions; they were out in force; and they were loud.

The 6-foot-7-inch Klitschko had a 32-2 record with 31 knockouts. But the two defeats told more about him than his triumphs. Three years ago, he fought Chris Byrd in Germany and was ahead 89-82, 88-83, 88-83 on the judges' scorecards when a torn rotator cuff in his left shoulder forced him to quit. Then, on June 21st of this year, he was leading Lennox Lewis after six rounds when the fight was stopped because of dangerous cuts around his eye.

Klitschko looked good in losing to Byrd and Lewis. And against Lennox, he showed that he has a chin, which is a valuable commodity in a heavyweight. But one learns to question fighters whose best appearances are in losing efforts. The idea is to win the big ones.

Meanwhile, Johnson has a lot of talent. Prior to meeting Klitschko, the only blots on his record were a 1998 draw against Al Cole (in which three points were deducted for low blows) and a 2002 disqualification against John Ruiz that resulted from similar transgressions. Were it not for low blows, he might have been undefeated a week ago.

But Johnson has a problem. He eats too much. As a young prospect, he fought in the 220s under the nickname "Bubba." Now he looks as though his day job is working as a food-taster for McDonald's. That view was confirmed when Johnson weighed in for Klitschko at 260 pounds. Yes, he was wearing a heavy warm-up suit at the weigh-in, but he was still grossly overweight. When Bubba entered the ring on Saturday night, his love-handles had love-handles and it was suggested that he change his nickname to Blubber.

Klitschko annihilated Johnson in two rounds. No one had walked through Johnson like that before. But then again, Johnson had never come into the ring in such poor shape.

So what comes next?

Mesi-Barrett was the first bout in a three-fight Mesi-HBO contract. The plan had been for an *HBO After Dark* encounter in late-winter followed by an HBO Championship Boxing extravaganza at Buffalo's Ralph Wilson Stadium next summer. Mesi was to step up in class to face a world-class opponent in one or both of those contests. Now the projected level of opposition might drop a bit. At the Garden, Joe showed heart, good hand-speed, and reasonable power in both hands. But if he can't handle the Monte Barretts of boxing more convincingly, it's hard to imagine him moving to the elite heavyweight level, even if today's elite heavyweights aren't so elite. Also, it should be noted that Mesi has been fighting now for nine years; six of them as a pro. He won't be able to cite the inexperience factor much longer.

Meanwhile, at night's end on December 6th, New York was talking about Vitali Klitschko and Joe Mesi was on his way back to Buffalo.❏

For his last show of 2003, Don King offered up a smorgasbord of personalities and fights.

DON KING DOES ATLANTIC CITY

The term "world champion" has a different meaning today than in the past. Boxing now has seventeen weight divisions and four primary world sanctioning organizations. That makes for a lot of belt-holders with relatively few television dates to go around. Don King promotes many of these belt-holders. And with no place to televise their fights as stand-alone bouts, he bundled them together into one pay-per-view extravaganza.

King's December 13th showcase in Atlantic City was entitled "Back-To-Back-To-Back." That was shorthand for "Back-To-Back-To-Back-to-Back-To-Back-To-Back-To-Back-To-Back-To-Back." There was no "must-see" fight on the card. But DK offered the world eight championship bouts including two super-championship fights, one unification championship fight, two mandatory championship fights, one interim championship fight, and two plain old ordinary regular championship fights. Despite the onset of Christmas, there was no partridge in a pear tree.

The key to the event was the blending of personalities involved. Bernard Hopkins, Ricardo Mayorga, Hasim Rahman, and Zab Judah are among the most quotable practitioners of the sweet science. And boxing's most cosmic personality hovered above it all.

On the night of December 11th, King was in Washington, D.C. at Dick Cheney's annual Christmas party, hobnobbing with the vice president and Donald Rumsfeld. Then he stormed Atlantic City, as much a force of nature as the angry windswept waves that crashed down beneath an overcast sky.

"This is the greatest card I've ever put together," King told the media. "It's a night in December that fans will remember. It's a card with no undercard. Every fight is a main event. Every fighter is a star." That was followed by a touch of humility. "This card came together in a spiritual manner," King explained. "I needed God's blessing to make it happen."

And there was patriotic fervor as well. "Hasim Rahman comes from Baltimore," King reminded his listeners. "Baltimore is where Frederick Douglass came from. William Joppy is from Washington, D.C., the home of our great national government. Bernard Hopkins is from Philadelphia, the cradle of American democracy. Zab Judah is from New York, where George Washington was inaugurated. This fight card is about America. My country tis of thee. If you love America, buy these fights. Don't be standing on shore when the ship goes out to sea. Order 'Back-To-Back-To-Back' now."

Listening to King talk, one got the impression that he might single-handedly extricate the United States military from Iraq by inviting all of the troops home to attend his fight card and then simply not send them back overseas.

Meanwhile, it was left to Bob Goodman (director of boxing for Don King Productions) and on-site coordinator Peyton Sher to iron out the details of eight championship fights. "My headaches have headaches," Goodman was quoted as saying. That's because there were four different sanctioning organizations. The unification bouts required a different supervisor and a different set of officials from each organization. All totalled, there would be twenty-four judges and eight referees.

DKP did its job well. On December 13th, Boardwalk Hall was sold out. In the opening bout, Rosendo Alvarez and Victor Burgos fought to a draw in a WBA-IBF light-flyweight unification contest. Then Wayne Braithwaite stopped Luis Pineda in the first round to successfully defend his WBC cruiserweight crown. That was followed by Luis Perez winning a unanimous decision over Felix Machado to successfully defend the IBF junior-bantamweight title. And Travis Simms cold-cocked Alejandro Garcia in the fifth round to capture the WBA super-welterweight championship just after referee Sammy Viruet did (or didn't) shout "break." But the night was dominated by the bouts that featured four of boxing's biggest talkers.

First up on the short list was Zab Judah versus Jaime Rangel for the WBO junior-welterweight crown.

Zab is only 26, but he has been boxing for twenty years under the tutelage of his father. "My father is the lifeline in my body," Zab says. "My father is the spine that holds me up. If he ever stops training me, I'm gone from boxing."

Judah was a much-honored amateur. At age 22, he won the IBF 140-pound title by knocking out Jan Bergman in the fourth round. Five defenses against undistinguished foes followed. Then, on November 3, 2001, he fought Kosta Tszyu in a title-unification bout. In the second round, Zab was knocked down, rose quickly, staggered, and fell. Referee Jay Nady stopped the fight. And Judah, who felt that he should have been given ten seconds from the time he first hit the canvas to compose himself, went berserk. Many people think that Nady stopped the fight prematurely; that the round had come to an end and the ring physician should have been allowed to examine Zab to determine whether he was fit to continue. But Judah went beyond the acceptable in his response, shoving Nady and throwing a corner stool at him.

"I know the way I acted was wrong," Zab acknowledged. "But what the referee did was wrong too. It was like everything I worked for my entire life was gone because Jay Nady took it away from me."

After his loss to Tszyu, Judah won a ten-round decision against Omar Weis. Then, in July of this year, he captured the WBO junior-welter-weight title with a split-decision victory over DeMarcus Corley. Zab has phenomenal physical gifts. He's quick and fast with a lot of charisma. Don King calls him "the hottest little super-hero out there." But the often-heard knock against him is that he's just not tough enough.

Judah approached his bout against Jaime Rangel with confidence. "It's going to be like a bank robbery," he advised. "I'm getting in quick and getting out quick." On fight night, he lived up to his words, whacking out Rangel with a straight left to the temple at the 72-second mark of round one. Still, putting Zab's victory in perspective, while Rangel came into the bout with a 29-4-1 record, only ten of his wins came against opponents who had ever won a fight.

Next up was Hasim Rahman versus John Ruiz for the "interim" WBA heavyweight crown. This was a bout that pitted two former champions, one real and the other alphabet, against one another. Before the fight, it was decreed that if Roy Jones (the current WBA champ) refuses to fight the winner, the "interim" would be removed from the victor's title.

Rahman was one of the more voluble personalities on the Atlantic City card. The former WBC champ has more than a little con in him, but he's inherently likeable. He's also easy to talk with and accepts the fact that the media's role isn't simply to write nice things about him. "I'm not into correcting the media," he said two nights before the fight. "If they get it, they get it. If they don't, they don't."

Rahman has three children, two sons (ages twelve and seven) and a five-year-old daughter. Prior to the Ruiz bout, he brought his family with him to training camp. And his concern for his children appears genuine.

"My household is strict," Rahman acknowledged. "I'm very much in touch with what goes on in my kids' lives. When I was four years old, I walked further on my own than my wife and I allow our son who's twelve to walk on his own now. I watch the company my kids keep. I want to know the parents of their friends. The question I'm teaching the kids to ask before they do something isn't, 'Will Daddy find out?' It's, 'What's right and what's wrong?' When I was a kid, I was very good at getting over on my parents so I know how it's done. No kid is perfect, but I think mine are pretty good. I expect them to be college graduates and successful in life. But as long as they're good people and happy, I'll be satisfied."

John Ruiz is a big strong guy who fights like his public persona: dull, plodding, and straight ahead. Rahman is a big strong guy with some skills. That was expected to give the edge to Rahman, but the fight didn't unfold that way.

In round two, Ruiz wobbled Rahman with a big right hand but failed to effectively follow up. That was as good as it got. The rest of the bout was a long display of grabbing, grappling, clutching, and holding. Ruiz's game plan seemed to consist of using his armpit to hold Rahman in a headlock. Hasim's primary offensive weapon was utilizing his forearm in clinches as an Adam's Apple compressor. Rahman also fought as though there were a clause in his contract that stipulated he couldn't throw more than two jabs a round.

Poor Randy Newman was the referee. His job was akin to separating two crabs that were fornicating on the beach. Meanwhile, for much of the night, the crowd exercised its constitutional right to boo.

The judges' scoring varied considerably (118-110, 116-112 and 115-114), all in favor of Ruiz. This discrepancy might have been due to the judges being too bored to watch the fight. This observer gave it to Ruiz 115-113.

"It was an ugly fight," Rahman admitted afterward. "It was an ugly fight," Ruiz opined.

Great minds think alike. Meanwhile, Hasim hasn't won in 32 months. He is 0-3-1 since defeating Lennox Lewis in April 2001.

Then came the most intriguing fight of the night: Ricardo Mayorga versus Cory Spinks for the unified welterweight crown.

Mayorga, who hails from Nicaragua, was virtually unknown at the start of 2003. But the WBC-WBA champion came to Atlantic City as a hot property by virtue of two wins over Vernon Forrest. Meanwhile, Spinks became the IBF 147-pound titleholder after a victory over Michele Piccirillo of Italy in March.

Spinks has good bloodlines. Father Leon beat Muhammad Ali, and Uncle Michael beat Larry Holmes. But Cory is a light puncher with only ten knockouts in 33 fights, and Don King had made Mayorga-Spinks with a Mayorga victory in mind. Indeed, preliminary contracts for a March 13, 2004, bout between Mayorga and Shane Mosley had already been signed.

Thus, King decreed a state of "Mayorga mania" in Atlantic City and declared, "Ricardo Mayorga has captivated the world with his explosive

style and indominitable courage. He's upsetting the entire boxing establishment. Ricardo is a true revolutionary peoples' champion."

Mayorga, who is known for chain-smoking, beer-drinking, and trash-
talking, lived up to his reputation by proclaiming, "Cory Spinks is a
nothing, a nobody. He doesn't know what he let himself in for when he
took this fight, but he'll find out when I rip his head off. This will be the
biggest purse and the biggest beating that Spinks ever gets. I'm going to
lay him flat on the canvas and dump his championship belt on top of
him. When I rip his head off, he'll realize what a mistake he made.
Instead of lifting weights, he should be doing push-ups because that's
what he'll be doing all night. As soon as I hit him, he'll go down."

Then, for good measure, Mayorga added, "He'll be crying for his
mama." That comment was particularly offensive to Spinks, who still
feels the loss of his mother Zadie May Spinks, who died in 1999.
Apprised of that fact, Mayorga sneered, "He says his family is pretty
much all gone and he doesn't have much else to live for. So I'm going to
reunite him with his whole family, who happen to be upstairs with our
Lord, Jesus Christ. I'll stay here with my family that's alive and well."

In other sports, Mayorga's trash-talking would have earned a summons to the commissioner's office. In boxing, it was treated like a breath
of fresh air. Meanwhile, Spinks said simply, "This will be my coming-out
party. Skills will be the difference. I can sit down and bang, or I can be
smart and box. I'm prepared to deal with anything he brings. Mayorga
is in for a rude awakening. He's just a tough rugged fighter. I think they
overrate him. He hasn't gotten any better. His head has gotten bigger;
that's all. They call boxing an art. Come December 13th, I'm going to
paint me a beautiful picture."

And legendary ring great Roberto Duran sounded a further note of
caution. "I've only seen Mayorga fight once," Duran offered shortly
before the weigh-in. "He didn't seem as good as people say he is. He
doesn't know how to box."

The Spinks plan was to outwork and outbox Mayorga. His lack of
power allowed the Nicaraguan to fight with abandon, and Ricardo was
the aggressor throughout. But Mayorga often fights on the edge of the
rules and it cost him. In round five, referee Tony Orlando deducted a
point for hitting after the bell. In round eleven, he took away another
point for holding and hitting Spinks on the back of the head.

Meanwhile, Spinks fought within himself, jabbing, circling, staying
in the center of the ring, and countering. He also received a big break;
two of them actually. In round eleven, Spinks went to the canvas twice,
and the second time, he appeared to have gone down intentionally to
extricate himself from a disadvantageous position. That's the equivalent

of taking a knee and should have been ruled a knockdown, but Orlando decreed that the incident was a slip. Then, in round twelve, Spinks visited the canvas again, apparently from a punch. But again, Orlando declined to call a knockdown. The earlier-referenced point deductions were appropriate. The missed knockdown in the twelfth round wasn't. Had that knockdown been called, it would have changed the outcome of the fight.

Arthur Ellison scored the bout a draw at 114-114. Eugene Grant leaned toward Spinks 114-112. John Keane had it 117-110 for Spinks. This writer scored it narrowly for Mayorga. Regardless, at the close of the fight, the "Spinks Jinks" was alive and well again and Cory's daddy was smiling.

Leon Spinks might be the saddest of all former heavyweight champions. He walks around looking as though he has been punched in the head by life. But December 13th was a good night for Leon. And it's worth noting that, whatever else happens, the record book will always show that he beat Muhammad Ali in 1978 to become the undisputed heavyweight champion of the world.

Mayorga-Spinks drained much of the energy from the crowd. The first bout had begun shortly after 5:00 p.m. and it was now midnight. Still, one fight remained; Bernard Hopkins versus William Joppy for the unified middleweight championship.`

Hopkins is one of boxing's great warriors but has little drawing power. This was a "mandatory" title defense that had gone to a purse bid. Thus, Bernard was fighting for $375,000 while Joppy received $125,000.

Perhaps the most interesting sub-plot surrounding the fight involved Hopkins's relationship with Bouie Fisher. Fisher trained Bernard from his second pro fight through his February 2002 victory over Carl Daniels. Then there was a falling out, and Bouie sued The Executioner for his rightful share of back purses.

"At one time, Bernard was like family to me," Fisher said at the time. "But my family has been raised and taught to be respectful and kind to other people; and Bernard just isn't that way. I always had it in the back of my mind that Bernard could be like this, but I didn't know it would be this bad. Bernard thinks money is everything. And money is good to have. You need it, but it's not everything. Right and wrong matter. Right is right, and wrong is wrong. And when you do wrong to other people and then try to justify what you've done, you wind up lying because the truth won't help you."

Meanwhile, Hopkins declared on an *ESPN2 Friday Night Fights* telecast that one of Bouie's sons, James Fisher, was "a bum who has never worked and has never wanted to work."

In response, Bouie observed, "I've had my glory. I've seen my children grow to be good men and women. I raised eight children in the middle of the ghetto and didn't have two hours of trouble with any of them. All my children finished high school and have good jobs. Four of them graduated from college. One of my daughters has been voted 'outstanding teacher of the year' two times at her high school. Another works with retarded children. James went to college and served in the United States Air Force. He has worked in our family's transmission shop and as a construction worker and salesman. Now I'm sending my grandchildren to college. So Bernard has his place in history, and I have a place in my family history."

Then, last month, Hopkins and Fisher reunited. "Every now and then, people can settle their differences," Bernard told the media.

"I always said Bernard was another son to me," Fisher added. "We were separated a little over a year ago and for one of his fights. But we're back together again, and it feels like I've reunited with a member of my own family."

Meanwhile, bad blood was brewing between Hopkins and Joppy. After fireworks between their supporters at a pre-fight kick-off press conference in New York, there was a pushing match between the fighters themselves at a press conference in Washington, D.C. Joppy was at the podium; Hopkins tried to take the microphone from him, and William gave Bernard a hard two-handed shove. That led Don King, who was hearing cash registers ring from enhanced pay-per-view buys, to declare, "It was a scintillatingly beautiful sight. There was hostility by geometric proportions."

Hopkins was more succinct in his comments. "This is a very simple fight to analyze," he prophesied. "Come Monday, December 15th, Joppy will have a squeegee in his hand and be on the twenty-eighth floor of some building doing windows."

Joppy was more optimistic about his fate. "I've been watching Bernard Hopkins press conferences for a while," he noted. "Bernard Hopkins is a coward who talks tough. He likes to dictate things; but as soon as you bring it back to him, he doesn't know how to act. He's a bully. I wasn't a bully growing up, but I like to bully bullies. Hopkins is a basic fighter, just a brawler," Joppy continued. "He doesn't have the boxing skills to touch me. With my natural ability I'm going to make him look like he doesn't belong in the ring with me. You're going to be able to count on one hand how many times he hits me."

At the final pre-fight press conference, Joppy revised his estimate upward, saying, "On two hands, you'll be able to count the number of times he hits me." Then, on Saturday night, William entered the ring to face reality.

Hopkins versus Joppy reduced boxing to its brutal essence. The bell for round one rang sixty seconds after midnight. And from that moment on, Hopkins and Joppy were predator and prey. Bernard methodically broke his opponent down and administered a merciless brutal beating. Joppy's corner should have stopped the fight after the tenth round, and so should referee Earl Morton. It was an extraordinary tribute to William's courage that he never went down. The judges scored it 119-108, 119-109, and 118-109. After the fight, Joppy's face was hideous. No part of his features looked right. Everything was lumpy, bruised, discolored, and swollen. And he took a horrible beating to the body too. Fighting Bernard Hopkins for $125,000 is a hard way to earn a living.

It was an exhausting night, almost eight hours of boxing. And when it was done, the victors planned for the future.

Zab Judah wants to fight Kosta Tszyu again. "There are still a lot of unanswered questions between us," Zab said. "It's two years old now, but what happened still bothers me. The fans were cheated. They weren't given a chance to see the real Kostya Tszyu against Zab Judah fight."

But in the next breath, Zab acknowledged, "I don't think he'll fight me. He's thirty-four; I'm twenty-six. He's slowing down; I'm getting better. Kosta Tszyu has everything to lose and nothing to gain if we fight again. For him to fight Zab Judah now would be a dumb move on his part."

"The big fight I'd like to make next is Arturo Gatti or Ricky Hatton," Judah continued. "They're talking about Floyd Mayweather coming up in weight to fight me, but the friendship between us is too strong to make that deal unless the money is really really big."

A Zab Judah title-unification bout against Vivian Harris is more likely. Or he could go up in weight to face Cory Spinks.

John Ruiz will become the WBA heavyweight belt-holder again if Roy Jones vacates the crown as expected. Ruiz might (or might not) be obligated to make an immediate mandatory title defense. If so, the WBA could massage its rules and rankings to require a bout against Vitali Klitschko, Wladimir Klitschko, Corrie Sanders, Joe Mesi, or David Tua. Don King could mastermind Ruiz against Fres Oquendo in Puerto Rico or Ruiz against Chris Byrd in an arena the size of a small cocktail lounge. James Toney appears to be out of the picture. Ruiz versus Lennox Lewis is an extremely long longshot. And of course, there's always the Mike Tyson wild card.

Suffice it to say for the moment that people now have a bit more respect for Roy Jones's performance against Ruiz.

Cory Spinks upset boxing's apple-cart when he upset Mayorga. The sweet science keeps looking for the next marketable mega-star between 147 and 154 pounds, but things can't get settled. Shane Mosley devalued Oscar De La Hoya twice. Vernon Forrest devalued Mosley twice. Ricardo Mayorga devalued Forrest twice. Now Spinks has devalued Mayorga.

There will be a lot of pressure on Spinks to fight an immediate rematch against Mayorga. Vernon Forrest and Antonio Margarito could also wind up in the mix. Zab Judah, Shane Mosley, and Winky Wright are also possibilities.

And last, but certainly not least, there's Bernard Hopkins. "I won't deny running my mouth," Bernard acknowledged. "But one thing nobody can deny is that I can fight my ass off. Love me or hate me; you've got to admit, I do my job."

Love him or hate him, one also has to admit that Hopkins is building an impressive legacy. He has now had seventeen successful title defenses. His last loss was to Roy Jones in 1993. He will be 39 years old in January. And nobody on the scene today who's his own size will beat him except Father Time.

"If I ain't loved, that's fine," Hopkins raged. "I don't need nobody in the media to kiss my ass or tell me they love me. And I don't need no television people giving me their phony line of shit. Just pay me and respect what I've done."

But Bernard has a problem. He can't make big money without a big-name opponent. He stirs passions within the boxing community, but the public-at-large doesn't know or care about him.

Also, for all his talk about going in tough, Hopkins has avoided the best available competition since beating Felix Trinidad and has settled for bouts against Carl Daniels, Morrade Hakkar, and William Joppy. Now, in all likelihood, his next big fight will be against Don King.

Three years ago, Hopkins signed a contract with Don King Productions to get into King's middleweight championship tournament. "I slept with the devil to get to where I am today," he explained after beating Trinidad. "It was the right choice."

But since then, Bernard has been an unhappy camper. "It's not like you go in and tell Don what you want and that's what you have when you leave," he complained recently. "Don's idea of being reasonable is, 'Yes, sir, boss . . . No, sir, boss . . . Thank you, boss.'"

Hopkins says that he's planning to establish his own promotional company, EX Promotions. "It cost me a lot of money to learn how to play this game," he explains. "Now I'm going to start making some of it back. All I've ever needed for big fights to happen for me is the leverage that comes with independence; the leverage not to have to pay a middleman before I get paid. I'm a free agent come January 24th, and that's no secret. My time is up. It's over; I'm paroled. As of next month, I'm gonna do it the Old Blue Eyes way—my way."

King, in turn, has proclaimed his loyalty to Hopkins with the pledge, "I'm sticking with Bernard irrespective of what anyone might say or do."

Translation: When Hopkins tries to opt out of his contract with King next month, look for a lawsuit.

Meanwhile, it should be said in closing that December 13th was a bad night for Don King. He lost big with Hasim Rahman (who had more money-making potential than John Ruiz) and bigger with Ricardo Mayorga. Those two decisions were both surprises. In the old days, fighters favored by Don King usually won the close ones.❑

When I was in Atlantic City for Don King's December 13th card, I also had the opportunity to talk with Roberto Duran.

ROBERTO DURAN REMEMBERS MADISON SQUARE GARDEN

Roberto Duran was born in El Chorrillo, Panama, on June 16, 1951, and made his professional debut as a boxer at age sixteen. His first 24 fights were in Panama or Mexico. Then he traveled to New York and fought Benny Huertas on September 13, 1971. More on that later.

Duran is arguably the greatest lightweight of all time. In his first 74 fights, "Manos de Pietro" (Hands of Stone) won 73 times against a single loss.

"Do you want to know how great Roberto Duran was?" asks Donald Turner, who trained Evander Holyfield and Larry Holmes. "Stevie Wonder could have trained Roberto Duran."

By the time an automobile accident forced his retirement from boxing last year, Duran had fought in five different decades. His ring career touched on the terms of eight presidents of the United States, beginning with Lyndon Johnson and ending with George W. Bush.

The world is familiar with the milestones of Duran's career. He won the lightweight title with a thirteenth-round knockout of Ken Buchanan on June 26, 1972. Eight years later, he went up in weight and handed Sugar Ray Leonard the first loss of his career, capturing Leonard's welterweight crown over fifteen hard-fought rounds. Then, in their November 25, 1980, rematch, Duran quit in the eighth round, uttering the infamous words, "No mas." It was only the second loss of his career, but he was never the same fighter again. From that point on, his record consisted of 31 victories against 15 defeats.

Many theories abound as to why Duran quit against Leonard. Roberto says that he'll carry the reason to his grave. There was vindication of sorts when he brutalized Davey Moore on June 16, 1983, to capture the WBA version of the junior-middleweight title. But championships were becoming fragmented by then due to the proliferation of world sanctioning organizations. And Duran's next two bouts resulted in losses. On November 10, 1983, he fought heroically but lost a decision to middleweight champion Marvin Hagler. Then he went back to challenge Thomas Hearns at 154 pounds and was annihilated in two rounds.

Duran's last gasp of greatness came on February 24, 1989, when he decisioned Iran Barkley to capture the WBC middleweight title. Nine months later, he lost his WBC belt to Sugar Ray Leonard in a dreary twelve-round rematch between over-the-hill boxers.

Young people today don't appreciate Roberto Duran. They know him only as a bloated fighter who entered the ring sporadically during the 1990s and beat just one world-class opponent (Iran Barkley) subsequent to 1983. But Duran in the 1970s brought a special blend of skill and savagery to boxing. And during the course of his career, he fought seven times at Madison Square Garden.

Duran claimed the first and next-to-last championships of his career at the Garden with his victories over Buchanan and Moore. MSG was also the site of the only loss in his first 74 fights: a ten-round verdict in favor of Esteban DeJesus in a 1972 non-title bout. Duran avenged that loss by knockout in 1974 and then again in 1978.

Adolfo Viruet, Monroe Brooks, and Carlos Palomino also lost to Duran at the Garden. But the MSG appearance that Roberto remembers most fondly was his first, when he knocked out Benny Huertas in one round.

"Madison Square Garden was the greatest place in the world to me," Duran said in Atlantic City, reminiscing about that long-ago time. "I was staying in the Hotel Pennsylvania. When the taxi took me there, we passed the Garden and I shouted at the driver, 'Stop! Stop! I want to see the Garden.' The driver told me, 'Take it easy. The hotel is only one block from here.' When the taxi stopped, I didn't even check into the hotel. I went right to the Garden and stared at it. I don't remember if it was cold or hot, day or night. There were a lot of people walking around me; no one knew who I was. And I told myself, 'Someday, when I stand here, everyone will know who I am.' Waiting for the day of the fight, I sat in my hotel room and just looked out the window at the Garden. Finally, the fight came and, in the dressing room, I was jumping around. People asked me, 'Are you nervous?' I told them, 'No, I want to go out and fight so I can see the inside of the Garden.' When the time came and I walked out of my dressing room and saw the arena, I couldn't believe it. It was like being in church for me. And I said to myself, 'This is good. Not everyone can fight in the Garden.'"❏

DON KING AND THE HEAVYWEIGHT ROLLERCOASTER

When Lennox Lewis retired earlier this year, it triggered a feeding frenzy that will continue into the foreseeable future. The heavyweight championship is a profitable commodity. As Ed Fitzgerald noted a half-century ago, "In the right hands, it generates money almost as fast as the United States Mint."

As for who would step into the void created by Lewis's departure, even before the first punches were thrown, a lot of people were conceding the belts to Vitali and Wladimir Klitschko.

The Klitschkos are remarkable individuals. Each has a Ph.D. in sports science from the University of Kiev. Their father was an officer in the Soviet Red Army; their mother, a school teacher. Vitali is 32 and compiled a 195-15 record as an amateur. He turned pro in 1996 and, at the time of Lewis's retirement, was 33-2 with 32 knockouts. Wladimir is 28. He won a gold medal in the super-heavyweight division at the 1996 Olympics and began his pro career with 42 wins, 2 losses, and 39 KOs.

Both Klitschko brothers are personable and charming. They now live in Los Angeles. Each speaks four languages: Ukrainian, Russian, German, and English. "But I'm married," Vitali noted, "so I go home to my wife and children and speak Russian. Wladimir is out meeting women, so his English is better."

In the wake of Lewis's retirement, the Klitschkos were not shy about voicing their aspirations.

"We have a dream to be world champions at the same time," Vitali stated. "After that, we have the goal to take the four most important world titles in the Klitschko family."

"This is about the heavyweight world title," Wladimir added. "This is about the story that we want to do. It has never been done in boxing history with two brothers holding the title at the same time. It is not easy and we know it, but we are ready to do it and we are on the way. Hopefully we get it."

One believer was Lewis's former trainer, Emanuel Steward, who began working with the Klitschkos as soon as the opportunity presented itself.

"I have always admired the Klitschkos because for such big men they have unbelievable coordination and they take their boxing very seriously," Steward said. "And I've never been in a camp where there's more hard work and serious training. The intensity that they bring to boxing combined with their size and skill is going to make it very difficult for anyone to beat them."

Not everyone agreed. Heavyweight contender James Toney grumbled, "It's like they [HBO] want a white heavyweight champ so bad, they're just trying to give these guys the belts."

One can argue about motives, but certainly HBO was planning to ride the Klitschkos. Gazing into the future, one insider at the cable giant declared, "Outside of Mike Tyson, the Klitschkos are the most marketable heavyweights in the world. How can we go wrong with four Klitschko title fights a year?"

Then came a two-week span starting on April 10th when all four heavyweight championship belts were up for grabs. And as one might expect, Don King was in the thick of it.

First up was Wladimir Klitschko against Lamon Brewster at Mandalay Bay in Las Vegas for the WBO crown. Brewster was in line for a title shot by virtue of his association with King, who promoted the bout.

Brewster's primary asset seems to be his inherently likeable personality. "When I was young, I tried everything other than being a fighter," he conceded shortly before the fight. "I'm not doing this because I want to. I'm doing it because I have to. I'm fighting to get out of boxing. I don't have a job at Microsoft with a check coming in every week. I'd like it if I could go to a big football game once a year and have everybody there give me five dollars. If I could make that happen, I wouldn't be here."

"I don't think I'm special," Brewster continued. "I'm just a good trier. I got determination; I got will; and above all, I got faith. What man gets up every morning and says he wants to be a fighter and have people hit him and maybe get knocked out? It has to be something in your spirit. I mean, you know you're gonna get hit."

Brewster said all the right things with regard to facing Klitschko. "I'm going to test him at every level," he claimed. "I'm going to test his skill; I'm going to test his body; and I'm going to test his spirit. I'm not going to say things where I'm stepping on other fighters that he's fought. But true American fighters, we fight. We move our head. We take punches and we give them back. When he hits me, he can expect to get hit back with everything I got, every second of every round. If his hand is raised at the end, it won't be luck. It will be because he's the better fighter."

Few members of the boxing intelligentsia took Brewster seriously as a threat to the Ukrainian giant. But Lamon took himself seriously, and it was his mindset that mattered. "I've done everything possible to get ready to win this fight," he said. "Now it's time to take the blanks out of the gun and put the real bullets in. I feel like the spirits of people who boxed before me are in me. And when I'm done, I hope my spirit carries on to the next generation."

Then Brewster voiced a refrain he had repeated often during the week. "Klitschko might think he's in for an easy night, but I plan on changing his mind. When the rabbit's got the gun, do you still want to hunt?"

In boxing, once the bell for round one rings, everything is up for grabs.

Despite his superior athletic ability, Klitschko looked like a fighter between styles. He fought with his feet wide apart; held on awkwardly when Brewster got inside; and bailed out whenever Lamon threw punches. Still, Wladimir was able to control the early rounds with his jab. Then, in round four, he landed a huge right hand that put Brewster on the canvas. Lamon rose from the first knockdown of his career and barely finished the round on his feet.

At the start of round five, Brewster looked like a man walking in waist-high water, but Klitschko was moving as though his legs were set in concrete. Then Lamon landed a solid left hook; referee Robert Byrd gave Klitschko an eight-count; the fight resumed, and Klitschko collapsed at the bell.

Lamon Brewster was the new WBO heavyweight champion.

Then the scene moved to New York for two more heavyweight "title" fights: John Ruiz versus Fres Oquendo (WBA) and Chris Byrd versus Andrew Golota (IBF). In reality, both titles were tainted. Ruiz got his by default when Roy Jones relinquished the WBA belt rather than fight a meaningless rematch against the man he'd thoroughly dominated in March 2003. And Byrd should have been on the losing end of the judges' scorecards in his bout against Fres Oquendo last September. Still, King was in his glory. Brewster's victory had given him control of the WBO crown, while the WBA and IBF titles were already in his pocket.

Don King fills up a room with his voice and his physical presence. With a Don King show, even if the fights are dull, the action that surrounds them is entertaining. Thus, DK began the final pre-fight press conference at Madison Square Garden by extolling Lamon Brewster's virtues and his own success: "It's great to be number one for three decades . . . HBO did such a great job of building up the Klitschkos that they started to believe their own press releases . . . Lamon Brewster is a black Rocky . . . I love talking. I'm so happy."

Where his upcoming fights were concerned, King tried to build enthusiasm for Ruiz-Oquendo. "It's not just Puerto Rico that's excited," he told the assembled media. "All of Latin America is talking about this fight. They'll be streaming across the borders to see it."

But no one except the Ruiz and Oquendo camps seemed to care about the WBA title fight. Byrd-Golota was the ticket-seller and also a source of controversy.

Golota's history is unsavory and well known. On July 11, 1996, he was disqualified for repeated low blows in a fight against Riddick Bowe at Madison Square Garden. A riot followed. Five months later in Atlantic City, the two men met in the ring again. Again, Golota was well ahead going into the late rounds. And again, he was disqualified for deliberately fouling.

Golota also quit after two rounds in an October 2000 fight against Mike Tyson and has bitten two opponents. An argument can be made that his fights should be officiated like NBA basketball games. That is, with three referees: one on either side of the fighters and a third moving around the ring.

Also, as of early March, Golota wasn't ranked by the IBF among its top fifteen heavyweights, a prerequisite to fighting for the IBF crown. Then, on March 13th, the IBF released its new ratings. Lo and behold, Golota was number fifteen. That led to a storm of protest over the besmirching of the cherished IBF crown. However, the controversy seemed a bit much given the fact that, at present, the IBF championship isn't a real heavyweight title. And let's not forget some of the championship-bout opponents for Joe Frazier (Terry Daniels and Ron Stander), George Foreman (Jose Roman), Larry Holmes (Lorenzo Zanon, Leroy Jones, Lucien Rodriguez, and Scott Frank), and Muhammad Ali (Brian London, Jean Pierre Coopman, and Richard Dunn).

Needless to say, King played on the controversy. After labeling Golota "the white Mike Tyson," he solemnly declared, "I must confess, I didn't make this fight. God made it. I thought that Chris Byrd would be fighting Derrick Jefferson, but Derrick got cut in his last fight. Right after that, I was staring at the clouds in despair when a bright religious light shone down from heaven and a voice said unto me, 'Put Chris Byrd in against Andrew Golota.' And that moved me deeply," King continued, "because coincidentially, Andrew had just come to me and confessed his sins and said he had been vilified, castigated, and humiliated, and that he had repented. And I said to myself, 'Give the white fighter a break.' So I signed Andrew and absolved him of all his sins. I know he had some wayward ways, but I love all people, and I know what it's like to suffer the slings and arrows of discrimination and be judged by people on the basis of perceived past wrongdoing rather than my present state. Nothing could be more fitting in this Holy month of April, the time of The Resurrection, than to resurrect the career of Andrew Golota."

In other words, God intervened and, through His grace, spared boxing fans the agony of Chris Byrd versus Derrick Jefferson. But would Golota go psycho in the ring again?

"Andrew has promised me that he'll fight fair and square," King assured the media. "And I promise you that Andrew will not hit Chris Byrd in the testicles. How do you prevent that from happening?" King asked rhetorically. And then he answered his own question. "You prevent that from happening by talking to Andrew and telling him to visualize that Chris Byrd's testicles have been taken out of his scrotum and are now in his chest."

And there was one more precaution as reported by Golota: "Don said to me, 'If you do that shit again, you don't get paid.'"

In the end, a surprisingly large crowd of 15,195 filed into Madison Square Garden. Then came the fights.

Ruiz-Oquendo was probably the most boring heavyweight "title" fight in boxing history and as bad as any bout that this observer has ever seen. Words like "dreadful", "stultifying", and "horrendous" come to mind, but it was worse than that. Fifty-nine seconds into round one, the crowd began to boo. Whistles and catcalls were heard at the two-minute mark. That was followed later in the fight by chants of "bullshit" and "Don King sucks." For ten rounds, all either fighter did was jab and hold. There wasn't one moment of excitement. Then, late in round eleven, Ruiz staggered Oquendo and drove him to the ropes with a right hand followed by a flurry of punches, and referee Wayne Kelly stopped the fight. The stoppage was premature, but Kelly should be forgiven since it spared fans three more minutes of agony. Also, it should be noted that Ruiz was going to win anyway. After ten rounds, he was ahead on the judges' scorecards 96-94, 96-94, 95-95; and round eleven had been a good round for him.

As for Byrd versus Golota, the pre-fight fear was that Andrew would be frustrated by his foe's elusiveness and resort to low blows. Lennox Lewis said as much when he opined, "Golota will be boxing against a guy who's going to frustrate him, and he doesn't react well to being frustrated."

But Evander Holyfield sounded a different note. "This is a dangerous fight for Byrd," the Real Deal observed. "Golota doesn't like pressure. That's the way to beat him; especially since, when you hit him, he freezes. But Byrd isn't the kind of fighter who applies pressure, and Golota's losses were against big guys or big punchers."

Golota isn't as good as he once was. But in recent bouts, Byrd seems to have lost some of his handspeed and quickness. As their fight progressed, Golota realized that his opponent couldn't hurt him, and that gave him confidence. Also, while Byrd had the faster hands, he consistently let Golota get off first.

Byrd spent most of the fight on the ropes, making Golota miss but rarely countering with much in return. In boxing, it's not enough just to avoid blows. You have to hit the other guy to win. The three judges scored the bout 115-113 Byrd, 115-113 Golota, and 114-114 even. This writer gave it to Golota by a point, but few observers quarreled with the draw.

After that, it was on to the Staples Center in Los Angeles for Vitali Klitschko versus Corrie Sanders for the vacant WBC crown. This one was promoted by Klaus Peter Kohl and K2 Promotions. And it was a grudge match of sorts, since Sanders had knocked out Wladimir Klitschko last year. That was a surprise, since Corrie had been ready to retire at age thirty-seven after working as a golf pro in his native South Africa and fighting only twice in the preceding two years.

Vitali came into the fight against Sanders as the most likely successor to Lennox Lewis, in large part because of his effort against the champion last June, when he gave the out-of-shape Lewis all he could handle before succumbing to cuts after six rounds. In the aftermath of that fight, many commentators dwelled on the fact that Klitschko was ahead on the judges' scorecards 58-56 when the bout ended. But as Lennox noted, "I didn't hug him to give him those cuts. I punched him."

In the days leading up to the fight, Sanders seemed like a man ready to retire with one foot already out the door. "Vitali is a good fighter," he said. "But I believe I'm better." Then, in the next breath, he added, "As long as I keep winning, I will probably be in the ring. But obviously, age is not on my side so the time may come to call it a day. Either way, whatever happens, I can now say I've had a nice career."

Klitschko, for his part, declared, "This fight is very important for me for two reasons. It's for a world title and also for Wladimir. I don't want to make the same mistake made by my brother. I don't want to underestimate Corrie Sanders. He is a very tough fighter. He has speed, power, and a hard punch."

But in truth, Sanders had fought only five rounds in the previous four years. And except for a knockout loss to Hasim Rahman, he had gone past the second round only once since 1997. His credibility was based almost entirely on his having knocked out Wladimir Klitschko; a credential that lost its luster after Wladimir was stopped by Lamon Brewster.

When D-Day arrived, Sanders was overweight and unprepared to fight four hard rounds, let alone twelve. Klitschko was in better shape but looked like a lumbering version of Jess Willard in old fight films. The result was an inartistic, sometimes entertaining brawl during which Vitali battered his foe until referee Jon Schorle stopped it in the eighth round without either man going down. Sanders showed courage but that's about all, as he was hit repeatedly with right hands and landed only six punches per round. Klitschko also tired badly at the end, which lent credence to the view that Lennox would have knocked him out had their fight not been stopped on cuts after six rounds.

So where do the past few weeks leave boxing?

For starters, there's a credibility gap in the heavyweight division and the heavyweight throne is now vacant.

There are two kinds of champions in the sweet science: alphabet-soup and real ones. At the moment, there's no real heavyweight champion and talk to the contrary is nonsense.

WBC titleholder Vitali Klitschko is champion of the Klitschko family but not of the world. He's big, strong, well-motivated, and probably the best of today's heavyweights. But at present, his credentials are based largely on a fight that he lost. Claims that Vitali is the "lineal" champion are spurious. Yes, the belt that Lewis relinquished last was the WBC title; but the WBC is no more credible than any of the other alphabet-soup organizations. If Vitali had fought Corrie Sanders for the WBO title and Juan Carlos Gomez fought Joe Mesi for the WBC crown, would the winner of Gomez-Mesi have been the lineal champion? Not at all.

WBA titleholder John Ruiz was thoroughly dominated by Roy Jones. IBF titleholder Chris Byrd lost his last two fights in the ring, if not on the judges' scorecards. WBO titleholder Lamon Brewster has shown no signs of greatness. It's a nice group of guys, but none of them rate recognition as the true heavyweight champion.

And more significantly, the public doesn't care. John Ruiz acknowledged as much when he recently declared, "People are losing their faith in the heavyweight division. Nobody knows who the champions are. Nobody knows who's coming up. Everyone used to know who was fighting for the title. Now you mention the name and everyone says, who the hell is that?"

Nor is there much hope for the immediate future.

A year ago, Wladimir Klitschko had dominated Chris Byrd, Jameel McCline and Ray Mercer and was being touted as the next great heavyweight. Now he's being mocked as "a white Michael Grant."

As for the rest of the heavyweight division—

Vitali Klitschko has a mandatory defense coming up against Joe Mesi. But Mesi is expected to retire because of head injuries, and Juan Carlos Gomez is next in line. Yuk!

John Ruiz faces a mandatory challenge in the form of a rematch against Hasim Rahman. Yuk again.

King has talked about a second fight between Chris Byrd and Andrew Golota. But the IBF has named Jameel McCline as the "leading available" mandatory challenger for Byrd and notified the fighters' respective camps that the fight must take place. McCline, one might recall, was previously discredited by Wladimir Klitschko.

Lamon Brewster would like to fight Mike Tyson, but that would require a settlement of the lawsuit between King and Tyson. Meanwhile, the WBO has ordered Brewster to face James Toney within 120 days or forfeit his title. Toney is recovering from surgery and says he'll be ready to fight in August.

There is, of course, no guarantee that any of the above-mentioned mandatory defenses will occur. King says that he wants to take the four current beltholders and match them in a heavyweight elimination tournament. But that won't happen unless Vitali Klitschko and Klaus Peter Kohl are willing to give King options, because DK isn't about to risk what he perceives to be his rightful share of the heavyweight crown. Meanwhile, Klitschko has said that he doesn't want to be tied promotionally to King.

In other words, the heavyweight division is up for grabs.

Parity might work in the National Football League. In boxing, it's not good. Still, as Chris Byrd noted recently, "Lennox is gone, and people have to get used to that." Thus, for the moment, there's one star in the heavyweight division and his name is Don King.

King thrives on situations like this. The two heavyweights he covets most are Mike Tyson and Vitali Klitschko. At present, he doesn't have either of them. But with three belts and the deft use of smoke and mirrors, DK will rule the heavyweight division for the forseeable future.

King's critics say that fighters sign with him out of desperation or to cheat their way to the top. King counters, "I'm in the hope business. A lot of these guys never would have had a chance if it weren't for me. These are the untouchables; the persona non gratas. I reach out and heal them."

Right now, the Mother Theresa of boxing is in the process of gathering as many toys as possible. Young fighters like Kali Meehan and Owen Beck are being groomed as cannon fodder. And at the other end of the spectrum, King just re-signed Evander Holyfield, who acknowledged, "I know I said I wouldn't sign with Don again, but it's a business decision. I can fight regular guys or I can sign with Don and fight for a title."

Look for King to keep those titles fragmented for a while. That way, as devalued as they might be, he'll control three of them. Lamon Brewster puts the matter in perspective when he acknowledges, "We're all pawns on a chess board." And King himself declares, "Like me or dislike me, I'm still here."

So sit back and enjoy the show. Don King has been on top for three decades and there's no end in sight.❏

Wladimir Klitschko and his attorneys came across as poor losers in the aftermath of Klitschko's loss to Lamon Brewster.

BOXING ISN'T EASILY EMBARRASSED BUT ...

Requesting that the United States Government conduct an investigation is serious business. Before doing so, one should, at the very least, get the facts straight.

After Wladimir Klitschko's loss to Lamon Brewster, an attorney sent a letter to the World Boxing Organization on his behalf expressing concern about "the possibility of foul play" and suggesting that an immediate WBO-mandated rematch was in order. Cutman Joe Souza was dismissed, and conspiracy theorists had a field day with rumors about foreign substances in Vaseline and switched water bottles. One report went so far as to claim that Wladimir's blood sugar level after the fight was "three to four times" normal levels. That was untrue. "Normal" is 130. Wladimir's blood sugar count was 240, which is high but explainable by virtue of body chemistry and the fact that doctors put an IV-line in him on the way to the hospital after he was knocked out.

Wladimir himself added fuel to the fire when he declared, "I have absolutely no explanation why I became so weak during the fight. From the middle of the first round, I was totally exhausted. My legs felt like rubber. I did not have the feeling as if I punched myself out. The feeling was much much different. I know fighters can punch themselves out and overpace themselves, but that doesn't happen in the first round."

But Klitschko didn't looked drugged when he put Brewster on queer street with a big right hand in round four. Rather, Wladimir appeared to fall apart in the manner of Shannon Briggs against Darroll Wilson.

Power matters in boxing, but not as much as having a chin. Wladimir has now been stopped by Ross Puritty, Corrie Sanders and Lamon Brewster, and the word on him is "no stamina, weak chin." Not a good combination for a fighter. Also, state of mind is huge for a boxer. A fighter can be physically superior and more skilled than his opponent. But if he's intimidated, he forfeits that edge. And some fighters can't seem to come back in a fight. Once they get hurt, they stay hurt.

Thus, Don King's gleeful rant. "The Klitschkos are complainers," DK chortled after Brewster's knockout triumph. "They complained after

Lennox Lewis beat Vitali, and they complained after Lamon Brewster
beat Wladimir. But it wasn't the water that Wladimir drank. It wasn't the
soup he ate. It wasn't the Vaseline they put on his face or the deodorant
he used under his arms. It was Lamon Brewster."

Then, on May 5th, Judd Burstein (yet another lawyer retained by
Klitschko) sent a letter to the United States Attorney for the District of
Nevada. In that latter, Burstein declared, "I am writing to respectfully
request that your office conduct an investigation into the highly suspicious events surrounding Mr. Klitschko's April 10, 2004, Las Vegas bout
against Lamon Brewster, and the equally suspicious frustration of Mr.
Klitschko's subsequent efforts to ascertain whether or not he had been
illicitly drugged or poisoned prior to or during the bout with Mr.
Brewster."

In many respects, the letter reads more like a press release than a serious call for an investigation. Indeed, one could be forgiven for believing
that its primary purpose is to gain an immediate rematch for Klitschko.

Burstein's letter references a series of irrelevancies concerning Robert
Mittleman's fixing of fights and Arnold Rothstein bribing eight members
of the Chicago White Sox to throw the 1919 World Series. Next, he
makes a mountain out of a molehill by referring to "a very suspicious
incident concerning fight credentials." Apparently, prior to the bout, a
member of the Klitschko team went to pick up his credential and was
told that it had already been picked up. This is construed to have created "a situation where an unidentified person secured an all-access pass
through fraud, thus providing himself unfettered access to the arena,"
which could have led to all manner of nefarious things.

Building block number three is gambling. Burstein's letter stated,
"The odds on the bout plummeted from 11 to 1 in Mr. Klitschko's favor
to just 3-1/2 to 1 by fight time . . . Mr. Brewster was understandably a
heavy underdog, and nothing in the public domain gave any cause for
such a drastic change in the betting line. On the other hand, if a drug-
ging of Mr. Klitschko was planned in advance, that fact would easily
explain why there was so much late money bet on Mr. Brewster."

However, in reality, very little money was bet on the fight, so one or
two wagers were capable of shifting the odds dramatically. Also, the
sports book at Mandalay Bay is reported to have changed the odds on its
own to engender more betting on the bout.

Then the Burstein letter gets to the heart of the matter: the suggestion that Wladimir Klitschko was either poisoned or drugged.

"Inexplicably, beginning in or about the second round," Burstein
wrote, "and prior to having been hit with any significant punches, Mr.
Klitschko exhibited and experienced a rapid loss of energy, coherence,

and equilibrium . . . As both Mr. Klitschko and his entire team, including Hall of Fame trainer Emanuel Steward, will attest, Mr. Klitschko was in extraordinary physical condition for the bout. Indeed, according to Mr. Klitschko, he had never trained so well or come into a bout so well-conditioned. Significantly, he had never shown himself to be a fighter who lacked conditioning or stamina. Thus, what happened on April 10 is wholly inconsistent with Mr. Klitschko's career."

This is known as rewriting history. Boxing fans will recall that the first loss of Klitschko's career came against journeyman Ross Puritty, when Wladimir all but collapsed from exhaustion and his own corner halted the fight. Let's also remember that Emanuel Steward assured everyone that Lennox Lewis was in great shape for Lewis-Rahman I. The difference is, when a poorly-conditioned Lennox got knocked out, the deposed champion didn't blame foul play; nor did he blame the altitude in South Africa (which was probably a factor). Instead, he said simply, "I got caught."

The Burstein letter next features a section entitled, "The frustration of Mr. Klitchko's efforts to learn the truth." Here, Burstein stated, "Out of concern for Mr. Klitschko, he was taken to the University Medical Center of Southern Nevada after the bout. At that time, blood and urine samples were taken from Mr. Klitschko. The next day, in order to ensure that he would have an opportunity to ascertain the truth, Mr. Klitschko arranged for additional blood and urine samples to be taken at Quest Diagnostics. Mr. Klitschko's team made it emphatically clear that they wanted the blood and urine specimens preserved so that they could be tested by an independent doctor of Mr. Klitschko's choosing. On April 14, 2004, both UMC and Quest were sent appropriate medical authorizations, signed by Mr. Klitschko, requesting that his medical records, including his blood and urine specimens, be sent to noted physician, Dr. Robert Voy. Quest has a policy of retaining blood and urine specimens for seven days after testing, and UMC has a policy of retaining blood specimens for ten days after testing. Hence, all of the blood and urine samples were in existence on April 14, when Quest and UMC received the medical authorization forms signed by Mr. Klitschko."

However—"incredibly," according to the Burstein letter—the blood and urine samples were destroyed. "Of course, there are a number of possible explanations, some innocent, for what occurred," Burstein wrote. "However, one of those possible explanations, and an eminently reasonable one, is that those specimens were destroyed in order to hide the truth of what happened to Mr. Klitschko."

There are myriad problems with this hypothesis. First, it presupposes that the University Medical Center and Quest Diagnostics were part of a massive conspiracy and cover-up. And second, it misstates the facts.

In truth, the Klitschko camp was told exactly what to do to get Wladimir's blood and urine specimens, but failed to follow up with the necessary paperwork in a timely manner. Klitschko signed an authorization for his representatives to receive all medical information and samples. But the lawyer who preceded Burstein on the case only requested information, not blood and urine samples, from UMC and Quest.

Let's also note that all of the drug screens tested "normal." And while it's technically possible that a drug not tested for was administered to Klitschko, there's no clinical evidence to support that hypothesis. Moreover, Wladimir left the hospital against medical advice hours after the fight. Behavior of that nature is hardly consistent with a belief that one has been poisoned or drugged.

Burstein acknowledges that, prior to writing to the United States Attorney, he did not contact the Nevada State Athletic Commission to confirm the factual statements contained in his letter. Rather, he stated, "Every fact in my letter came from a memorandum prepared by Ron DiNicola's office."

However, Mr. DiNicola is hardly a disinterested observer. He is one of Wladimir Klitschko's attorneys and, on April 16, 2004, sent the aforementioned (and equally flawed) letter regarding the fight to WBO president Francisco Valcarcel.

So what happened to Wladimir Klitschko in his fight against Lamon Brewster?

The truth may lie in another HBO offering. Anyone who watches *The Sopranos* knows that Tony Soprano suffers from panic attacks.

A panic attack has nothing to do with courage. No one should question Wladimir Klitschko's bravery. Rather, a panic attack is a physiological response during which a person experiences a range of symptoms such as light-headedness, dizziness, rapid heartbeat, hyperventilation, fatigue, and shortness of breath. One scenario far more likely than the conspiracy theory advanced by the Klitschko camp is that, as the fight progressed, Wladimir Klitschko suffered a panic attack. Then he got whacked and suffered a concussion.

Wladimir and Vitali Klitschko are likeable, intelligent individuals. There was every reason to believe that they would be a breath of fresh air for boxing, and they still might be.

But for the moment, it's hard to escape the conclusion that Wladimir is in denial and that there are certain hard truths that he is simply unable to accept.

There are enough bad occurrences in boxing to obviate the need for creating imaginary ones. Marc Ratner (executive director of the Nevada State Athletic Commission) says as much, when he declares, "I'm saddened by this whole state of affairs. We have a wonderful fight this weekend and another one coming up. And instead of concentrating on these fights, we're spending time dealing with nonsensical allegations that have no validity whatsoever."

Let's also consider the fact that all of this is insulting to Lamon Brewster. Lamon fought a courageous fight, and it's wrong to tarnish his victory in this manner.

Judd Burstein is an excellent lawyer but this is one time when he has overstepped his bounds.

As for Wladimir Klitschko, there's no embarrassment in his having been knocked out by Lamon Brewster. But Wladimir is dangerously close to embarrassing himself now.❏

At present, Roman Greenberg and Yuri Foreman are curiosities. But each hopes to become a force in the world of boxing.

THE HAIFA CONNECTION: ROMAN GREENBERG AND YURI FOREMAN

On the first Saturday in December, two young men made their way through fourteen inches of snow in New York. They were familiar with harsh winters, having spent their early years in the Soviet Union. Then they'd left the cold behind and moved with their families to Israel. For a while, they'd lived under the same roof in Haifa. Later, they'd gone separate ways. Now one lives in New York and the other in London. They hadn't seen each other for four years.

There was an embrace. The snow continued to fall.

"I'm very happy to see you," Roman Greenberg said.

"You've gotten a lot bigger," Yuri Foreman told him.

What made their reunion noteworthy is that Greenberg and Foreman, both Jewish and Israeli citizens, are undefeated professional fighters.

Between 1901 and 1938, there were 26 Jewish world champions, most of them from New York and Chicago. Abe Atell was the first. Benny Leonard and Barney Ross followed. But great Jewish fighters have been few in number. As legendary trainer Ray Arcel once noted, "Punching people in the head isn't the highest aspiration of the Jewish people."

The last Jewish world champion was Mike Rossman, who knocked out Victor Galindez of Argentina twenty-five years ago to capture the light-heavyweight title. But in reality, Rossman fought under his mother's maiden name, rather than that of his father-manager Jimmy DiPiano.

"It doesn't matter," Rossman said when the discrepancy was noted. "My mother's a Jew. And in the Jewish religion, whatever your mother is, that's what you is."

That brings us to Roman Greenberg and Yuri Foreman.

Greenberg was born in Russia in 1982 and speaks fluent Russian, Hebrew, German, and English. When he was ten, he moved with his parents and infant brother to Haifa.

"Some parts of my life were not so nice," Greenberg recalled. "When we arrived in Israel, it was quite hard. We lived on the streets, my parents, my little brother Alex, and me. It was not good in Russia, but those early days and nights in Israel were an absolute nightmare. There were times when we had nothing to eat. Those are the experiences that push people to get to the top. You do not even want to remember that something like that happened. My ambition is that my children will not have the same problems I had when I was young."

When Greenberg was eleven, some friends who had started boxing invited him to a gym. Two years later, Roman had his first fight. "It was very exciting and very frightening," he remembers. "But I won on a knockout in eighteen seconds. Then the referee put my hand up in the air and said I won, and I told myself, 'I like this. I want to do this again.'"

Greenberg won a silver medal at the World Junior Championships in Budapest in July 2000. Overall, he compiled an amateur record of 47 wins and 5 losses. "I was knocked out once," he says. "It happened when I was fifteen years old. I fought a guy who was twenty-six and the national light-heavyweight champion. He knocked me down. I got up. He hit me again. And then there was a blackout."

Greenberg turned pro in 2001 after serving for seven months in the Israeli Army. He now divides his time between London and Tel Aviv, where his parents live with his 12-year-old brother.

"You have to be careful in Israel," Greenberg says. "You never know when or where something bad might happen."

Greenberg himself escaped tragedy two years ago when he and some friends wanted to go to a discotheque in Tel Aviv but were short of the funds required for admission. That night, a suicide bomber killed 21 people in the same discoteque and injured hundreds of others. "Sometimes it's good not to have money," Roman acknowledges.

Greenberg is promoted by Evans-Waterman Boxing Promotions. His record stands at 14 wins and 0 losses with 11 knockouts. But critics note that he has fought only one opponent with a winning record, and there's an assumption in some circles that Roman is little more than a promotional gimmick. That view stems in no small measure from the fact that he's white, Jewish (from Israel, no less), and a small heavyweight (221 pounds).

The contrary view is expressed by Robert Waterman, who says, "When I first saw Roman training in Israel in 1999, I saw raw talent. Then he turned pro, and I realized that we were onto something special. Roman has a good boxing mind and incredibly fast hands. None of us claim that he has been fighting world champions. We wouldn't be doing our jobs right if we rushed Roman before he became more skilled as a boxer and matured physically. But in each of his fights, we've stepped up the level of competition to give him a test. And the truth is, based on his experience to date, Roman couldn't be doing any better than he is now. In fact, on three occasions, Roman has fought an opponent that Audley Harrison fought. And each time, Roman won more decisively than Audley won."

Greenberg himself admits, "Soon, I need to fight opponents who have better skills and different kinds of styles to see how I deal with them." Then he adds, "When I move up in class, people will see how good I can be. Size isn't everything. It's what you do with your ability that matters."

Meanwhile, Yuri Foreman is pursuing his ring career on the other side of the Atlantic.

Foreman was born in Belarus in 1980. When he was eleven, his family moved to Haifa. "At first it was difficult," he remembers. "I was missing my friends. And sometimes in Israel, there was discrimination between the Russians and the Jews. The Russians were also Jewish, but the Israelis would call us Russians and say we didn't deserve to be there, so there would be fights in school between the immigrants and the Israelis."

In Israel, Foreman learned the rudiments of the sweet science under the watchful eye of another Russian immigrant who taught adolescents to box in an outdoor lot. There was no ring and no heavy bag.

"They wouldn't give us a gym because we were just Russians," says Foreman. "We went to City Hall and begged for a place to hang a bag and put up a ring. All they told us was, 'Go box with the Arabs.' So finally I went to the Arab gym. The first time I walked in, I saw the stares. In their eyes, there was a lot of hatred. But I needed to box; and boy, did they all want to box me. After a while, the wall that was between us melted. We all wanted the same thing. I traveled with them as teammates. It helped that I won almost all the time. And finally, we became friends."

But outside the ring, there were constant reminders of the divisions within Israeli society. "Sometimes it was hard with the suicide bombings," Foreman says philosophically. "But after so many, it becomes kind of normal. I wasn't scared because I believe in destiny. If you're supposed to be on one of those buses, there's nothing you can do. So when a bombing happens, you feel sad and then you go on with what you have to do."

Foreman compiled a 75-5 amateur record and was a three-time Israeli national amateur champion. Then, like all Israelis, he received notification at age eighteen that he was required to serve in the Israeli Army.

"That would have ended the dream of boxing for me," Yuri remembers. "For three years, no boxing. So the first letter, I ignored it. Then comes a second letter, and I ignore that one too. Finally, I get a blue letter; the one where they say they're coming to pick me up. That was when I left Israel and came to America. Someday, I hope to go back to Israel to visit. But I cannot go now because the Army wants me."

Foreman's first job in New York was in a clothing store in the heart of Manhattan's garment district. He swept the floors, made deliveries, and did whatever else was necessary. Meanwhile, he began training at Gleason's Gym in Brooklyn. He turned pro in January 2002 and now has a record of 13 wins against no losses with 6 knockouts. His trainer is Tommy Brooks.

"One of the happiest things in my life is to train with Tommy Brooks," Yuri acknowledges. "In my first fights, I was too amateur, too straight, too open with no head movement. When you go to better competition, the good opponents will take advantage of it. The first few months with Tommy, I had to think to do what he was telling me, like angles and bending and throwing more combinations. Now it's natural to me. I still make mistakes, but I'm making them less."

Foreman is also a newlywed, having married a 29-year-old model from Hungary. They met at Gleason's Gym, where the future Mrs. Foreman was training for her first amateur fight, which she won on a second-round knockout. "There's a big age difference between us," Yuri acknowledges before adding, "There's a big experience difference too."

In truth, neither Greenberg or Foreman is particularly religious. Roman was bar mitzvahed and attended religious schools in his youth but is no longer observant. Yuri has little religious training and admits, "I don't really follow the traditions. I go sometimes to synagogue with my ex-boss from the clothing store, but that's all."

Still, boxing, more than any other sport, thrives on ethnic confrontations. Thus, Greenberg has engendered interest from promoters on both sides of the Atlantic, and Foreman is also considered marketable. Both fighters, in turn, have held onto their Jewish identity for reasons that go beyond the commercial.

"Right now, there is no support for boxing in Israel," says Foreman. "Roman and I had no support at all. If we're successful, it will bring support for boxing in Israel."

And Greenberg adds, "It's important to me that I'm a Jewish fighter. The Jews have had a hard life for all of our history. If there's a Jewish heavyweight champion of the world, it would be good for Jewish people around the world."

But lest one think that Greenberg is too parochial, it's worth noting one final thought from him. "My heroes are Roy Jones and Muhammad Ali," says the heavyweight from Israel. "Roy Jones is from a different planet. I think he's the greatest fighter ever. And Muhammad Ali, what can I say? I like everything about him."❏

This was typical of the slice-of-life moments that make boxing a great sport.

JEFFREY RESTO'S FIGHT FOR REDEMPTION

One of boxing's small dramas played out last week in Manhattan.

Being a fighter requires fortitude that most people only fantasize about.

"Have you ever been whacked in the ribcage hard by someone who can punch?" asks veteran cutman Al Gavin. "Have you ever stood there with your eyelid sliced open, dripping blood, knowing that there will be punches coming for another twenty minutes before you can even think about getting stitched up? That's a little bit of what's involved in being a professional fighter. You're tested every minute of every fight."

Nine months ago, Jeffrey Resto failed the test. The 27-year-old Bronx native is married with three children and works forty hours a week as a receiving clerk at Mt. Sinai Hospital. He began boxing at age eleven after being mugged on the street. He won a 1996 Golden Gloves title, turned pro the following year, and was being groomed for stardom. Then, last September, he took his 17-0 record into the ring against Carlos Maussa in a fight that was nationally-televised on ESPN2. Maussa gave as good as he took. And in the sixth round, Resto quit.

"I don't know how it happened," Resto said afterward. "I got hit in the eye and I couldn't see his punches. Then I got hit in my other eye. Both times, it felt like his thumb. It became very frustrating for me because I couldn't see anything. All I could do was pick up my hands to protect myself. Carlos knew I was hurt and let his hands go, and I kept getting hit by everything he was throwing. Things just got worse and I didn't know what to do."

Resto took seven weeks off after the Maussa fight. Then he went back to the gym; not to spar, but to work out and see how things felt. Now, nine months after quitting against Maussa, he was returning to the ring.

The opponent was Michael Warrick, a tough 140-pounder with a record identical to Resto's 17-1 mark.

"Jeffrey knows what he's facing," promoter Lou DiBella said shortly before the fight. "He's heard it more than anyone. He made a bad decision. But he's a good person; he's a talented fighter; and everyone deserves a second shot. He has to prove that what happened in the ring that night was an aberration. If he beats Michael Warrick convincingly, if he comes back after that and beats Maussa or a seasoned veteran, then he deserves another shot at the big time. But I don't think Jeffrey can ever turn his back again," DiBella added. "If he ever shows anything less than the courage of a lion, he's gonna be nowhere."

"This fight means everything to me," Resto acknowledged. "If I lose, I'm out of boxing. But I believe in myself and I believe I can go far in this sport."

Then came the fight. The first round was a feeling-out process with the edge to Resto. But in round two, Warrick decked him with an overhand right. Jeffrey rose; Warrick was on top of him with a barrage of punches; and you could all but see the wheels turning in Resto's head. Eight more painful rounds lay ahead. He could fight back or quit.

"All I thought about was surviving," Resto said later.

Surviving as a fighter. Which meant weathering the storm until his mind cleared, his strength returned, and he was able to mount his own assault.

Thereafter, Resto fought back. And Warrick fought with him. At times, their encounter resembled a barroom brawl. Warrick led with his head and lost a point for hitting on the break. Resto was penalized for low blows. In the middle rounds, Resto seemed to regain control of the battle, breaking Warrick's will rather than the other way around. But Warrick came out hard for round eight, put Jeffrey down with a vicious body shot, and followed with a heightened two-minute assault. Again, Resto fought back in a grueling struggle marked by sustained action until the final bell.

All three judges scored the bout 94-92 for Warrick (the same as this observer's scorecard). The knockdowns were the difference. The fight called Resto's physical strength into question. He looked like a good tough club fighter; not the potential superstar he was once thought to be. But there were no questions about his heart.

"It was a good fight," Resto said afterward. "I gave it my best. I feel good about myself. I proved that I wasn't a quitter. I got my honor back."❏

Bill Cayton was in the final stages of terminal lung cancer when he asked to meet with me about his fighter.

THE LEGACY FIGHTER

His name has been changed, mangled, and mispronounced. It's Lenord (accent on the second syllable as in Le-nord) Anasta. Fight fans call him Leonard Pierre.

Lenord was born in Haiti on July 6, 1979. He came to the United States in 1991 and settled with his family in Hudson, New York, six miles from the town of Catskill. His father is a house painter. His mother works in a factory. His first language is Creole, and there's a melodic ring to his voice.

"My father got me started in boxing," Lenord says. "He saw Sugar Ray Leonard and Mike Tyson making so much money from one fight. So when I was twelve, he took me to the gym in Catskill."

Kevin Rooney, who learned his trade from the legendary Cus D'Amato and trained Mike Tyson during the glory years in Catskill, recalls his early work with Lenord.

"I started showing him the things I learned from Cus," Rooney says. "And what I remember most is, when I held the pads for him, he had what I call a Tyson punch. He kept coming to the gym, which is important. He was serious about it. Then I put him in a local tournament and he stopped his opponent in the first round. Next fight, he knocked the opponent out; literally out, unconscious, in the first round. And he was only twelve years old."

"At first," Lenord admits, "I didn't like boxing because I got hit. But when I knocked that kid out, when I hit him, I discovered my abilities. I felt a vibration going from my arm to my heart."

Lenord graduated from Hudson High School in 1998 and earned an associate degree in fine arts from Columbia-Green Community College in 2001. He's now trained as a graphic designer and also makes ceramic vases and busts. Meanwhile, after going 86 and 5 as an amateur, he has compiled a 9 and 0 record with eight knockouts in the middleweight ranks as a pro.

Lenord is carrying two legacies on his shoulders. The first is that of Cus D'Amato.

"I don't know much about Cus as a person," Lenord acknowledges. "But I know his technique and I believe in what Kevin teaches me. If I follow the Cus D'Amato technique, I don't have to worry about my opponent."

The second legacy is that of Bill Cayton, boxing's consummate sales-man and a brilliant manager who guided Mike Tyson, Wilfred Benitez, and others to stardom.

"This is my last hurrah," says Cayton, whose managerial duties will eventually be assumed by assistant manager Steve Lott. "But I honestly believe that, as of today, Lenord is the most exciting fighter in the world. And within a year, he'll be good enough beat Oscar De La Hoya. If Ross Greenburg was really smart, he'd put Lenord on HBO every chance he got."

But given the fact that De La Hoya is HBO's franchise fighter, why would Greenburg want to knock him off?

"There, you have it," Cayton answers. "That's our slogan. Lenord Agasta: He's too good for HBO."

The other ghost wrapped up in all of this is, of course, Mike Tyson. During his glory years, Iron Mike fought out of Catskill, trained with Rooney, and was managed by Cayton.

"I met Tyson once," Lenord says. "It was in Hudson in 1995 after he got out of prison. I shook his hand and told him I was a fighter. It was short, but he was polite."

Still, in terms of personality, Lenord is the anti-Tyson.

"The way people see me is important to me," Lenord elaborates. "I want to be a good citizen. My heroes are people like Gandhi, Martin Luther King Jr., and Nelson Mandela; people who made a difference. I hope someday I can be influential in a positive way, helping poor people and uneducated people get knowledge. Being middleweight champion of the world and rich and famous without making a difference wouldn't mean anything to me." And then he adds, "Bill Cayton, Kevin Rooney, Steve Lott. Tyson left all of them like he never knew them, and I think that's bad. I want to be with this team forever."

Like Tyson, Lenord is an aggressive fighter with power in both hands. He has never been knocked down as an amateur or pro although, once, he was dropped by a body shot in the gym. He's well-conditioned and doesn't lose his strength as a fight goes on.

"Lenord breaks his opponent's will," says Rooney.

"Things change when they get hit," Lenord says, confirming Rooney's thought. "The look on their face changes, and I say to myself, 'Yes, I got him.'"

All of Lenord's fights to date have been scheduled six-rounders.

Rooney plans three eight-rounders by the end of the year and ten-rounders against top-ten opponents in early 2004.

Rooney, Cayton, and Lott are believers. Most people around undefeated young punchers are. Still, it should be noted that Lenord has less polish than might be expected from someone who has fought for twelve years. He has experienced difficulty cutting off the ring against opponents who move. And he has yet to demonstrate that he can deal with a fighter who jabs, punches well, and takes a good punch.

Also, let's not forget that, when Mike Tyson was Lenord's age, his time of glory had already passed. At age twenty-three, one year younger than Lenord is now, Iron Mike was dethroned by Buster Douglas.❏

The Observer (of London) commissioned this stateside view of today's American heavyweights.

THE DECLINE OF THE AMERICAN HEAVYWEIGHT

On June 9, 1899, James Jeffries knocked out Bob Fitzsimmons in the eleventh round to claim the heavyweight championship of the world. For the next hundred years, the most treasured prize in sports was largely American property.

Max Schmeling of Germany won the title by disqualification over Jack Sharkey in 1930, but lost it to Sharkey in a rematch. Sharkey was defeated by Primo Carnera of Italy whose short-lived reign was ended by Max Baer. In 1959, Ingemar Johansson of Sweden defeated Floyd Patterson but was knocked cold by Patterson in his first title defense. And that's it, unless one counts Gerrie Coetzee and Frans Botha of South Africa, Trevor Berbick of Jamaican heritage, and England's own Frank Bruno, all of whom held alphabet-soup title belts but weren't really regarded as champions.

Then Lennox Lewis came along and things changed. The heavyweight champion of the world and the best heavyweight of his time was no longer an American.

King Lennox's reign has now ended, but there's no sign that America is about to reclaim the heavyweight throne. The man most likely to be recognized as the world's best heavyweight in the near future is 32-year-old Vitali Klitschko. Klitschko was born in the Ukraine, turned pro after compiling a 195-15 amateur record, and is now the World Boxing Council heavyweight champion. Critics note that Klitschko has yet to beat a quality American fighter. His signature wins have come against Kirk Johnson of Canada and South African Corrie Sanders. But he's big and strong and can take a punch.

In recent years, ten heavyweights born outside of the United States have attracted notice on the boxing scene. Lennox Lewis is first among them. Then, after Vitali Klitschko and his brother Wladimir, comes David Tua.

Tua was born in Samoa. Managerial problems have kept him out of action since a March 2003 draw against Hasim Rahman. But with the exception of Mike Tyson, Tua remains the hardest puncher in the heavyweight division. His record is 42-3-1 with 37 knockouts, and he's still only 31 years old.

Former cruiserweight champion, Cuban-born Juan Carlos Gomez, is undefeated as a pro and now campaigns as a heavyweight. Polish-born Andrew Golota was beating Riddick Bowe in both of their encounters before being disqualified for low blows. Golota recently fought International Boxing Federation champion Chris Byrd to a draw in a fight that many ringside observers thought he won. Olympic gold-medal winner Audley Harrison of England and Samuel Peter of Nigeria are also regarded as potential titleholders.

And then there's Ike Ibeabuchi of Nigeria, who many thought was destined for greatness. Ibeabuchi compiled a 20-0 record with 15 knockouts and was the second-ranked heavyweight in the world. He handed David Tua his first defeat and was the only fighter to knock out Chris Byrd.

In July 1999, Ibeabuche called a telephone service and asked that a lap dancer be sent to his room at The Mirage Hotel & Casino in Las Vegas. According to courtroom testimony, the dancer insisted on cash payment in advance, at which point the 245-pound fighter became enraged and raped her. This came on the heels of similar allegations against Ibeabuchi made by two other outcall dancers in Nevada and Arizona. Ibeabuchi was sentenced to five-to-thirty years in prison as the result of a plea deal with prosecutors.

Meanwhile, America's heavyweights are faltering. Mike Tyson and Evander Holyfield are long past their prime. Michael Grant, who was supposed to be the next great American heavyweight, folded like an accordian when faced with adversity in the ring. John Ruiz, Hasim Rahman, Jameel McCline, Lamon Brewster, Monte Barrett, Calvin Brock, Dominick Guinn, Joe Mesi, and Fres Oquendo are all viewed as fighters of less-than-true-championship caliber.

Chris Byrd admits the decline and acknowledges, "I suppose it's true. Look at me. I'm not a big guy; I'm not a true heavyweight. Roy Jones, James Toney, me. Right now, all of us could get down to cruiserweight. In fact, Roy is fighting at 175 pounds again. There's no way we should be the top American heavyweights, but we are."

And trainer Emanuel Steward, who guided Lennox Lewis to greatness, takes things a step further when he declares, "The next generation of elite heavyweights is going to come from Europe and Africa. It's happening already. You can look ahead now and see that America simply is not developing heavyweight boxers anymore in the amateurs. In fact, the last outstanding class of American amateur heavyweights was in 1988 when Riddick Bowe and Ray Mercer came out of the Olympics.

And the amateurs is where your future heavyweight stars come from."

"The American heavyweights today are terrible," adds former champion Larry Holmes. Then, with a touch of hyperbole, Holmes proclaims, "I'm 54 years old and I can kick their butts. I've forgotten more about boxing than these guys know."

How did this sorry state of affairs come about?

Things didn't happen overnight. It was a long slow process.

There was a time when boxing and baseball were America's two national sports and virtually everyone in the western world knew the heavyweight champion's name. Indeed, Alex Haley (who co-authored *The Autobiography of Malcolm X*) recalled being introduced to Joe Louis and blurting out, "I feel like I'm finally meeting with God."

But in recent decades, the talent pool for American heavyweights has vastly diminished. The first reason for this is that boxing is no longer part of the social fabric and dreams of America's underclass. It has been supplanted by basketball and American football.

"There are hundreds of great American heavyweights out there," says HBO boxing commentator Larry Merchant. "But they're all playing power forward in the National Basketball Association or linebacker in the National Football League."

The average salary for a National Basketball Association player is now almost $3,600,000 annually. For Major League Baseball players, it exceeds $2,430,000. In the National Football League, the number is $1,235,000 per year. Yes, the heavyweight champion of the world is well paid. But very few fighters make as much money in an entire career as an American team athlete makes in a single season. In fact, most professional boxers hold a second job because they can't make a decent living from their primary trade.

Also, big money comes more quickly for athletes in other sports than it does in boxing. It's no longer uncommon for elite high school basketball stars like Kobe Bryant and LeBron James to skip college altogether and go directly to the professional ranks for tens of millions of dollars.

Money is a great motivator. Thus, Emanuel Steward opines, "If Vitali and Wladimir Klitschko had been born in the United States, with their size and coordination, they probably would have become basketball stars."

And Lennox Lewis concurs with the acknowledgement, "If I had grown up in the United States with its football and basketball culture, I might not have become a fighter. But I grew up in Canada, where I was surrounded by hockey. I got to the level of being able to skate and even skate backwards, but my feet kept growing and skates were expensive, so I took up boxing."

In America today, there's also more glory in being a star football or basketball player, even at the college level, than there is for most professional fighters.

"Seeing something on television makes kids want to get into it," says Emanuel Steward. "Television is a great motivating factor. All young men want to be on television, but there's almost no boxing on free television anymore. It's all on cable and pay-per-view."

And the glory once bestowed upon fighters has been further diminished by the proliferation of world titles. There are now four major sanctioning organizations with seventeen weight classes in each. That's sixty-eight "world champions." Vitali Klitschko, John Ruiz, Chris Byrd, and Lamon Brewster all presently claim a heavyweight title.

Having four heavyweight champions is like having four kings of England. It doesn't work.

In sum, boxing simply isn't very popular in America anymore. And you can't attract large numbers of athletes to a sport that isn't popular; particularly when that sport involves getting punched in the nose. Most of today's top American fighters (like Roy Jones, Oscar De La Hoya and Shane Mosley) are in boxing because their fathers put them into it. And many of the top American heavyweights are guys like Joe Mesi, Fres Oquendo, Jameel McCline, and Michael Grant, who started out playing other sports in high school, failed athletically when they got to the next level, and turned to boxing relatively late in life.

So the problem with American heavyweights begins with a dwindling supply of talent. Next, there's an ever-diminishing opportunity to learn.

Heavyweights like Lennox Lewis, Ike Ibeabuchi, Andrew Golota, and the Klitschkos still come to the United States for the training they need to become "more like American fighters." But there are fewer opportunities for American fighters in general to learn their trade.

Great fighters start young. In the United States, when a child is athletically gifted, he or she can develop in most sports by participating on a school team. But very few Americans have access to a gym where they can learn to box.

Moreover, as noted by Teddy Atlas who helped shape Mike Tyson's early career, "Quality trainers are rare; and when you don't have good teachers, you don't learn."

Roy Jones is in accord and declares, "My father taught me how to box, but there are very few people around now who can teach the fundamentals from the ground up."

And it's not just heavyweights. There's an overall deterioration of the skill level of boxers in the United States. The middleweights have been called boxing's second glamour division. During the reign of Sugar Ray

Robinson, it was said that the division was divided into Sugar Ray and everyone else. Now, middleweights in the United States are divided into Bernard Hopkins and no one else.

There's also the matter of character.

Joe Frazier, as honorable in the ring as any man who ever lived, once declared, "I was never big with words. I wanted to fight, not talk. I wasn't no philosopher or poet. No, sir, I was a fighter."

But the truth is, being a fighter requires a unique commitment and special character. People "play" football and basketball. Nobody plays boxing. It's hard getting punched in the head day after day in the gym. And being a fighter requires certain intangibles that are missing from many American lives today.

HBO boxing commentator Jim Lampley observes, "There used to be a societal reverence in the United States for working hard to overcome hard circumstances. Now the reverence is for getting over on someone and making money without working hard. In fact, I'll go so far as to say that the talent pool for boxing is diminished by the fact that, in some areas where fighters traditionally come from, there's easy money to be made on the streets, dealing drugs and engaging in other criminal activity. The guy who works hard is thought of as a sucker."

Trainer Bouie Fisher, who has been with Bernard Hopkins since the second fight of "The Executioner's" career, has a similar view.

"You have to live right between fights," Fisher declares. "But the way things are today, there's parties here and parties there and vices everywhere. A young man today makes a few thousand dollars, and the first thing he wants to do is to go partying. And if you don't have proper discipline, you get caught up in partying and hanging out and you wind up cheating yourself; particularly if, like most of the top heavyweights today, you only fight once or twice a year."

"Too many times," Fisher continues, "when you try to tell young men something today, they become resentful and don't want to listen. They say, 'What's this old gray-haired guy talking about!' And I tell them, 'You know, I didn't just dye my hair gray. I earned my gray hair. You should go out and earn yourself some gray hair too.' But what makes me want to pull my gray hair out sometimes is when a young man with all the talent in the world doesn't want to do the work and make the sacrifices that are necessary to reap the rewards that his talent can bring him."

And according to Donald Turner, who trained Larry Holmes and Evander Holyfield, the requisite intangibles are particularly lacking in the heavyweight division.

"It's a lack of toughness and a lack of discipline," says Turner.

"Generally speaking, the smaller fighters are tougher than heavy-weights. That's because, growing up, they had to fight to survive; whereas with the heavyweights, people said, 'Don't mess with him; he's big.' Then you come to the discipline issue," Turner continues. "No one is harnessing the thug in a lot of these guys. And on top of that, there's a lack of pride. In the past fifty years, there are only five heavyweights I can think of who gave their all every time out. Rocky Marciano, Muhammad Ali, Joe Frazier, Larry Holmes, and Evander Holyfield. The rest of them, forget about it."

And last, on top of everything else, it's not just that American heavy-weights are in a period of decline. The rest of the world is getting better.

During George Foreman's first reign as champion, Big George declared, "People talk about my title, but it isn't mine. It belongs to the world. It's the same title that was around before me, before Muhammad Ali, before Joe Frazier; and it will be there when we're all gone."

Note that Foreman didn't say that the title belonged to America. His words were, "It belongs to the world." And the world is learning how to compete on a higher level in most athletic endeavors.

Take tennis as an example. The Davis Cup was inaugurated in 1900, and each of the first 27 competitions was won by the United States, Great Britain, or Australia. Then, after a brief French reign, the same three nations won every competition through 1973. Contrast that with the past nine years during which six different nations have won the Davis Cup.

Baseball, the quintessential American game, has seen an influx of Latin American players during the past two decades. The National Hockey League is rife with European stars, as is the National Basketball Association. Why should anyone be surprised if the next generation of great fighters comes from Eastern Europe or Africa?

Still, it should be noted that Lennox Lewis remains the only domi-nant non-American heavyweight of the past century. And for most fans, the heavyweight division is defined by its champion. For example, the division was pretty thin for most of Joe Louis's tenure, but no one talked about the decline of American heavyweights because Joe was there. Jack Johnson, Jack Dempsey and Rocky Marciano were also great heavyweight champions but had few true inquisitors during their respective reigns.

Moreover, boxing, like most sports, tends to run in cycles. After Gene Tunney retired, there was a dreary nine-year period during which the title was held by Max Schmeling, Jack Sharkey, Primo Carnera, Max Bear, and James Braddock. Then "The Brown Bomber" arrived. After Joe Louis, there were thirteen years when title was in the hands of Ezzard

Charles (really a light-heavyweight), Jersey Joe Walcott (37 years old), Rocky Marciano (the real thing), and Floyd Patterson (he of the glass jaw). But that was followed by Sonny Liston, Muhammad Ali, Joe Frazier, George Foreman, and Larry Holmes. Holmes was beaten by Michael Spinks in 1986; the same year that Mike Tyson annihilated Trevor Berbick for the WBC crown. If Tyson had reigned into the next millennium as expected, there would be less talk now about the decline of American heavyweights. Rather, people would be comparing Tyson, Evander Holyfield, Riddick Bowe, and Lennox Lewis with Muhammad Ali, Joe Frazier, George Foreman, and Larry Holmes.

So let's give the final word on the subject to the man most responsible for occasioning this dialogue.

"I don't agree that there's a decline in American heavyweights," says Lennox Lewis. "If you look at history, during what some people call Golden Eras, very often there was one great heavyweight and not much else. The 1970s with Muhammad Ali, Joe Frazier, George Foreman, and Larry Holmes were an aberration. Depth like that is rare in the heavyweight division."

"In the era that's passing now," Lennox continues, "you had Mike Tyson, Evander Holyfield, and Riddick Bowe. Those are three A-list American fighters. In fact, if Tyson and Bowe hadn't self-destructed, you probably wouldn't be writing this article. So be patient. What might seem like a decline now is just the period before a new era. The next great American heavyweight will come."❏

In June 2004, when Oscar De La Hoya and Bernard Hopkins fought on the same card in separate bouts, the fights were over-shadowed by a controversey over referee Joe Cortez.

DE LA HOYA WINS BUT LOSES; HOPKINS LOSES AND WINS

A fighter got old overnight this past weekend at the MGM Grand in Las Vegas, but it wasn't 39-year-old Bernard Hopkins.

On Saturday, June 5th, Hopkins and Oscar De La Hoya engaged in separate bouts in what was widely viewed as an infomercial for their scheduled September 18th showdown. Bernard defended his many middleweight belts against journeyman Robert Allen, while Oscar vied for a 160-pound title of his own against World Boxing Organization "champion" Felix Sturm.

Hopkins-Allen was a tactical fight, with the champion content to counterpunch for most of the night. In round seven, he decked his foe with a sharp overhand right and followed with a vicious body attack. Meanwhile, Allen fought like a fighter who had no belief in himself. He survived, but that's about all he did.

The twelve-round "punch-stats" showed Hopkins landing 156 blows to only 71 for Allen. The judges' scorecards were equally one-sided: 119-107, 119-107 and 117-109 for Hopkins.

The fight solidified Hopkins's claim to the top spot in boxing's "pound-for-pound" rankings. Bernard carries an aura of menace with him whenever he enters the ring. And more to the point, he's incredibly disciplined when it comes to boxing, both in his training regimen and in fights themselves. He fought cautiously against Allen, but he usually does. And with a $10,000,000 payday in September at stake, caution was to be expected.

Meanwhile, De La Hoya came out hard against Sturm, throwing more than a hundred punches in the first round. But if he thought he would blow Felix away, he was mistaken.

Sturm showed a nice jab and a quick left hook. By contrast, Oscar was less than sharp and looked soft at 160 pounds. Sturm bloodied De La Hoya's nose in the opening stanza, and the claret trickled down for most of the night. By round four, Oscar was visibly tired, and Felix dominated the late rounds. Overall, he outlanded De La Hoya 234 to 188.

But Sturm lacked two essentials: punching power and a scheduled multi-million-dollar fight against Bernard Hopkins that is considered crucial to the economy of Nevada. Thus, as De La Hoya versus Sturm unfolded, HBO commentator Larry Merchant remarked that the judges' scoring would be "the ultimate test of the officials in Las Vegas."

If so, the judges flunked the test. All three gave the nod to Oscar by a 115-113 margin.

There have been worse decisions. Most observers felt that Sturm clearly won five rounds and De La Hoya clearly won four. That meant all three of the close rounds were awarded to Oscar.

"That's what a hometown decision is," Merchant later noted.

After the fight, De la Hoya was remarkably honest. "Everything went wrong tonight," he acknowledged. "I stepped into the ring and, nothing. Sturm is an ordinary fighter. I don't know what it was. I'm very disappointed with my performance."

Sturm, for his part, said simply, "Everyone saw who won the fight. If Oscar really loves the sport, he will give me a rematch. If Oscar loves the money, he will fight Bernard."

One might add that, in the eyes of the betting public, if Oscar values his health, he won't fight Bernard. Prior to last weekend, Hopkins was an 8-to-5 betting favorite over the Golden Boy. By Sunday morning, the odds were 3-to-1.

But there was another fight that took place in Las Vegas last week; one that occurred outside the ring.

Marc Ratner (executive director of the Nevada State Athletic Commission) says that, on May 25th, he told a representative of the Hopkins camp that he planned to recommend Joe Cortez as the referee for Hopkins-Allen and that there was no objection. The following day, Cortez was formally designated at a public hearing of the commission. Then, on June 3rd, two days before the fight, Hopkins advised the NSAC that he would pull out of the fight if Cortez was not removed as the referee.

Hopkins said that he had objected to the use of Cortez in previous fights and that those past objections would prejudice Cortez against him. He also claimed that Cortez, who is of Puerto Rican ancestry, might be prejudiced against him because he beat Felix Trinidad three years ago and because, on two occasions during promotion for that bout, Bernard threw a Puerto Rican flag to the ground.

Having lodged his objection, Bernardo Hopkins (as he's known to his adoring fans in Puerto Rico) went to the airport and threatened to board a flight out of Las Vegas. "I'm always paranoid," he proclaimed. "But I'm not crazy paranoid. This ain't a bluff or a ploy. There are two guys in the ring punching, but the third guy in there can make or break the fight. A referee can control a fight and he can interfere with a fight. I won't stand for this. I'm not saying give me somebody I want, just anybody but him. My mind has to be clear for war. I shouldn't have to worry about the referee. I'm adamant about my instincts. I don't want Cortez. I ain't a fool. They're trying to get rid of me by any means necessary."

Ratner called Cortez on Thursday morning and told him, "We have a problem with Bernard Hopkins."

"Behind the scenes after that," Cortez said later, "there was a lot of pressure on me to step aside; telephone calls from certain people and things like that."

Ratner was quoted as saying that he believed there would be no problem switching Cortez with Tony Weeks, who was slated to referee the lightweight title fight between Juan Lazcano and Jose Luis Castillo on the same card, should Cortez request the change.

Promoter Bob Arum claimed that, if Hopkins pulled out, the entire card would be cancelled and declared, "Nobody is attacking Cortez's integrity, but he's got to understand what's at stake here. There is an easy solution, and that's simply for Cortez to step aside and work one of the other fights. For him to take the position that he won't step aside is absolutely ludicrous." Then, for good measure, Arum added, "If he doesn't [step aside], maybe there's something to what Bernard is saying."

HBO and the MGM Grand let their interests be known. Meanwhile, John Bailey (chairman of the NSAC) declared, "Joe Cortez has done nothing wrong and is one of the finest referees in the world. I have not heard one credible shred of evidence why Joe Cortez should not officiate this fight. As a regulatory body, we can not allow fighters and promoters to dictate who we appoint as officials."

And most important, Cortez held firm. "I know what's right and I know what's wrong," the referee said. "My integrity is impeccable. If I step down, it would be like admitting the things Bernard is saying about me are true, and they're not. You just can't have people changing officials," Cortez continued. "That would set a bad precedent and make the commission look weak. If Bernard Hopkins obeys the rules, he has nothing to worry about with Joe Cortez."

Cortez's refusal to step aside was proper. Bernard's claim of ethnic bias was nothing more than ugly character assassination.

In the end, Hopkins backed down. Most bullies do when met with a show of commensurate force. Bernard tried to put a positive spin on his surrender, saying, "What I have done is the right thing. I can fight one person in the ring, but not two. Now it's open. The eyes of the world are going to be watching the fight."

However, in truth, Bernard's record in squabbles outside the ring is less illustrious than his record in physical combat. In recent years, he has lost a $610,000 libel judgment to Lou DiBella. And after he dismissed his longtime trainer Bouie Fisher, Fisher sued and was rehired.

But there's a larger issue at stake here. Ring officials should be appointed by state athletic commissions at the discretion of state athletic commissions, period.

The Los Angeles Lakers don't tell David Stern who the officials will be for the NBA Finals. When the New York Yankees play the Boston Red Sox, Joe Torre doesn't get to veto the home plate umpire because "Pedro Martinez is pitching, and this guy likes Hispanics," or "This guy lets Pedro get away with throwing high and inside."

In boxing, too many jurisdictions bow to the will of promoters, managers, and fighters when it comes to the selection of ring officials. Nevada has a mixed record on this point. It stood up for Jerry Roth (who scored Jones-Tarver I a draw) when the Jones camp objected to Roth's selection as a judge for last month's rematch. But on many occasions, it has bowed to Top Rank in inappropriate ways, most notably in the assignment of ring physicians for Top Rank fights.

Allowing a promoter, manager, or fighter to influence the selection of officials in any way has a horrible chilling effect. It increases the possibility that a referee or judge who wants lucrative high-profile future assignments will give the edge to a fighter backed by powerful interests. And it increases the possibility that a fighter will be seriously injured or killed in the ring as the result of a referee or ring doctor being reluctant to stop a fight.

If a ring official is considered "pro-Puerto Rican" or "anti-black" or biased in any other way, then he or she lacks the character necessary to be an official and shouldn't be assigned to any fight. But absent a showing of incompetence or bias, the rules are the rules and all ring officials should be presumed capable of effectively and impartially enforcing them. ❏

Oscar De La Hoya versus Bernard Hopkins was heralded as the 2004 "super-fight of the year."

DE LA HOYA - HOPKINS: GOLD VS. CONCRETE

When Oscar De La Hoya versus Bernard Hopkins was announced earlier this year, there were a lot of naysayers who said the fight would never happen. Now the only potential stumbling block appears to be the possibility that Hopkins will pull out because of laryngitis.

Barring the unexpected, September 18th will see an updated version of Sugar Ray Leonard versus Marvin Hagler: a Golden Boy with Olympic pedigree going up in weight to challenge a dominant blue-collar champion.

De La Hoya bristles at that categorization. "A lot of people think I had everything handed to me on a silver platter," he says. "People see the actual fight and say, 'Wow, he won all this money in one night.' Or they think it was easy and that they can do it. But it's not that easy. I started when I was four years old. People don't realize how many sacrifices I've had to make over the years. It was a long road to where I'm at now. It's not easy being an athlete, especially at this level; and on top of that, being a fighter."

Both men are fighting for immortality. And both men have such strong personalities that their ethnic differences have hardly been noticed.

The contract weight is 158 pounds, two pounds below the middleweight limit. But that shouldn't be a problem for Hopkins, who is rarely more than a few days away from making weight.

"Bernard Hopkins is very, very dangerous," De La Hoya acknowledges. "This guy is strong, an animal. I know I'm in deep water, but I'm willing to put my life on the line to make history. I was born to fight. Boxing runs through my veins; it just won't go away. It's not for money; I can make money against anyone. I love to fight and to rise to the occasion. What's bigger than beating Bernard Hopkins?"

This is Hopkins's second coming-out party. The first was three years ago when he devastated Felix Trinidad, knocking him out in the twelfth round. As Patrick Kehoe later wrote, "To fight the fight of your life in your most momentous outing defines a champion."

If there's a knock against Hopkins as a fighter, it's that he always seems to get in the ring against littler guys. But he has successfully defended various versions of the middleweight crown eighteen times. And in the process, he has stamped his persona on boxing.

"Hopkins," Tom Gerbasi observes, "is all about what's right for him. That has burned a lot of people; from promoters to managers, from the media to his own trainer. It wasn't personal. They served their purpose and were let go. He travels light. You're either with him or against him. There is no room for dissent or questions. That's business; and business is not about friendship, loyalty, or doing the right thing by those who have done right by you."

Hopkins stands for the proposition, "Life is tough, but I'm tougher." He's self-absorbed with emotional wounds that scar over but never really heal. He's an angry man, and his anger fuels him. He acknowledges as much when he declares, "Motivation can come in all shapes and forms with me. If I go outside and all my tires are slashed, that's motivation. When things run smoothly, somebody has to break a glass. Some people need bumps in the road to make things happen. It don't always have to be downright dirty ignorant stuff. It just has to be some type of motivation. I need that. Maybe, in some cases, I've interacted and made it to the point where I brought it upon myself."

"I don't think a lot of people will get ulcers or cry all day if Bernard Hopkins don't come up with a win," Hopkins continues. "I was born with something that everybody ain't born with—my heart. Not just a heart that's beating, but a heart to stand up and balls to stand up and courage to stand up. It's easy for me to stand up because that's me. They call me an ingrate. Why is that? Is it because I refuse to be fucked, or is it because I prefer to be the one fucking?"

One denizen of the boxing world who has crossed swords with Hopkins is promoter Dan Goossen. When reminded of the Will Rogers saying—"I never met a man I didn't like"—Goossen responds, "Obviously, Will Rogers never met Bernard Hopkins."

Still, as Hopkins observes, "People can say what they want about my character. One thing everyone agrees is, in the ring, I'm not a liar. When it gets hot, I'm not jumping out of the kitchen."

That's true. As his trainer, Bouie Fisher, notes, "Bernard is a throwback fighter when it comes to dedication in and out of the ring. Boxing never leaves his thoughts. He lives, eats, and dreams boxing. He puts in the work that's necessary to be great."

To date, Hopkins has been respectful of De La Hoya. "Oscar is known as the darling boy of boxing," he acknowledges. "But you can't hate him for that. Oscar brings a lot to boxing and Oscar is a great competitor.

You can say a lot of things about him, but the man comes to fight and he's never ducked anyone. He's the money-man, the big draw. He got more money for fighting guys you all say shouldn't have even been in the ring with him than most of us do for fighting the biggest and most difficult challenge of our lives. He didn't have to take Bernard Hopkins; that was strictly Oscar's call. This fight is happening because Oscar wanted it to happen, and that tells me a lot about the man."

But then Hopkins adds, "Twenty successful middleweight title defenses is my goal. I think it would be a long time before anyone beat that record. To me, Oscar is number nineteen; that's all."

On September 18th, De La Hoya will be going into the ring as an underdog for the first time in his professional career. Most pundits think Hopkins will win. Many of them don't even think it will be a competitive fight.

"I have a lot of respect for Hopkins," says De La Hoya. "He's a great champion, but I believe that my speed will be the difference. I'm not Trinidad. Trinidad is a one-dimensional fighter, easy to figure out. I'm not that easy, and I guarantee that Hopkins won't figure me out. People expect that I'll stick and move and run a lot, like Leonard did with Hagler. But I'm going to have to take it to Hopkins, at least a little bit. I have to get that respect. If I don't, he'll run right over me. But once I have his respect, I'll make it my fight. I don't have to have a big punch. I am not counting on a knockout. My focus is on going the distance and winning. Don't underestimate the little guy."

Then there's the matter of Hopkins's age. On fight night, he'll be four months shy of forty.

"Do I get more aches and pains than I did five or six years ago?" Bernard asks rhetorically. "Absolutely. Do I get more rubdowns, more chiropractors? Absolutely. We all deteriorate. I hate to say it like that; but the longer we live, the more we're going to hurt."

But then, in the next breath, Hopkins declares, "My body has been put together different by God than any other body that's living. Once you start thinking old, you become old. I haven't started thinking old yet."

De La Hoya might think that, against Hopkins, he can revert to the fighting style of his youth. But he won't be able to. Bernard won't let him. And more significantly, Oscar no longer has the physical tools to fight the way he once did. He's not young anymore.

De La Hoya's record is 6 and 3 in his last nine fights. One can argue that the decisions he lost to Felix Trinidad and Shane Mosley (in their second encounter) were questionable, but so was his victory over Felix Sturm. And other than Sturm, the only fighters Oscar has beaten over the past five years are an overmatched Derrell Coley, a blown-up Arturo Gatti, a one-dimensional Javier Castellejo, a drug-ridden Fernando Vargas, and a shot Yuri Boy Campos.

Hopkins hit the nail on the head when he assessed De La Hoya's performance against Sturm. "He wasn't moving to his left or his right quickly," Bernard notes. "And Sturm was just eating him up with those jabs. I thought Oscar was using some kind of macho thing, which is unprofessional because you don't want to show that you can hang in with the middleweights by taking punches. Then, as the rounds went on, I said, 'Wait a minute. He can't get past this guy's jab.'"

Moreover, Hopkins might be stretching reality when he proclaims, "I'm perfect when it comes to boxing." But his fists are nasty weapons, and he has both the skills and attitude to use them to maximum effect.

"I'm not shy when it comes to inflicting pain on people," says Hopkins. "Nothing is fair, what fighters do. You hit behind the head? It's not legal, but it happens. There's no such thing as a dirty fighter to me. It's just an opportunity. You're dirty only when you get caught. In the ring, there's a chance you can die or become a vegetable. And the reality is, I would rather it be him than me."

"De La Hoya won't see twelve rounds," Hopkins continues. "Somewhere along the line, his corner will have to make a decision. He'll still have his movie career if they stop the fight in time. They'll be smart enough to know that we'd better stop it right now while we still got an eye left or a lip left. It's up to them; it's their call. I don't think they're going to let De La Hoya get punished like Joppy did [in his fight against Hopkins last year]. I think that his corner has enough sense to do what Joppy's corner didn't do; throw the towel in."

In sum, De La Hoya versus Hopkins has the markings of a man beating up a boy. On paper, Oscar doesn't have the tools to win. But this is boxing. And regardless of what has happened in the past, fighters who face one another in the ring start from scratch each time out and must perform every time.

If, as expected, Hopkins wins, neither man's legacy will change. But if De La Hoya finds a way to prevail, historical perspectives will be revised. Is an upset possible? Hopkins himself noted last month, "It only takes one shot to shatter your dreams." ❏

De La Hoya-Hopkins presented a unique opportunity to look behind the scenes at a big Las Vegas fight.

DE LA HOYA, HOPKINS, AND THE
FIGHT CAPITAL OF THE WORLD

"New York," Jerry Izenberg once wrote, "was the greatest fight town that ever was and ever will be."

But Las Vegas power brokers take a contrary view. When there's a super-fight in New York, they note, only fight fans are aware of it and the action takes place on fight night at Madison Square Garden. When there's a big fight in Las Vegas, the action is all week and excitement crackles through the entire city.

Las Vegas was founded in 1905 as a railroad town. Thirty years later, the state legislature legalized gambling and changed its domestic relations law to allow for "quickie" divorces. Thereafter, the casino industry took hold as the primary business in Las Vegas and organized crime rose to a position of power. Then, in 1967, the laws changed to permit publicly-traded companies to obtain gambling licenses and a new breed of corporate owner moved in. In 1950, Clark County (where Las Vegas is located) had 48,589 residents. In 2000, that number was 1,428,690.

The first big-name boxer to fight in Las Vegas was Archie Moore, who won a fifteen-round decision over Nino Valdes on May 2, 1955. The city's first world championship bout saw Benny "Kid" Paret take the welterweight crown from Don Jordan in 1960. Its first heavyweight championship contest was the 1963 rematch between Sonny Liston and Floyd Patterson. That was followed by Muhammad Ali versus Patterson in 1965. It wasn't until December 6, 1969, when Sonny Liston was knocked out by Leotis Martin at the International Hotel, that a fight was held in a Las Vegas hotel-casino.

Once the casinos realized that major fights attracted high rollers, boxing began to receive billing on the neon signs that had once been reserved for entertainers like Elvis Presley and Frank Sinatra. But the fight that changed everything was Larry Holmes's title defense against an aging Muhammad Ali on October 2, 1980. Caesars constructed a huge temporary outdoor arena evocative of historic nights at Yankee

Stadium and Comiskey Park. The fight sold out and the casino "drop" was unprecedented. That night, Las Vegas was crowned the new "Mecca of Boxing."

Boxing's negative image scares off most corporate sponsors but not hotel-casinos. To the contrary, Las Vegas has a collective corporate commitment to boxing that is unmatched anywhere in the world. Entertainment to a casino is only as good as the excitement it brings to the gaming floor; and nothing creates excitement like a big fight. Other events, be it a NASCAR race or corporate convention, lure millions of people to Las Vegas each year. But those visitors are less likely than high-rolling boxing fans to drop tens of thousands of dollars at the tables in a single night.

The risk and exitement generated by boxing parallels the risk and excitement of gaming. A big fight doesn't just bring in high rollers. It creates an environment that encourages gambling. The situation becomes combustible. There's an explosion of money. And the benefits of a big fight go far beyond that one event. A big fight reinforces the view that the host site is a place where exciting things happen. A million pay-per-view buys with four or five people sitting around each television set is excellent branding.

Las Vegas will never host the World Series, Super Bowl or NBA Championships. But it regularly snares the biggest and best in boxing. It lost Holyfield-Lewis I to Madison Square Garden and De La Hoya-Mosley I to the Staples Center in Los Angeles. But generally, the city gets what it wants.

Logistically, no site can duplicate Las Vegas. The infrastructure at the big hotel-casinos is incredible. They offer lodging, meals, meeting rooms: the entire fight center under one roof. The MGM Grand and Mandalay Bay have their own large arenas. Taxes are low. Site fees are high because the money will be made back on ticket sales, at the gaming tables, and from other revenue streams such as rooms, restaurants, and shows. Direct flights to and from McCarran Airport are plentiful. And once Las Vegas says 'yes' to a fight, the entire city supports the promotion because a big fight at one casino benefits all of them.

Marketing a mega-fight is a well-coordinated effort in which the major players are the venue, the television network, and the promoter. Everything is ratcheted up. There's a nicer-looking ticket (although new ticketing systems are sometimes incompatible with works of art); commemorative chips in the casino; better food in the media center; and lavish fight-night parties. Gifts to high-rollers are more elaborate than the norm, from boxes of fine cigars with bands bearing the fight logo to gloves autographed by both main-event fighters.

For Holyfield-Lewis II, Don King created media credentials that were shaped like his crown logo and cost ten dollars each to manufacture. More memorably, on the night of Holmes-Norton, DK hosted a "Sportsman's Ball." Legend has it that the guest list was comprised largely of drug dealers, numbers operators, pimps, and others who were personally acquainted with King from his younger days. The "sportsmen" didn't have credit lines with Caesars, but arrived with bundles of cash and gambled liberally on the casino floor.

The idea is to create a mindset that the host site is the place to be and be seen and have a good time. On fight night, there's a parallel between the anything goes atmosphere of Las Vegas and the anything goes ethic of boxing. Every major casino is jammed. Room rates double. Restaurants are full. There's traffic everywhere. Hot women are running around and more hookers than usual are seated at the bars. Patrons at strip clubs have to wait their turn just to get a lap dance. Every limousine is contracted out. The issue of which high rollers get which ringside seats has been more carefully charted and fought over than who sits where at a presidential inauguration. Closed-circuit fight parties have been booked at hotels for guests who don't rank high enough on the pecking order to merit a ticket to the fight. And when the fight is over, the site hotel is mobbed; not just with regular customers, celebrities, and high-rollers, but also with pick-pockets and hustlers. Extra security is needed to keep guests safe and, equally important, make them feel safe. Otherwise, they'll go to their rooms instead of gamble.

It was in this milieu that Oscar De La Hoya and Bernard Hopkins became business partners.

For twelve years, De La Hoya has been boxing's "Golden Boy." Earlier this year, *Sports Illustrated* ranked him #6 on its list of the world's highest-paid athletes with earnings of $32 million in 2003.

Oscar has endorsement contracts with Visa and Nestle and a licensing deal for his own line of clothing. More significantly, he's the principal shareholder in Golden Boy Sports and Entertainment Group, which has five subsidiaries: (1) Golden Boy Promotions, which promotes fights; (2) Golden Boy Management, which represents fighters; (3) Golden Boy Television and Film, which produces various programs; (4) Golden Boy Videos, which owns visual rights to many fights, including Oscar's; and (5) Golden Boy Music, which owns the rights to De La Hoya's CDs and music videos. Then there's Golden Boy Real Estate Group, which is the majority owner of an office tower in downtown Los Angeles and has a minority interest in a second office tower in New York. Another entity, Golden Boy Corporate Holdings, has an interest in CPK Media, which gives it a stake in *La Opinion* (the largest Spanish-language daily in the United States) and *El Diario - La Prensa* (the nation's oldest Spanish-language newspaper).

Over the years, De La Hoya, Mike Tyson and Evander Holyfield have been the primary pay-per-view attractions in boxing. Hopkins was Oscar's sixteenth pay-per-view fight. The first fifteen engendered 8,515,000 buys with gross revenues of $388,300,000. There were 1,400,000 buys for De La Hoya against Felix Trinidad, more than any non-heavyweight fight ever. De La Hoya-Mosley II and De La Hoya-Vargas rank second and third on that list. By contrast, there were only 440,000 buys for Hopkins-Trinidad, which was Bernard's lone previous mega-fight.

Hopkins understood those realities and agreed to fight De La Hoya for a ten-million-dollar purse despite the fact that Oscar would be getting three times that amount. "We all got egos," Bernard said. "Tarver, Roy, me; we all got egos. But sometimes you need to put that to the side. There's ego and there's business. To make money, you've got to be bigger than just a champion today. Oscar De La Hoya is the pot of gold at the end of my rainbow."

How did Hopkins feel about getting only ten million dollars to Oscar's thirty million?

"Since when is ten million dollars 'only'?" Bernard countered.

An Oscar De La Hoya fight is always more than the fight itself, and this one was no exception. The MGM Grand (which paid a $12,000,000 site fee to host the bout) did its best to create an atmosphere that said this was a unique event. Images of De La Hoya and Hopkins were on everything from the felt tops on blackjack tables to computerized room-key cards. Back-lit fight posters and video walls featuring the combatants were on display throughout the hotel.

The timing was good. Boxing was desperate for a big event; there was nothing to compete with this one; and with the heavyweight division in a slump, De La Hoya-Hopkins was this year's Super Bowl for Las Vegas.

Still, the buzz seemed to be manufactured rather than spontaneous. When Oscar fought Felix Trinidad and Fernando Vargas, his opponents brought their own constituencies with them. Hopkins didn't. De La Hoya-Hopkins never caught fire as east versus west or black versus white. There was no rivalry between Mexican-American castes or Hispanic-Americans and Puerto Ricans to play off of. It was simply Oscar and Bernard.

Presiding over it all was Bob Arum, a power in boxing for forty years. In recent decades, most of the non-heavyweight mega-fights have belonged to Arum, including Marvin Hagler versus Ray Leonard and Hagler against Thomas Hearns.

Arum did his best to promote De La Hoya-Hopkins as the reincarnation of Hagler-Leonard. In each instance, an Olympic gold-medalist and darling of the boxing establishment was stepping up in weight to challenge a foreboding blue-collar champion. Hagler had been unbeaten for eleven years before he fought Leonard. Hopkins hadn't lost since he was defeated by Roy Jones eleven years ago.

At the final pre-fight press conference on Wednesday, September 15th, the big-fight rituals were all in place. Arum was throwing around terms like "fever pitch" and proclaiming, "Our goal is to make this the biggest fight in the history of pay-per-view boxing."

When it was his turn to speak, Hopkins began with the declaration, "I'm not playing De La Hoya cheap. Oscar had a different road to get here, but I don't underestimate his trials and tribulations." He then sounded a humorous note, responding to De La Hoya's claim that his poor performance against Felix Sturm this past June was the result of not being properly motivated for the fight. "How can you not get motivated," Bernard asked rhetorically, "when a guy is coming to punch you in the face?"

De La Hoya made a point of saying that, this time, he was in superb condition and had trained eleven weeks for the fight. But Hopkins had trained for it his entire adult life. "Five o'clock in the morning, every morning," Bernard told the media, "a 39-year-old man is up, going out to do roadwork. This night has been on my mind for twenty years."

"I have a better right hand and left hook than Oscar," Hopkins continued. "Out of everybody Oscar De La Hoya has fought, I'm the best fighter, talent-wise, strength-wise, and more versatile. Everything Oscar De La Hoya has done in the ring, Bernard Hopkins can do better. Oscar has to be perfect to have a chance in this fight. I only have to be Bernard Hopkins to win." Then Hopkins pointed directly at De La Hoya. "Dead man walking," he said.

At that moment, De La Hoya-Hopkins looked like Little Red Riding Hood versus the Big Bad Wolf. But there was one compelling argument to be made in favor of Oscar emerging victorious. He didn't have to take the fight; no one had expected him to take the fight; no one would have held it against him if he hadn't; and he didn't need the money. Ergo, he must think he can win.

On Thursday, the fighters' respective trainers visited the media center. Floyd Mayweather Sr. began his remarks with the declaration, "Most of the media just repeats what it hears; it doesn't understand boxing." He then stated the case for a De La Hoya victory, saying, "Hopkins is bigger and stronger than Oscar, but Oscar has more talent than Hopkins. Oscar just has to keep Hopkins from imposing his will on him. He has to frustrate Hopkins; jab and get out. And there will be times when Oscar has to stand his ground and exchange punches."

But there was a caveat. "Oscar is in the best condition he's ever been in," Mayweather posited. "If Oscar gets tired, it's just in his head. And if that's what's in his head, there's nothing that anyone can do about it. No matter what anyone tells you, no one can go into another person's mind."

Bouie Fisher (Bernard's trainer) had no such reservations. The foundation stone of hope for most De La Hoya supporters was the belief that, against Oscar, the 39-year-old Hopkins might somehow grow old overnight.

"I know a thing or two about growing old," the 76-year-old Fisher said. "And I can tell you that no one grows old overnight. As long as a fighter is properly conditioned, his age won't show all at once."

Then Fisher was asked who would have won a fight between Hopkins and Sugar Ray Robinson. "Oh my God; it would have been no contest," he answered. "Ray Robinson was so great. He was a beautiful fighter."

By Friday, the media center had become a giant social gathering place and also a bizarre bazaar. Boxing is a great laboratory for the study of human behavior, and the petrie dish was overflowing.

The National Hockey League season seemed to be going down the drain because of a lockout. Thus, promoters and managers were scrambling to see if TSN (Canada's version of ESPN) wanted to fill a portion of its schedule with boxing. Hurricane Ivan was decimating the Florida panhandle, which led to thoughts of Roy Jones and the question of how one evacuates forty pit bulls and seven hundred fighting cocks from a farm. Visions of *The Birds* combined with *Cujo* came to mind.

Legendary ring great Roberto Duran was holding court in a corner of the media center. Bob Arum had wanted to bring Ray Leonard and Marvin Hagler to Las Vegas to promote the fight. But Leonard was busy taping *The Contender* for NBC, and Hagler had demanded $25,000. The 53-year-old Duran fit within the promotion's budget.

Duran has come a long way from his days as a boy who slept on the streets of Panama. "I don't miss fighting," he said. "When I got older, it was a chore. When I got old, everybody wanted to beat Roberto Duran. Now my life is good. I play dominoes. I play ball with children in the street. If someone tries to pick a fight with me in a bar, I call security. I love cooking; I'm a pretty good cook. And I go to the movies a lot. When I was a boy, I used to shine shoes to get enough money to go to the movies."

What kind of movies?

"John Wayne was always my favorite. When they showed John Wayne movies in Panama, every time it was a full house. The first movies I bought when I got a Betamax were a John Wayne movie and *King Kong*."

Duran voiced the opinion that Carlos Monzon would have beaten Hopkins, and Hagler would have beaten both of them. Then "Manos de Piedras" was asked about politics and turned surprisingly thoughtful. "I'm worried about the world," he said. "It's very sad. Soon, people are going to burn the whole world down. I never like war; innocent lives are lost. And now it's war all the time. Four years ago, I was invited to the Middle East to see the Pyramids and the Wailing Wall. I wanted to see them, but I was afraid to go."

Meanwhile, in another part of the hotel, the HBO production team was conducting its pre-fight meetings with the main-event fighters. The interview with De La Hoya went as planned, but the session with Hopkins turned ugly. Bernard launched into a diatribe that included a whack at Larry Merchant, whom he has been at odds with since his March 2003 title defense against Morrade Hakkar. Emanuel Steward, wanted to talk about Hopkins versus De La Hoya and grew weary of it all.

"Look," said Steward. "Larry calls things the way he sees them. And besides, Larry has always given you credit for being a great fighter."

That earned a withering look from Hopkins, who told Emanuel, "This is 2004. You don't have to defend him anymore."

Merchant then joined the act, demanding, "Why are you starting that black-white stuff?"

At 3:30 on Friday afternoon, Hopkins and De La Hoya weighed in at the MGM Grand Garden Arena before an estimated 5,000 fans. Both men came in light; Bernard at 156 pounds, Oscar at 155. Hopkins looked like one of the raptors from *Jurassic Park*. But as Bouie Fisher noted, "If you're in a mean, vicious business, it helps to be mean and vicious."

Then came a twist, a bad one. At 5:30 p.m., well after the pre-fight physicals and weigh-in, Tony Daly (De La Hoya's personal physician) told Marc Ratner (executive director of the Nevada State Athletic Commission) that Oscar's left hand had been cut on Wednesday and that he'd received eleven stitches. According to Daly, the cut was sustained when assistant trainer Joe Chavez pierced De La Hoya's hand with a scissors while cutting off his training wraps. Biff McCann was the plastic surgeon who sutured the wound.

Why was the information being made available to the commission two days after the fact?

Because, according to Daly, Oscar had received an injection of lido-caine.

Lidocaine is illegal under the rules and regulations of the Nevada State Athletic Commission. Tylenol is the only pain medicine that a fighter is allowed to take before a fight. Daly was telling Ratner in case Oscar's urine sample came up "dirty."

That raised a host of questions giving rise to a range of conspiracy theories. De La Hoya-Hopkins was happening because Oscar had won a questionable decision over Felix Sturm in Las Vegas three months earlier. All three judges scored that bout 115-113 in De La Hoya's favor. Two of those judges (Dave Moretti and Paul Smith) were now being rewarded for their wisdom with the plum De La Hoya-Hopkins assignment. Also, for the first time in recent memory, the medical director and chief ringside physician for the Nevada State Athletic Commission had been passed over for a ringside assignment at a Las Vegas mega-fight. Many observers took that as a sign of Bob Arum's influence with the commission. Arum and Dr. Margaret Goodman have been feuding in recent years over such issues as Goodman's advocacy of mandatory MRI testing for fighters and her decision to place at least one fighter promoted by Arum on medical suspension. And last, Joe Cortez (Nevada's top referee) had been passed over in favor of Kenny Bayless.

In sum, the biggest fight of the year was about to take place. And the NSAC had chosen not to assign it's number-one referee, its two top judges (Jerry Roth and Duane Ford), or its premier doctor.

Goodman's absence meant that De La Hoya's pre-fight physical had been conducted by Dr. Albert Capanna, a presumably capable neuro-surgeon and self-described "friend of Bob Arum."

How does a doctor conducting a pre-fight physical not notice eleven stitches in a fighter's hand; particularly when the fighter is known to have undergone hand surgery in the past? Isn't it odd for a cornerman to be so careless that he slices open a fighter's hand while cutting off tape after a pre-fight workout; particularly when the fighter is Oscar De La Hoya on the verge of a thirty-million-dollar payday? And lidocaine disappears from a person's system within seven or eight hours. Was it possible that the De La Hoya camp was simply looking for a way to inject lidocaine into Oscar's troubled hand on fight night? Just by announcing that a fighter has been given an illegal drug doesn't make it right.

The affair brought some pointed comments on HBO the following night. Jim Lampley spoke of "unusual issues." Larry Merchant was more direct, referencing "the appearance of a cave-in to business interests." In reality, the problems appear to have been the work of a minority of commission members, who failed to consult with their peers on important matters. The Nevada State Athletic Commission is now balanced on a precarious fulcrum. One hopes that Governor Kenny Guinn will push it toward good government rather than something less in the months ahead.

Meanwhile, the Hopkins camp was philosophical. James Fisher (Bouie's son) expressed its collective view regarding De La Hoya's hand when he said, "If you're on death row, slip in the shower, and get cut, it doesn't make much difference."

In the end, the fight fell short of selling out. Capacity for the arena was 16,270, and 158 tickets went unsold. But all of those were single seats, and 9,384 more fans watched the fight at closed-circuit parties in the MGM Grand.

There were 850 requests for media credentials; 550 were granted. Two hundred reporters sat at ringside and 60 in auxiliary positions. 290 more watched the fight on television in the media center. There were 16 photographers on the ring apron and 41 in the upper reaches of the arena.

The odds had opened at 11-to-10 in favor of Hopkins and moved quickly to 5-to-2. By fight time, they were down to 2-to-1. The big money (i.e. wagers by professional gamblers) came in on Bernard. The small bets were mostly on Oscar. Six days after the fight, HBO announced that the telecast had engendered one million pay-per-view buys, but more than one insider questioned whether the real number was that high.

Spectators at ringside included Mike Tyson, Evander Holyfield (who got the loudest cheers), Vitali Klitschko, Roberto Duran, Thomas Hearns, Arturo Gatti, Shane Mosley, Winky Wright, Floyd Mayweather Jr., Antonio Tarver, and Marco Antonio Barrera. The NBA was represented by Magic Johnson, Charles Barkley, Patrick Ewing, Phil Jackson, Kevin Garnett, LeBron James, Scotty Pippin, Rasheed Wallace, and Chauncy Billups. John McCain, Larry King, Sylvester Stallone, Billy Crystal, Michael J. Fox, Mark Wahlberg, Chris Tucker, Jamie Foxx, and Nicole Kidman were also there.

Moments before the main event, *Thus Spake Zarathustra* (more commonly known as the theme from Stanley Kubrick's *2001: A Space Odyssey*) sounded. Then De La Hoya entered the ring in the wake of a seven-man mariachi band. Hopkins followed to the strains of Frank Sinatra's *My Way* which segued into *The Champ Is Here*.

As for the competition, the action was sparse as each man fought a cautious tactical fight. The crowd was heavily pro-Oscar. But as Bouie Fisher observed, "The crowd can't throw a punch and they can't duck a punch. They can't block a punch and they can't land one."

Hopkins always comes prepared, and this night was no exception. He's a fighter who bides his time, breaks his opponent down, and does what he has to do to prevail. De La Hoya knows how to win rounds but isn't always willing to pay the price.

For the first six stanzas, Bernard chose to counterpunch, like a cat who has baited a mousetrap with cheese. Then, in round seven, he stepped up the pressure behind a more aggressive jab. The feeling then was that De La Hoya would be slowly beaten down. Instead, one brutal body punch (a left hook to the liver in round nine) spared him that fate. Two of the three judges had Hopkins comfortably ahead at the time of the stoppage. This observer had him leading 77-75 (five rounds to three) when the end came.

"I have no excuses," Oscar said afterward. "He caught me with a good shot. When you get hit to the body, it's not just how hard you're hit; it's where you're hit. It was a perfectly placed shot."

As for the future, both men have myriad options. De La Hoya maintained that he'd been so focussed on Hopkins that he hadn't thought about what comes next. If he continues to box, he could look to a B-level opponent for his next fight or seek a lucrative rematch against Felix Trinidad or Shane Mosley.

Hopkins made it clear that he wants his next fight to be the twentieth defense of his middleweight-championship reign. Then, he says, he'll seek big fights out of the middleweight division. That could mean someone like Antonio Tarver. But given Bernard's history of fighting smaller men, he's more likely to continue in the ring against Felix Sturm or the winner of Winky Wright versus Shane Mosley. A rematch against Felix Trinidad is also possible. If he fights Jermaine Taylor, he'll want to do it before too much time goes by.

Bernard Hopkins is a remarkable fighter. When he turns forty on January 15th, he'll be the undisputed middleweight champion of the world. One hopes he remembers that champions fight champions and that he will show as much courage in seeking out future opponents as Oscar De La Hoya demonstrated in challenging him.❏

When SPORTClassic Books published The Italian Stallions, *an illustrated history of great Italian-American champions, I wrote the following introduction for the book.*

WHEN BOXING MATTERED

In 1922, Jack Dempsey was heavyweight champion of the world. Babe Ruth was patrolling rightfield for the New York Yankees. And Knute Rockne was the head football coach at Notre Dame. But as "the Roaring Twenties" were blossoming, a wave of xenophobia was sweeping America.

The previous year, Italian-born anarchists Nicola Sacco and Bartolomeo Vanzetti had been tried and found guilty of killing two men in a Massachusetts payroll robbery. Despite substantial evidence of their innocence, they were later executed. Also in 1921, Congress passed legislation that sharply curtailed immigration to the United States. Much of the impetus for this legislation came from anti-Italian sentiment. Shortly thereafter, Benito Mussolini marched on Rome and formed the fascist government that would be forever identified with his name.

It was into this world, in 1922, that Guiglielmo Papaleo, Giuseppe Berardinelli, Thomas Rocco Barbella, and Giacobe LaMotta were born. In 1923, Rocco Francis Marchegiano joined them. Ultimately, these five men would become known as Willie Pep, Joey Maxim, Rocky Graziano, Jake LaMotta, and Rocky Marciano. They would win world championships as professional boxers. And in doing so, they would shape the way in which America viewed the Italian-American community and also the manner in which the Italian-American community viewed itself.

Boxing belongs to the underclass. When the Irish came to America in large numbers, John L. Sullivan was their standard bearer. In the early twentieth century, the Jewish ghettos of New York gave rise to Benny Leonard and Barney Ross.

Giuseppe Carrora emigrated to the United States from Sicily with his parents. Fighting under the name of Johnny Dundee, he won the junior-lightweight title in 1921 and, a year later, the world featherweight crown. Dundee was regarded as the first of the great Italian-American fighters.

Italian-American champions born in the United States followed in

Dundee's wake. Frankie Gennaro and Midget Wolgast won the world flyweight title. Battling Battalino and Petey Scalzo held the feather-weight crown. Sammy Mandell and Sammy Angott ascended to the lightweight throne. Tony Canzoneri reigned as featherweight, light-weight, and junior-welterweight king.

These men represented the struggle of first-generation Italian-Americans born in the United States who were trying to fight their way out of the ghetto. And they fought at a time when boxing truly mattered.

In the first half of the twentieth century, boxing and baseball were America's two national sports. On Saturday afternoons, hundreds of people would go to Stillman's Gym in the Bronx just to watch the fighters train. At one time, there were twenty-two fight clubs in New York City; each one in a different neighborhood. And unless someone was boxing an opponent from another part of New York or had risen to world-class status, he fought guys from his own neighborhood. There was no such thing as bringing in an opponent from out-of-state for a four-round preliminary fight.

Fighters were connected to the community in a meaningful way. People in the neighborhood knew them and saw them on a regular basis. And for Italian-Americans, boxing had special meaning because there were few Italian-American heroes on a national scale.

Fiorello LaGuardia was elected mayor of New York in 1933, but Italian-Americans were largely excluded from the high councils of polit-ical power. It wasn't until Lyndon Johnson designated Anthony Celebrezze as Secretary of Health, Education, and Welfare in the mid-1960s that an Italian-American served in the president's cabinet.

Meanwhile, Angelo Bertelli starred on the gridiron for Notre Dame. Hank Lusetti excelled in basketball for Stanford. And of course, there was Joe DiMaggio. But the sport that was most open to Italian-Americans was boxing. Willie Pep reigned as featherweight champion for seven years. Joey Maxim won the light-heavyweight title and is in the record books as the only man to knock out Sugar Ray Robinson. Rocky Graziano and Jake LaMotta captured the middleweight crown.

LaMotta is an icon today because of the movie *Raging Bull*. But in his heyday, his standing within the Italian-American community was a complex matter. LaMotta was born to Italian immigrant parents on the Lower East Side of Manhattan. After a brief sojourn in Philadelphia, his family moved to the Bronx. LaMotta attended Public School 55 and got as far as ninth grade. Then he was sent to a juvenile detention center. Subsequent to his ring career, he spent six months in prison for a con-viction on charges that he operated a cocktail lounge for purposes of prostitution.

LaMotta wasn't the only "bad boy" among Italian-Americans in boxing. Rocky Graziano had dropped out of school after fifth grade and resided in correctional institutes for six of his first twenty years. Drafted into the United States Army during World War II, Graziano then spent ten months in military prison for going AWOL and assaulting an officer.

Willie Pep had been arrested for illegal gambling. Joey Giardello, who later reigned as middleweight champion, also spent time in prison. But to his neighbors, LaMotta's crime, the one the community reviled him for, was worse than any of the aforementioned offenses.

In 1947, LaMotta signed to fight Billy Fox, a Philadelphia light-heavyweight with a record of forty-eight wins, one loss, and forty-eight knockouts. The "Bronx Bull", as LaMotta was known, was the number-one middleweight contender. He had never been knocked out. On the afternoon of the fight, the odds jumped from even money to 12-to-5 in Fox's favor. Madison Square Garden was completely sold out. The fight, as LaMotta later admitted in testimony before Congress, was fixed. Fox hit him unanswered blows for four rounds. Finally, the referee halted the bout.

LaMotta had committed the ultimate sin. People had believed that he was an honest fighter. His neighbors were certain that he would always do his best. Now that belief was gone. Men and women who worked hard for their money, neighbors who had known him for years, had bet on him and lost. He had betrayed them.

Nineteen months later, LaMotta won the middleweight title, but he was an unpopular champion. Many fans disliked his abusive personality. Others despised him for having thrown the Fox fight. *Newsweek* described him as "more hated than any other two champions." W.C. Heinz wrote an article entitled "The Most Hated Man in Sports" that closed with the words, "Jake LaMotta will go into the books as one of the most unpopular sports figures of all time."

But as a counterpoint to LaMotta, there was Rocky Marciano.

Marciano was embedded in the consciousness of Italian-Americans in the same way that Joe Louis lived in the hearts of his people. Born in Brockton, Massachusetts, the son of an immigrant shoemaker, Rocco Marchegiano left high school during tenth grade. For a while, he worked in the same shoe factory as his father; but he couldn't stand being indoors, so he took a job as a landscape gardener and then went to work clearing land. In 1943, he was drafted into the United States Army. Two years after World War II ended, he turned pro. In 1952, Marciano knocked out Jersey Joe Walcott to become heavyweight champion of the world. Four years later, he retired with 49 victories in 49 fights.

There had been an Italian heavyweight champion before Marciano. But Primo Carnera, who wore the crown for less than a year in the mid-1930s, was mob-controlled. Many of his fights had been fixed, and there came a time when the public knew it.

Marciano was the real thing, and he reigned at a time when the heavyweight championship was the most coveted title in sports. It was also a time when the sports media was very different from today. Fans got most of their information from newspapers and magazines. The fights themselves were experienced by attending in person or by listening to the radio. On occasion, they were witnessed on a new medium called television. And for the most part, reporting on athletes was innocent in the extreme.

Thus, Ed Fitzgerald wrote in the pages of *SPORT*, "All the boys from Brockton identified themselves with their champion. His victories became their victories. They rejoiced that success hadn't taken Rocky away from them. He still lived among them. Rocky is a neighborhood kid who married a neighborhood girl and who thinks the old hometown is the greatest place in the world. Rocky's social activities are confined largely to entertaining friends and relatives at home or making the rounds of their houses, and to the Ward Two Club and the Seville Council, Knights of Columbus. The priests and nuns of St. Colman's parish where he worships call on him again and again to serve as a model for their lectures to the neighborhood kids."

The profligate womanizing that marked Marciano's life went unreported. So did other instances of anti-social behavior. And for Italian-Americans, Rocky Marciano became the ultimate status symbol; in part, because he was seen as the stereotypical Italian-American.

To the community, Marciano was "one of us." Joe DiMaggio had a passport to a higher level of society. DiMaggio was the essence of style and grace, but DiMaggio was aloof. He gave the impression of being above it all and on a level that other Italian-Americans could never reach. DiMaggio married Marilyn Monroe. Marilyn Monroe would not have married Rocky Marciano.

There were several Italian-American champions after Marciano. Carmen Basilio's parents emigrated to the United States from Italy. Basilio's father became an onion-farmer in upstate New York. Basilio became the welterweight and middleweight champion of the world. Joey Giardello followed suit as far as the middleweight title was concerned.

But assimilation and upward mobility were ending the glory years for Italian-American fighters. And while there have been fighters who mattered a lot during the past half-century—Muhammad Ali foremost among them—boxing as a sport has receded in the public consciousness.

Still, a final look at Johnny Dundee, Midget Wolgast, Frankie Gennaro, Sammy Mandell, Tony Canzoneri, Battling Battalino, Sammy Angott, Petey Scalzo, Willie Pep, Rocky Graziano, Joey Maxim, Jake LaMotta, Carmen Basilio, Joey Giardello, and Rocky Marciano is in order.

The term "champion" has been devalued in recent years with seventeen weight classes and four world sanctioning bodies. But these men were true champions. And they were tough. Their composite record reveals 2,101 professional fights; many against world-class competition, often against one another. Yet in 2,101 professional fights, they were knocked out only 44 times. Discount the inevitable late-career knockouts by removing 48 fights from the end of their composite record, and the totals show a mere 26 knockout losses in 2,053 fights. That's extraordinary.

Want more? In world championship fights, these seventeen men compiled a composite record of 77 wins, 36 losses, 7 draws, and 1 no contest. In fourteen of the fifteen years between 1945 and 1959, at least one of them was involved in *Ring Magazine*'s "Fight of the Year."

And one final note. Sugar Ray Robinson is the gold standard against which all other fighters are judged. Four of these men (Jake LaMotta, Joey Maxim, Carmen Basilio, and Joey Giardello) beat Robinson.

But statistics can be cold and hard, so let's give the final word to another Italian-American fighter. Vito Antoufermo was born in Italy and came to the United States as a child. During a career that lasted from 1971 to 1985, he had 50 wins, 7 losses, and 2 draws. Antoufermo was as honest as a fighter can be. Strong, plodding, always moving forward. His curse was that he cut easily. Time and again, his face betrayed him.

In 1977, the great Carlos Monzon retired as middleweight champion. He was succeeded by Rodrigo Valdez, who gave way to Hugo Corro. On June 30, 1979, Antoufermo won a fifteen-round decision over Corro to capture the 160-pound crown. Antoufermo's first defense was against Marvin Hagler. It was a foregone conclusion that Hagler would win. Except, at the end of the bout when the judges' scorecards were tallied, Antoufermo had retained his title on a draw.

"Sometimes I wish I could have fought against those guys," says Antoufermo. "You know, against guys like Basilio, LaMotta, and Graziano. It would have been an honor to get in the ring with them and to test myself against them."

Antoufermo is part of a tradition: Italian-American champions who share a common bond dating to a time when boxing truly mattered.❏

Felix Trinidad's return to the ring on October 2, 2004, gave boxing a much-needed boost.

THE RETURN OF FELIX TRINIDAD

Felix Trinidad is one of the few fighters in boxing today who inspires true passion among his followers. "Tito" is a hero in his homeland of Puerto Rico. When he fights in New York, it's like carnival time and the Puerto Rican Day Parade rolled into one.

Twenty-nine months ago, Trinidad retired at age 29 with a record of 41 wins against a single loss. On October 2nd at Madison Square Garden, he returned to the ring against Ricardo Mayorga, whose signature victory was a 2003 knockout of Vernon Forrest for the WBC and WBA welterweight titles.

There were times when it looked as though the fight might not happen. Mayorga missed the kick-off press conference in New York, and news agencies in Nicaragua reported that he had been arrested on a charge of punching a man in the face and threatening him with a pistol. Ricardo denied the accusations. "I did no harm," he told the local press. "Actually I was the victim."

Next, in mid-August, Mayorga halted training for an undisclosed period of time due to (choose one) flu-like symptoms or injuries suffered in an automobile accident in which he (did or didn't) drive his red BMW into a ditch. "It wasn't me," Mayorga said of the accident. "Yes, there was an accident; and yes, it was my car. But I was not the driver. I loaned the car to a friend and he was in the accident."

Then, on September 2nd, an arrest warrant was issued for Mayorga in Nicaragua after he was accused of raping a 22-year-old woman in a hotel room in Managua. That day, police searched for the fighter at his house, his parents' home, and the homes of several family members without success. The alleged victim told police that Mayorga had asked her out to dinner, taken her to several night-spots, invited her back to a hotel room, and raped her. Hotel employees confirmed to police that Mayorga was a regular patron and had taken a room with the woman. A hospital examination revealed that she had bruises inflicted by punches on her ribs and chest. In response, Mayorga issued a statement saying, "I had normal sexual relations with her, and the hotel employees can testify on my behalf that she left the hotel very happy. I gave her two 500 córdobas bills (about 30 dollars) and we said goodbye."

That led some observers to question why the New York State Athletic Commission would license Mayorga after signalling its intention earlier this year to deny licenses to Floyd Mayweather Jr. and Paul Spadafora because of criminal charges pending against them. More than one cynic suggested that Don King's extensive campaigning on behalf of George Bush was a factor in earning Governor George Pataki's favor.

Meanwhile, as is his custom, Mayorga was shooting off his mouth. "Trinidad is scared to fight me," he told the media. "Trinidad's father will have to throw him in the ring or else he will not enter to fight. If I have to, I will go to the back and drag him out myself. His corner will have to push him out after every round because that sissy will try to run back to his hotel room. The minute he plants his feet on the ground is the minute that I send him back to retirement. Tito has been knocked out since the day he signed the contract to fight me."

"I like that he talks," Trinidad responded. "It just makes me want to hit him harder. His chin might be made out of granite, but I will chisel it. Mayorga is a good actor. But when he hits the canvas, he won't be acting. It will be real."

The prognosis was for an exciting fight. Mayorga is a non-stop brawler who throws punches from all angles. And Trinidad is a happy warrior, who is more of a puncher than a boxer. But there were other ingredients in the stew as well.

Trinidad-Mayorga took place in the long-term shadow of 9/11. Three years ago, Tito had been scheduled to meet Bernard Hopkins at Madison Square Garden on September 15th. Then disaster struck; the fight was postponed, and Hopkins went back to Philadelphia to train, while Felix stayed in New York and got emotionally involved in the communal mourning. On September 29, 2001, Bernard dealt Trinidad the only loss of his career by systematically dismantling him en route to a twelfth-round stoppage. The Trinidad camp believes that, but for 9/11, Felix would have prevailed.

Then there was the 2004 presidential campaign, which is of major interest to Don King.

Samuel Johnson once observed, "Patriotism is the last refuge of a scoundrel." Be that as it may, King has raised large sums of money for George Bush and campaigned for him in inner-city neighborhoods.

"I'm supporting George Bush because he believes in human dignity and respect and bringing people of all different colors and religions and creeds together in this great nation of ours," King proclaimed on the day of the fight. "And I understand what George Bush is going through now with all the terrible things people are saying about him, because people have been unfairly attacking me and vilifying me for years."

One can only begin to imagine the thoughts that run through King's mind on the subject of politics . . . "Why were our military commanders in Iraq so stupid that they authorized eighteen hundred photographs and videotapes of the Abu Ghraib prison torture? In boxing, when someone does something illegal like giving money under the table to a world sanctioning organization, they don't pose for the camera. Bobby Lee taught us that . . . John Kerry and George Bush both suffered injuries that epitomize the spirit of America. Kerry was awarded the Purple Heart for combat wounds suffered in Vietnam. Bush passed out and suffered a bruised lip when he choked on a pretzel while watching a football game on television." And no doubt, King admires the current administration for putting a dyslexic spin on the war in Iraq to convince Americans that the Iraqi people regard us as the Great Santa rather than the Great Satan.

But back to Trinidad-Mayorga. The big question prior to the fight was, "How much does Trinidad have left?"

"Once you retire from boxing, boxing leaves your heart," said Mayorga. "That's something a fighter never gets back again."

The bout was scheduled for twelve rounds. Trinidad was a 12-to-5 favorite. Each man weighed-in comfortably below the middleweight limit: Tito at 157-3/4 pounds, Mayorga at 158.

The crowd of 17,406 was heavily pro-Trinidad. It booed the Nicaraguan national anthem, joined in singing the Puerto Rican anthem, and was largely indifferent to "The Star-Spangled Banner." They weren't just fight fans; they were idolators.

The night belonged to Trinidad. "I want to hear the crowd roaring and chanting my name," he said several months ago in explaining his comeback. "'Tito, Tito, Tito.' I want that moment again."

He got it.

Mayorga was the aggressor in the first two minutes of the fight, with Trinidad throwing next-to-nothing. Then Felix landed a big left hook and Mayorga stuck out his chin, daring him to do it again. So Tito did it again and followed with a straight right hand that wobbled his foe.

Thereafter, fans were treated to a marvelously entertaining, action-packed brawl. Trinidad's best weapon was a straight right hand, but he scored with a variety of blows. Mayorga's primary weapon was his left hook; but when it landed, Felix stood up to it.

There was a fluke knockdown in round three, when Mayorga landed a clubbing right to the top of Trinidad's head and Felix's glove touched the canvas. That created a quandary for the judges. As a general rule, when a fighter scores a knockdown, it's a 10-8 round in his favor. But here, except for the "knockdown," Trinidad dominated the round. One could have scored the stanza even (as this observer did) or 10-9 in Mayorga's favor. What one should not have done was score it 10-8 for Mayorga, which was what each of the three judges did.

Other than that, Trinidad won every round, systematically and brutally beating Mayorga down. Mayorga is tough. He took blow after blow and stayed on his feet despite being battered, literally, from post to post. By round eight, his left cheek was split open and the eye above it was a bloody mess. Then Trinidad put him down with a horrific left hook to the body. Two more knockdowns followed, and at 2:39 of the stanza, referee Steve Smoger stopped the fight.

Trinidad landed twice as many punches as Mayorga (290 to 141). And he connected on an extraordinary 63 percent of his punches thrown.

As for what comes next, Trinidad has myriad options. One possibility is a rematch against Oscar De La Hoya, whom Felix defeated on a questionable decision five years ago. Trinidad versus the winner of the November 20th match-up between Winky Wright and Shane Mosley would also be attractive. But the fight that most fans want to see is a rematch between Felix and Bernard Hopkins.

Hopkins will be forty years old in January. And Trinidad appears to have been rejuvenated by his time away from boxing. Hopkins-Trinidad II would be an intensely interesting fight.❏

I was in Roy Jones's dressing room again on the night of May 15, 2004, when he fought Antonio Tarver for the second time.

ROY JONES: A SUPERSTAR GROWS OLDER

There's a stylish edge to Roy Jones and nothing phony about him. He says what he thinks and does pretty much what he wants to do. His talent as a fighter has earned him that right.

It wasn't always that way.

"My father had his way of control." Jones remembers. "It wasn't nice; and when I was in his house, I had to take it. But I vowed that, once I got out from under my father's control, I'd never be controlled by anyone again."

Jones delights in his freedom. "I'm wild," he acknowledges. "I'm not a savage, but you can't domesticate me. I'm wild like a bird is wild; I'm free."

But at times, Jones's freedom is curtailed. The demands of his profession require that he step into a cage and conform his movements to the dictates of a clock. Three minutes on, one minute off; three minutes on, one minute off, until the outcome of the conflict that he's engaged in is resolved.

"A lot of people think boxing is a game," Jones says. "Boxing isn't a game. It's a deadly violent sport. But God put fighting in me. It's what I was born to do."

Jones burst upon the scene as a 19-year-old prodigy at the Seoul Olympics in 1988. Pound-for-pound, he has been the best fighter in the world for the past decade. There's still a youthfulness about him, but he's not a kid anymore and the signs of age are evident around his eyes. Now he's at a crossroads in his life as a consequence of last weekend's fight against Antonio Tarver.

Jones and Tarver first met in the ring as 13-year-olds at the Sunshine State Games in Gainesville, Florida. It has been said that, when boxers talk about long-ago amateur fights between them, there are three versions of what happened; one from each fighter and the truth.

"I beat his ass," Jones says of their 1982 encounter. "I chased him around the ring, beating on his ass, and won all three rounds."

"We had a very very competitive fight," Tarver counters, "and Roy won a split decision."

Last November, they met again. This time, both men agree that the encounter was competitive, although they disagree on the outcome. Jones was physically debilitated from oral surgery gone wrong and the rigors of making weight. Later, he acknowledged, "In the seventh round, I told myself, 'This ain't working.' And in the eighth round, I was so tired; I told myself, 'This dude could stop me. If he ever could stop me, it would be now.'"

But Jones dug deep in his desperate hour and won a majority decision on the judges' scorecards. Later, Tarver complained, "In all of Roy's fights, if neither fighter is doing anything, the judges think that Roy is doing something. I watched the tape of that fight several times. Every time, I scored it seven rounds to five for myself, and that's giving Roy the benefit of the doubt."

Jones, for his part, responded, "I'm judged by what I've done in the past. People remember a lot of my other fights and how good I looked; and they feel like, if I don't look that good in every round, something is wrong."

In truth, Jones won Jones-Tarver I. At least, this observer gave it to him by a 115-114 margin. But his trainer, Alton Merkerson, conceded, "Roy wasn't what he should have been. He was hit more by Tarver than he'd been hit in his whole boxing career. It was a close fight."

Thus, the question of what might have been.

"When I look back on that fight," Tarver said, "the one thing I regret not doing is going more to the body and being more aggressive."

Had he done so, Tarver's partisans believe, he would have won the fight. But could he really have stepped things up that night, or had Jones's body shots taken more out of him than Antonio cared to admit? And how much of a factor was Jones's weight loss? Jones-Tarver II was slated for May 15th to get some answers.

In the days leading up to the fight, Tarver was his usual voluble self. "It doesn't matter which Roy Jones shows up," he proclaimed. "As long as Antonio Tarver is in front of him, he's in a world of trouble. I'm the most grossly underestimated fighter in the world today. Everybody has their nemesis; everybody has their match. I just happen to match Roy Jones; speed for speed, skill for skill, talent for talent. I know my way around the ring. I'm confident in my ability. I have a devastating left hand. I can outbox anybody and I can outfox anybody. Any way you want to measure up, I measure up."

"I don't like being second best," Tarver continued. "I don't want to be remembered as the man who gave Roy Jones his toughest fight. I want to be remembered as the man who beat Roy Jones twice. Even though

Roy got the decision last time, in my mind, I'll be coming into the ring as champion. Roy Jones didn't do a damn thing last time except survive. I made the guy look average in the ring. This time, I'm going to finish the job. I'm going to put the finishing touches on Roy Jones once and for all. It's not trash-talking; it's conviction. I'm going to kick his ass all night long."

Jones, in turn, had a few thoughts of his own. "Roy is back to being Roy," he said. "My state of mind is fantastic. I'll fight the same fight I fought before, except this time I'll have more energy. Last time, I took a lot of punches, so I know I can take whatever Tarver has to give. He couldn't whup me when I was damn near dead. You think I'm worried about him whupping me healthy? If Antonio Tarver is so tough, let's go twelve rounds toe-to-toe. I love a good fight. It's what God put me here for. This time, Tarver is gonna understand that he got beat."

Where the issue of weight was concerned, Tarver had come to training camp at 190 pounds and worked his way down to the 175-pound light-heavyweight limit. His trainer, Buddy McGirt, took that as a good sign, since Antonio had reported to camp at 210 pounds for Jones-Tarver I.

Jones also came to camp at 190 and worked with conditioner Mackie Shillstone for six weeks prior to the fight. When they began their regimen, his body fat was 11.5 percent. By fight night, that number had been cut in half.

Meanwhile, all the talk about weight aggravated Tarver. "Roy Jones is the pound-for-pound king of excuses," he proclaimed. "Weight was never an issue for the rematch. They never came to me and said, 'Let's do it at 180 or 185.' That tells me that Roy's excuse about looking bad because of all the weight he had to lose is a crock of shit."

The fighters' respective camps were equally confident.

"Roy will probably be stronger this time," said McGirt. "And he'll try to impose his will on Antonio early. But when he finds out he can't, it will play games with his mind and he'll start to weaken; maybe more than last time. I expect anything and everything from Roy. That's what we're preparing for: anything and everything. We have strategies with a plural to offset any type of attack that Roy has. But the most important thing is, everybody Roy fights backs away or covers up when he starts punching. But when Roy throws punches, what you have to do is punch back. If he starts gun-slinging, you have to shoot bullets with him."

As for Team Jones, the word was, "Roy has a lot of pride. He's not fighting this fight to look like he did last time." The surest sign that Jones was feeling himself again was that he played basketball twice in the three days before the fight. "All Tarver has is his left hand," opined

Billy Lewis, Jones's longtime friend and sparring partner. "Antonio will be entering *The Matrix* with just one gun."

Still, Jones knew that he was in for a hard fight. "The best two fighters I've fought are Antonio Tarver and Bernard Hopkins," he acknowledged. Then, shortly after the Friday weigh-in, he added the following thought: "Tarver is good, but I'm better. The only chance he has is to catch me with one of those wild haymakers."

The first arrivals in Jones's lockerroom on Saturday night were Alton Merkerson, former Olympic boxing coach Kenny Adams, cutman Richard Lucey, and Mackie Shillstone. Jones, wearing a black Air Jordan warm-up suit with red and white trim, arrived at 6:30 p.m. with a half-dozen entourage members in tow.

On a silent television monitor at the far end of the room, Bruce Seldon and Gerald Nobles were engaged in an inartistic heavyweight brawl. The room was quiet. Jones seemed confident and relaxed. "I'm good tonight; ready to go," he announced.

"Some classic basketball games this week," he was told.

Roy's face lit up. "A lot of them," he said.

At 6:55, Larry Merchant came into the room to conduct a short interview for HBO. That was followed by referee Jay Nady's pre-fight instructions. By seven o'clock, two dozen people were on hand, many of them constant presences in Jones's life: Billy Lewis, Derrick "Smoke" Gainer, Mario Francis, Lemuel Nelson, Al Cole.

Seldon-Nobles ended and was replaced on the screen by Zab Judah versus Raphael Pineda. Roy began changing into his fighting clothes. Gray trunks with red and white trim. Gray-and-white shoes with red, white, and gray tassels.

At 7:20, John McClain (Laila's Ali's husband and one of Tarver's seconds) entered the dressing room to watch Merkerson tape Roy's hands. Ten minutes later, the rap music began.

"The champ is here! The champ is here! The champ is here!"

Jones pulled up a chair beneath the television monitor and watched impassively, arms folded across his chest. From time to time, he chatted with Gainer, who was standing beside him.

Judah versus Pineda ended. Jones rose and walked the length of the room, back and forth several times. Then everyone gathered into a prayer circle with each person reaching forward so the outstretched arms were like the spokes of a wheel with their hands forming the hub.

Al Cole led the group in prayer.

Jones circled the room and embraced everyone, one person at a time. Minutes later, he and Antonio Tarver were in ring center, facing one another.

"I gave you your instructions in the dressing room," referee Jay Nady told the fighters. "Do you have any questions?"

"I got a question," Tarver sneered. "Do you got any excuses tonight, Roy?"

The bell for round one rang, and the fight began with Jones stalking and Tarver keeping his distance. Two natural counterpunchers.

"In the ring," Jones once said, "you adjust to what people do and make them do what they don't want to do."

Not much happened, although Roy had an 8-to-2 edge in punches landed and it was his round.

In round two, Tarver began to stand his ground. Then, midway through the second stanza, Jones scored with a quick righthand and followed with a hook that was more of a slap than a punch. As he did, he drew his head back a bit and raised his right hand in a defensive posture. He thought that the right side of his face was protected.

It wasn't. And Tarver landed with the precision of a gangland hit.

"We both threw at the same time," Antonio said later, "and I turned it over shorter than he did. It was an overhand left, right on the kisser. I would have knocked anyone out with that shot. It was a perfect punch."

Jones went down, tried to rise, pitched forward onto his right shoulder, and forced himself to his feet at the count of nine through an act of incredible will. But Jay Nady waved his arms. The fight was over.

In boxing, as in the rest of life, one moment of violence can change everything.

One of Jones's cornermen put a stool beneath him. Dr. Margaret Goodman entered the ring, knelt beside the fighter, and took his hand.

"Are you okay?"

"I'm cool, baby," Jones told her.

"I'm so sorry."

"Hey, it happens."

Then Goodman began to probe.

"Do you have a headache?"

"I don't have a headache."

"Are you dizzy?"

"I'm not dizzy."

"Are you nauseous?"

"I'm not nauseous."

From a neurological standpoint, Jones was responsive and alert. His pupils were equal and reactive.

Derrick Gainer stood nearby, visibly shaken and crying. "Is he okay?"

"He's fine," Goodman assured him. Then she turned her attention back to Jones. "I want you to sit here," she instructed. "A lot of people will want to talk with you, but I want you to rest for a minute. Let's take your gloves off."

The gloves were a way of buying time. Cornerman Mario Francis removed them and, as he did, Jones watched a replay of the knockout on one of the giant screens above.

"How are you doing now?" Goodman queried.

"I'm cool."

When a fighter is knocked out, there's physical damage and also the anguish of losing. It's a humbling experience to be knocked woozy by another man in front of millions of people.

There were a lot of broken hearts in Roy Jones's dressing room afterward.

Jones sat on a chair, looking straight ahead with a pile of towels beside him. Conversations were going on around the room, but he was the focus of attention.

"I had him where I wanted him," Roy said. "I was doing what I wanted to do. I was faster than last time. I was stronger than last time. I just got caught. I guess God wanted me to go through this at least one time." He took a breath and let it out slowly. "One shot. I know exactly what happened. I threw a righthand and tried to come back with the left. He read it and fired his gun first. My right hand was up and I couldn't see the punch coming. No excuses. He caught me with a good shot."

Felix Trinidad, who suffered his own disappointment at the hands of Bernard Hopkins three years ago, entered the room. There's a fraternity among great fighters. "I'm sorry," Trinidad said. Jones rose and the two men embraced. "You are a great fighter," Trinidad told him.

Jones sat down again. "Nothing like this ever happened to me before. It hurts. It feels hard, but there's no physical pain . . . Hey, that's how life goes sometimes. I'll deal with it. Take it as it comes . . . Shit."

One of the entourage members sought to boost Roy's spirits.

"The referee was looking to stop the fight. He never gave you a chance."

Alton Merkerson shook his head. "Coach Merk" has been a stabilizing presence throughout Jones's career. He's also a man who has known combat throughout his life: growing up on the streets of Chicago, as a career military officer in Vietnam, and in boxing. On the night that Roy was disqualified against Montell Griffin, Merkerson had to be physically restrained in the ring. "If I had to go to war," Jones has said, "I'd want Coach Merk with me first."

As the diatribe against Jay Nady continued, Merkerson shook his head. "The guy that's talking to Roy now doesn't know shit about boxing," he said. "Believe me, if something happened that was wrong, I'd be the first one to let everyone know about it. But I can't fault Nady. He was looking after Roy's best interests. Roy was hurt. There's a chance he could have weathered the storm, but he was still shook when they stopped it." Merkerson shook his head again. "No use crying over spilt milk. Tarver's a good fighter."

"What do you think about the stoppage?" Jones was asked.

"When you're in there, you want to go on," Roy answered. "But I can't say the referee did the wrong thing. Hey, it happened. In your heart, you always know it can happen, even though you hope it never will." Then he repeated words that would sound throughout the night. "Nothing like this ever happened to me before."

"This doesn't change who you are," a friend told him. "You're still every bit as good a person as you are a fighter."

Jones smiled. "Tonight, I'm a better person than I was a fighter." Then he turned toward Derrick Gainer, who had begun crying again. "Don't be sad. God is good."

● ● ●

So what happens next?

For Antonio Tarver, the future looks bright. Before beating Jones, he told the media, "What's mind-boggling to me is that people have never looked at my career as a whole. Who has beaten me? Who has dominated me? Who has kicked my ass? I had one off-night when I came up short against Eric Harding, and I came back and defeated him." Then Tarver added, "My dreams don't stop with Roy Jones. My dreams go way past Roy Jones."

Now Tarver has his chance. Apart from a rematch with Jones, his options range from trying to unify the light-heavyweight title to a heavyweight bout against one of the alphabet-soup beltholders. A match-up against Vassiliy Jirov, who bested him in the semi-finals of the 1996 Olympics, is also possible.

For Jones, the future is more complicated. The disqualification against Montell Griffin and the Olympic robbery he suffered in Seoul weren't really losses. One had to go back to a defeat on points at the hands of Gerald McClellan in the 1988 National Golden Gloves semi-finals to find a fight that Roy really lost.

Now he has lost again; decisively. And no one can know with certainty what would have happened without that one punch.

"Roy is like a wounded soldier," says Alton Merkerson. "Not a dead one. He can fight again if he wants to."

If he does, there are myriad options.

Immediately after being knocked out, Jones said that a third Tarver fight wasn't of interest to him. It's possible he'll change his mind. But styles make fights, and Antonio has the tools to always make things difficult for him. Also, at 6-feet-2-inches, Tarver is three inches taller than Roy. If they were to fight at, say, 185 or 190 pounds, it might accentuate Tarver's size advantage. Indeed, on fight night, Antonio weighed 189 pounds on the HBO scale [reported as 187] while Jones weighed in at 180.

Next, there's the possibility of Jones fighting at heavyweight, although the loss to Tarver takes much of the shine off that prospect. Prior to his defeat, Roy was talking about fighting Mike Tyson. But a lot of people thought that wasn't a good idea, and Roberto Duran was one of them. Even before Jones got knocked out, Duran opined, "If Jones fights Tyson, that will be the biggest mistake he ever makes. Roy Jones is a great fighter, but he doesn't have the punching power to hurt Tyson. He thinks he can fight Tyson like he fought John Ruiz. He thinks he'll be able to confuse Tyson in the ring and make him look stupid. But in the ring, Mike isn't stupid."

When Jones returned to 175 pounds, his explanation for leaving the heavyweight division was, "There was more risk than money." Now, the heavyweights offer the same risk and less money than before.

Option number three is for Roy to continue fighting as a light-heavyweight against someone other than Tarver. One opponent who has been mentioned within the Jones camp is WBA light-heavyweight "champion" Fabrice Tiozzo. Tiozzo sports a 46-2 record and moves more slowly than molasses on level ground. Once Jones beats Tiozzo, he could plan his future from there.

Or Roy Jones can retire from boxing.

Jones is 35 years old now. That's the same age as Tarver, but the two men have different types of skills. It's an axiom in boxing that speed and reflexes go before power. And as Buddy McGirt noted hours before Jones-Tarver II, "If you take away Roy's speed, he's not spectacular."

Jones himself evaluates a fighter's greatness based on physical skills (including age), technical knowledge, and state of mind. Then he says, "My physical skills were at their peak around the time I fought James Toney."

That was ten years ago. Adding fuel to the fire, earlier this month, Alton Merkerson noted, "I worked with Roy in 1988 on the Olympic team, and I'll tell you what I see in Roy at the age of thirty-five. The ring generalmanship; he still has it, but it's not as sharp as it used to be. He's just getting older. He can't do the things that he did when he was younger. You just lose it after a time when you get older. It's going to happen, as sure as you live and die."

The move to, and from, heavyweight might also have hurt. At first, it was a plus. Jones had begun to slow down by the time he fought John Ruiz, but Ruiz was so slow that no one noticed. Then, in the first Tarver fight, the assumption was that Roy's problems were the result of making weight. But Roy Jones is getting older. His speed and reflexes are slowing.

Also, the older a fighter gets, the more it takes out of him to go up and down in weight. Indeed, one can posit that, even if he chose not to fight John Ruiz a second time, Jones should have stayed at heavyweight. Once stripped of his WBA belt, he still would have been regarded by the public as a champion. Then he could have fought an interim heavyweight bout instead of the two Tarver fights and, after that, gone after even more profitable game. But from a physical standpoint, large fluctuations in weight aren't good. And gaining and losing muscle mass is worse.

In sum, Roy Jones has been the best fighter of his time, but it might not be his time anymore. Even if he summons up greatness in future fights, he'll never again be the dynamic young fighter that he once was. When Roy stepped into the ring against Antonio Tarver for the second time, he was the same age to the day that Muhammad Ali was when he fought fifteen dreary rounds against Alfredo Evangelista. One might also recall the famous words of Joe Louis after his 1947 bout against Jersey Joe Walcott. "I saw openings I couldn't use," the Brown Bomber acknowledged. "A man gets old; he don't take advantage of those things as fast as he used to."

Louis was 33 years old at the time.

"I've been fighting since I was ten years old," Jones said earlier this month. "That's a twenty-five year career. It's time to walk away, really. Twenty-five years of boxing can be bad for your health."

Add to that the fact that the three most revered fighters in history (Joe Louis, Sugar Ray Robinson, and Muhammad Ali) fought longer than they should have. And each of them wound up in a seriously debilitated physical condition.

From now on for Roy Jones, the risks in the ring grow. The risk of losing; the risk of injury. Thus, Jones might say to himself, "If I don't have the speed and reflexes I once had, if I'm not Roy Jones in the ring anymore, then it's time to put boxing behind me." If so, he could do what Marvin Hagler did; walk away with his head held high, knowing that he was still one of the best fighters in the world after a loss that hurt.

But regardless of what happens next, thoughts now turn to Jones's legacy. That legacy was at its peak after Jones-Ruiz, but what happened against Tarver leads to a reevaluation. Should Roy fight Tarver again and win the third fight between them, the lustre would be restored and then some. But that's speculative, so let's examine things the way they stand now.

Jones says that he doesn't think much about his place in boxing history; that he has always been more concerned with pound-for-pound recognition in the present tense. Also, as previously noted, styles make fights. Muhammad Ali had trouble with Joe Frazier and Ken Norton every time out, while George Foreman obliterated Frazier and Norton but was stopped by Ali.

Moreover, as a general rule, the losses that great fighters suffer at the end of their career become unimportant from a historical perspective. Sugar Ray Robinson was close to perfection as a welterweight. But as he moved up in age and weight, he was beatable; trading wins and losses with Randy Turpin, Carmen Basilio, and Gene Fullmer, before suffering unavenged defeats at the hands of Memo Ayon, Ferd Hernandez, and others.

Pernell Whitaker (the man Jones calls "the last guy who deserved to be called pound-for-pound before me") never won a fight after age thirty-three. Evander Holyfield has won two of eight fights since age thirty-five. Few people hold it against Muhammad Ali that he lost three of his last four fights. Fewer still even remember that Joe Frazier ended his career on a draw against Jumbo Cummings.

The criticism of Jones for years was that he'd punk out if the going ever got tough. But as Evander Holyfield, boxing's consummate warrior, noted after Jones-Ruiz, "You don't get down on a person because he's so talented that he hasn't been put in a position where he has to go through fire to win."

Then Holyfield was asked if, in his view, Jones would in fact walk through fire. His response was, "I don't know. It don't matter how good a fighter is or what he has done before. Until he's faced with that moment for the first time, you don't know what he'll do because he doesn't know himself. He might think he knows, but he don't."

Then, in Jones-Tarver I, Roy walked through the fire to win. Now his critics are saying, "Great fighters don't get stopped by one punch."

But one-punch knockouts happen in boxing. Ask Lennox Lewis, who was starched by Oliver McCall and Hasim Rahman. Ask Larry Holmes, who, in today's world, wouldn't have been allowed to continue after being knocked woozy by Earnie Shavers and Renaldo Snipes in fights that he ultimately won. Ask Roberto Duran, who, one day shy of his thirty-third birthday, suffered a one-punch knockout at the hands of Thomas Hearns.

The most famous one-punch knockout in boxing history is the left hook that Sugar Ray Robinson placed on Gene Fullmer's jaw. Fullmer was one of the most durable fighters in the sport. Other than a loss to Dick Tiger in the final fight of his career, it's the only time he was ever stopped.

"I still don't know anything about the punch," Fullmer said years after the fact, "except I watched it on movies a number of times. The first thing I knew, I was standing up. I asked my manager, 'What happened?' and he said, 'They counted ten.' Up to then, I probably got to thinking I couldn't be knocked out. And all at once, I realized that anybody can. It's just got to be in the right place at the right time and you're gone."

Boxing's legacies are written in the ring. Roy Jones won his first world title by beating Bernard Hopkins and his second by defeating James Toney. Those are two legitimate Hall of Fame fighters. He has won championship bouts against opponents who weighed anywhere from 160 to 226 pounds and beaten fifteen men who held world titles.

Moreover, Jones's record is all the more remarkable given the fact that the better fighter doesn't necessarily always win. The best tennis player, the best golfer, the best track-and-field star, all lose occasionally to lesser foes. That's true of fighters too.

Lennox Lewis puts the matter in perspective best. "I feel for Roy," Lennox said this week. "I've been there, so I understand the sadness he's feeling now. But in boxing, there has to be a time when you lose, and Roy shouldn't get down on himself. It's like falling off a horse. And what you do is, you get up and ride again if you want to, which is what I did. Or if the hunger isn't there anymore, you retire. I honestly believe that Roy would beat Tarver in a rematch," Lewis continued. "But no matter what happens next, Roy is a great fighter. There will be arrogant ignorant people who try to take credit away from him and belittle his accomplishments. But to be as good as he's been for as long as he's been; ask the fighters. We know how great Roy Jones is."

Meanwhile, Roy Jones's loss is a reminder that no fighter is spared the hardships of boxing. All fighters grow old in the end.❏

The following article was written after Roy Jones's September 25, 2004, knockout loss at the hands of Glencoffe Johnson.

ROY JONES: POSTSCRIPT

In February 1997, I was in Pensacola, Florida, when Roy Jones and Muhammad Ali engaged in a mock sparring session. No blows were struck but a lot of strategizing went on.

Afterward, Roy told me, "When I'm fighting, the first thing I do is, I want to see my opponent's jab to find out if there are any flaws in it. The first time my opponent makes a mistake, I pick up on it. The moment Ali and I started sparring, I could see he was searching for the hole, looking for a flaw in my jab. Right away, he picked up on something I do that I can get away with because of my speed. He thought it was a flaw and he found it."

Times change. Roy Jones can no longer overcome his technical flaws with speed. The end isn't near. The end is here.

Boxing commentator Teddy Atlas once commented on Jones's ring greatness with the observation, "For years, Roy Jones was Secretariat in the Belmont, winning by thirty lengths."

Jones dominated the middleweight, super-middleweight, and light-heavyweight divisions in a way that few fighters ever have. Then he moved up to heavyweight and, on March 1, 2003, defeated John Ruiz for the WBA heavyweight crown.

For years, one could ask a hundred boxers, "Who's the best fighter in the world pound-for-pound?" Virtually all of them would answer, "Roy Jones." And when they spoke his name, it was with a mixture of admiration and awe.

Last November, Jones returned to 175 pounds to challenge Antonio Tarver for the light-heavyweight title. He struggled to make weight, was debilitated by dental surgery gone awry, and prevailed on a majority decision.

"Roy looked human for a change," World Boxing Organization 168-pound champion Joe Calzaghe noted afterward.

Then, showing a champion's heart, Jones gave Tarver an immediate rematch. Tarver scored a one-punch knockout in the second round. The Roy Jones aura of invincibility was gone. But Jones had an explanation.

"God brings even the best people down," he said, "to see if they'll remain faithful and go back up."

On May 22nd of this year, one week after he was knocked out by Tarver, there was a "Support Roy Jones Rally" in his home town of Pensacola. Clearly moved, Jones took the microphone and told the crowd, "I need you all. I need somebody to pick me up, and you all came to energize me. People wonder why I say, 'Pensacola is in the house' when I fight. This is the reason. If you see tears in my eyes today, don't think I feel bad. It's because I feel love."

Then Jones asked the question, "Do ya'll want some get-back?"

The crowd roared.

"Okay. I'm gonna go get some get back."

But instead of a third fight against Tarver, Jones signed to fight Glencoffe Johnson, who through a series of fortuitous events had become the International Boxing Federation 175-pound titleholder. Over the previous five years, Johnson had won only eight of nineteen bouts.

Jones spoke confidently before the fight. Yes, he had lost to Tarver; but in his eyes, he was still The Man. "Who beat John Ruiz since I beat him?" Roy demanded. "[Hasim] Rahman didn't beat him. [Fres] Oquendo didn't beat him. No one could beat him. Who beat Bernard Hopkins since I beat him? No one. It starts right here."

And it ended against Glencoffe Johnson on Saturday night in Memphis. Johnson pressed the action in every round and outlanded Jones 118 to 75. Roy scored with some good left hooks to the body, but that was all. Johnson won six of the first eight rounds. In round nine, he knocked Jones cold with an overhand right. Roy hit his head hard on the canvas when he fell. He lay there for eight minutes and sat on his stool for 24 minutes more before leaving the ring.

I've been at ringside for twelve Roy Jones fights. Other than Muhammad Ali in his prime, Jones was the most beautiful fighting machine I've ever seen.

I wasn't in Memphis for Jones-Johnson. I watched it on television. Whenever I think I might write about a fight, I scribble notes on a yellow pad between rounds. My notes on Jones-Johnson tell the tale:

Round 1: Roy on the ropes. He isn't moving like he used to. But he's 35 years old and a fighter has to play the cards in his hand.

Round 2: In the past, Roy went to the ropes as a way of luring opponents into punching range; but this is different. He's there by necessity; not out of choice.

Round 3: Roy looks weak and slow. And apart from looking old, it seems like getting knocked out by Tarver changed him. Is there a crisis of confidence?

Round 4: More of the same; Roy against the ropes getting hit.

Round 5: Roy's greatness was built on reflexes and speed, and they're simply not there anymore.

Round 6: In the old days, Roy would have won every minute of every round against Johnson. Now he's losing the fight.

Round 7: Roy getting hit with a lot of overhand rights. He looks like a shot fighter.

Round 8: This is like Muhammad Ali against Larry Holmes; except unlike Holmes, Johnson is an ordinary fighter.

Round 9: Roy KO'd at 48 seconds. He should never fight again.

Roy Jones once told me, "My father is a genius, but his ego ruined it for him." I hope that Roy is smart enough and has enough pride to retire from boxing.❏

ROUND 2

NON-COMBATANTS

There's more to Michael Buffer than meets the eye, as I explained in this profile.

MICHAEL BUFFER

Shortly before Oscar De La Hoya and Shane Mosley answered the bell for round one last Saturday night, a tall, slender, impeccably groomed man wearing a tuxedo entered the ring. There were a few perfunctory introductions followed by the moment that everyone in the arena was waiting for.

"Now, for the thousands in attendance and the millions watching on television around the world . . . LET'S GET R-R-R-READY TO RUMBL-L-L-E . . ."

The crowd roared in a Pavlovian response now common on the boxing scene. "Let's get ready to rumble" has become part of the vernacular, and its practitioner is regarded by many as a sports icon.

Michael Buffer was born in Philadelphia in November 1944. His natural father was in the Navy during World War II and got married at age nineteen. Then, after the war, Buffer's natural father and mother went separate ways, and he was sent to live with foster parents.

"I was eleven months old at the time," Buffer explains. "So growing up, my foster parents were the only parents I knew. Their name was Huber, and they were a great mom and dad. My foster father, who I think of as my father, was a bus driver. My name was Michael Huber. Then, at age twenty, I enlisted in the Army. But because I'd never been formally adopted, my legal name was still Michael Buffer, and that's what the Army used."

Buffer wed at age twenty-one and had two sons in a marriage that ended after seven years. More than a quarter-century passed before he remarried in 1999. He and his second wife recently separated.

Meanwhile, in 1967, Buffer was discharged from the military and went to work as what he calls "the worst car salesman in the world." In 1976, a friend suggested he try modeling. "The next thing I knew," Buffer remembers, "I was on a runway doing a show for Gucci, and I haven't had a real job since."

At the time, Buffer was six feet tall, 165 pounds, fifteen pounds below his current weight. As for modeling, he was a natural. More runway and print work followed. Then, one afternoon in 1982, he was at home watching a fight on television with his son when the ring announcer botched a decision.

"Dad, you could do that," Buffer's son told him.

"That sounded great," Buffer remembers. "So I sent my resume and an eight-by-ten headshot to all the hotels in Atlantic City with a letter saying that their image would be better served by a ring announcer with a James Bond look. The Playboy Hotel and Casino liked the idea and recommended me to Alessi Promotions, which gave me a shot. My first time in the ring, I was very scared even though I'd gone over what I was going to say a hundred times. And I was atrocious; absolutely horrible. That was it. My moment in the sun as a ring announcer was over. But in March 1983, Frank Gelb gave me another chance on a fight card at The Sands. Gelb handled all of Bob Arum's fights on the East Coast and, in those days, Top Rank provided ESPN with all of its boxing. Frank liked my work and, before long, I was a fixture on ESPN, which gave me a national identity at a time when ring announcers were strictly local. Then Bob Halloran at Caesars championed my cause, and I was on my way."

As for the origins of "let's get ready to rumble," Buffer explains, "I don't remember the first time I used it. I think it was in 1984. I used to watch films of old fights on television. In the old days, the ring announcer would introduce the important fighters who were in attendance. But that had evolved to announcing five commissioners, three sanctioning-body officials, two ring doctors. And it chilled the crowd. I wanted something comparable to 'Gentlemen, start your engines' at the Indy 500; a hook that would excite people and put some energy back into the arena. I tried 'man your battle stations' and 'batten down the hatches' and 'fasten your seat belts,' but none of them worked. Then I remembered Muhammad Ali saying, 'Float like a butterfly, sting like a bee; rumble, young man, rumble.' And when Sal Marchiano was the blow-by-blow commentator for ESPN, he'd say, 'We're ready to rumble.' So I took those ideas and fine-tuned them."

"I wasn't impressed," recalls Bob Arum. "It was another trite kind of expression. He didn't put the pizzazz into it that he does now."

But over time, Buffer altered his tempo and began rolling his "R"s and stretching out his "L"s and "M"s until virtually everyone in the arena was waiting for the magic words.

Then fate intervened.

"In 1989," Buffer remembers, "I got a message that a man named Joseph Buffer had telephoned. He'd seen me on television, heard my name, and wondered if I might be the son he'd given up for adoption forty-five years earlier. I called him back; we got together, and I met his wife and sons from his second marriage."

One of those sons was Bruce Buffer, who recalls, "I was thirty-two years old at the time, and I approached our meeting with a mixture of excitement and curiosity. I'd seen Michael before on television. In fact, people had asked me from time to time if we were brothers because our looks are similar. And I'd always answered, 'I don't know.'"

Bruce Buffer had started a telemarketing company at age nineteen. His later business ventures included selling nutritional products, founding a home security company, and motivational speaking.

"Bruce was a pretty good businessman," Michael elaborates. "He saw the potential in what I was doing and suggested we work together. So we made up some business cards; I started referring offers to him, and we obtained a trademark and copyright on the phrase. My job was to keep my face in front of the public, and Bruce did the rest."

Just as George Foreman's work as an HBO commentator amounts to free advertising for an entire line of products, so too, Buffer's status as the premier ring announcer in boxing does wonders for his checkbook. By virtue of his signature phrase, he has managed to turn himself into a marquee brand name.

Each year, Bruce Buffer sends a letter to every team in each major sport reminding them that "Let's get ready to rumble" and related phrases like "Let's get ready for roundball" are protected by copyright and trademark. In the same mailing, he offers Michael's services for a price.

Over the years, Buffer has worked his magic at the World Series, Stanley Cup Finals, NBA Championships, and NFL playoff games. He has been a guest on *The Tonight Show* with Jay Leno close to a dozen times in addition to appearing with David Letterman, Arsenio Hall, Jimmy Kimmel, and virtually every other major television talk-show host. He has been featured on *The Simpsons* and in movies like *Ocean's Eleven* and *Rocky V*. Riders in New York City taxis have heard Buffer's voice advising them to get ready to rumble and fasten their seatbelts.

There was a time when Buffer served as the ring announcer for eighty to a hundred boxing cards a year. Now, he limits himself to roughly two dozen fight shows annually plus twenty to twenty-five appearances at conventions and other events. For a boxing card, he generally receives expenses plus $3,500 to $5,000. Corporate appearances are likely to net $15,000 to $25,000. His fee for other sports events varies.

"When you're on television at the NBA finals in front of hundreds of millions of people, sure there's a lot of money being generated," Bruce Buffer explains. "But we also consider the fact that it's wonderful exposure for Michael. It gives us fuel to expand his following and it's nice to be part of a historic event, so a discount is called for."

In recent years, sales of a "Ready To Rumble" boxing video game have grossed more than $150,000,000. Other "Let's Get Ready To Rumble" merchandise includes T-shirts, hats, key chains, action figures, a talking wrestling ring, microphones, and Rumble Robots. "Let's Get Ready To Rumble" slot machines will be available to casinos throughout the world by the end of 2004. All totalled, "Let's Get Ready To Rumble" products have a retail gross in excess of $350,000,000, which Buffer notes, "is why my soon-to-be-ex-wife and I now have his and her's Mercedes convertibles."

Given the world we live in, Buffer is constantly called upon to protect the rights to "Let's get ready to rumble."

"It's on ongoing issue," says Bruce Buffer, "because people constantly violate our copyright and trademark rights by using the phrase without authorization. We investigate every reported violation. Then, if warranted, we send a letter notifying the violator of our rights and demanding that the infringement cease and desist. After that, we try to negotiate a settlement. If necessary, we sue."

In the past, Buffer has sued Columbia Pictures, New Line Cinema, Oliver North, Don Imus, and a minor league hockey team in Louisiana for trademark and copyright infringement. Settlements have run well into six figures.

Meanwhile, like every other fan, Buffer usually has a rooting interest when he goes to a fight but it's his job not to let it show. He's also quite knowledgeable about the sport and business of boxing, although he tends not to voice his opinions publicly in an effort to maintain his neutrality.

As for his success, Buffer says simply, "Everyone is capable of succeeding in life. It's just that they might not know what their skills are and which road to follow. I've never been a driven person. I've always accepted the fact that I'm lazy. But I've had a lot of luck; I've been very blessed, and I'm a survivor."

In sum, those who think of Michael Buffer as a Ken Doll are wrong. Buffer is smart and very good at what he does. He has become an important part of the pageantry of boxing. Fights are more exciting for everyone if there's a highly-charged atmosphere, and he contributes to that. He makes a fight seem important simply by virtue of his presence. No other ring announcer in history has done that.❏

Randy Neumann was never a world champion, but he's one of boxing's success stories.

RANDY NEUMANN

When Chris Byrd and Andrew Golota face off against one another at Madison Square Garden on April 17, 2004, the third man in the ring will be Randy Neumann.

The 55-year-old Neumann was born and raised in New Jersey. He might have had an idyllic childhood, but for a cruel twist of fate.

"My father was a scholar-athlete and my mother was an incredibly beautiful woman," he remembers. "They could have been the king and queen at any high school senior prom. But my father was a tragedy of World War II. He was in the Air Force; he saw a lot of his friends killed. After he came back from the war, he had a nervous breakdown. And when I was five years old, he moved away from home. My mother was a tough independent woman," Neumann continues. "She never remarried. Instead, she went to work as a model and earned enough money to raise my sister and me well."

In high school, Neumann played offensive and defensive tackle in football and, his junior year, was undefeated while wrestling at 190 pounds. He also worked as a lifeguard at Palisades Amusement Park, which boasted of having the largest salt-water swimming pool in the world. "But I spent a lot of time at a place called Lester's Poolroom," he acknowledges, "and my grades were not good."

In 1967, after graduating from high school, Neumann enrolled at New York Institute of Technology and began exercising at the West Side YMCA. "Some amateurs in their thirties used to box there," he recalls. "They didn't do much, only punched to the body. I started sparring with them and, after a while, they told me to get out. I was beating them up. So I went to Gleason's Gym in the Bronx to see what real boxing was like. My first day there, I watched what was going on; and it was very different from what went on at Y, so I left."

Then Neuman went back to Gleason's.

"I didn't know it at the time," he says. "But in hindsight, I was looking for the hardest thing I could do this side of the law to prove to a father who had left me that I was tough. Hitting other people is easy.

Getting hit in the face is hard. Most athletes believe they won't get hurt in competition. Boxers know they will."

Neumann's first trainer was a man named Pat Colavito. "He kept me on the floor for three months," Neumann remembers. "Teaching me that my left foot should precede my right foot when I was going forward and my right foot should precede the left going back. Finally, he told me, 'Okay, chief; let's go,' and put me in the ring with a fighter named Wendell Newton. I started flailing away, and Wendell was nice to me. Basically, he was just babysitting which, when I got experienced, I did for other kids who were starting out."

After eighteen months as an amateur, Neumann turned pro. His first fight was a preliminary bout at Madison Square Garden against an opponent named Jeff Marx, who was making his pro debut too.

"Marx was a big strong football player from Long Island," Neumann recalls. "Basically, we were two kids who didn't know anything. Early in round one, we banged heads and I got cut. Then, at the bell, I landed a good right hand and Marx went down. Tony Perez was the referee. It was his first pro fight too. They had just established a new rule in New York that, in the event of a knockdown, the referee's count would continue after the bell. I was the first beneficiary of that rule."

Neumann's first six opponents had a combined total of two wins. Eighteen months after turning pro, he was 11 and 0 when he stepped into the ring against 1 and 6 Jimmy Harris. After the fight, Harris's record was 2 and 6.

"Against Harris," Neumann acknowledges, "I learned that just because a guy can't fight doesn't mean he can't punch. In the first round, I gave him a boxing lesson. I was playing with him. Second round, same thing. Then I got sloppy and threw a righthand lead, and his righthand landed first. I went down and got up. But I didn't know what planet I was on, and the referee stopped the fight."

One month later, Neumann decisioned Harris in a rematch. After that, he won five more fights to bring his record to 17 and 1. Then, on December 12, 1971, he fought the first of three bouts against Chuck Wepner.

"Chuck and I were great rivals," Neumann recalls. "We were New Jersey's version of Tunney and Dempsey. He was the tough guy from the streets, and I was the young college-kid whippersnapper."

Wepner remembers, "The first time we fought, they told me, 'Don't worry about this kid; he's nothing.' But I found out otherwise. Randy beat me. It was an honest decision. I was bigger than he was, but he was tough. He was in shape, he had a good jab, and he could box. No doubt about it, Randy won our first fight."

Neuman lost to Wepner on points in an April 15, 1972, rematch. "It's the only decision I ever lost," he says. "And it was a lousy decision."

Wepner, for his part, says simply, "the second bout was real close. Randy thought he won; I thought I won; and they gave it to me seven rounds to five."

On March 8, 1974, they met for the third time in a bout that was stopped after Neumann suffered an ugly gash from a clash of heads in the seventh round. "That's the only fight I ever won on a cut," Wepner acknowledges. "Usually, I was the guy who did the bleeding."

One year later, Wepner challenged Muhammad Ali for the heavyweight championship of the world. Meanwhile, in retrospect, the Neumann-Wepner bouts were notable for the brawling tactics that both men employed.

"If the other guy started something," Neumann acknowledges, "I'd fight dirty too. And Chuck being the kind of fighter he was . . ." A whimsical smile crosses Neumann's face. "Al Braverman [Wepner's manager] accused me of biting Chuck's ear in one of our fights."

Was the accusation true?

"I might have nibbled on it," concedes Neumann. "But Chuck and I get along well now. In boxing, old adversaries become new friends."

"I didn't like Randy when we fought," Wepner says in response. "But I like him a lot now. He's a good guy."

In addition to Wepner, Neumann fought two other men who battled Muhammad Ali. He won a ten-round decision over Jimmy Young at Madison Square Garden. "I gave Young a boxing lesson," he remembers. "I out-jabbed him all night, which was all either of us did. It was a terrible fight."

And he was stopped by Jerry Quarry.

"The Quarry fight broke my heart," Neuman recalls. "In the sixth round, I was ahead on points when he hit me low. It wasn't your ordinary low blow. Jerry lowered his shoulder and came up from the bottom where there's no protection. That was before they gave a fighter five minutes to recover from a low blow. Tony Perez was the referee. All he did was say to Quarry, 'Don't do it again.' After that, Jerry beat on me like a punching bag. My corner stopped it after the sixth round."

Neumann's overall ring record was 31-7 with 11 knockouts. "My best weapons as a fighter were my jab and the fact that I could think well in the ring," he says. "I had a pretty good chin. I didn't have much of a punch. I fought at 200 pounds, but could have made 190 easily. I was a cruiserweight before there was a cruiserweight division. I trained well, so I was almost always in better shape than my opponent. And I loved boxing. In my soul, I believe it's not a bad thing to do. Some people might want to ban it, but that's their problem."

Meanwhile, in 1975, the same year he was the ninth-ranked heavyweight in the world, Neumann graduated from Farleigh Dickinson, where he'd majored in business. "I figured it was time to use my degree," he recounts, "so I retired from boxing." Today, he's a certified financial planner, and Randy Neumann & Associates, Inc. is a ten-person company that oversees roughly $55,000,000 in assets.

"People need financial planning for security and cash flow," Neumann says, explaining his current livelihood. "That involves decisions with regard to investments, insurance, pensions, long-term health care, and estate planning. I don't pick stocks. I use money managers for that. I just do the planning, and I've been doing it for a quarter-century. A lot of the clients I started with are at a point now where they're ready to retire, and it's a good feeling to know that I've helped them get there."

As for his continuing role in the sweet science, Neumann is one of the few fighters of note who has had success as a referee.

"After I retired," he remembers, "I stayed away from the sport for several years. Then, in 1982, I called John Condon [president of Madison Square Garden Boxing] and told him I wanted to referee. John put in a word for me with the New York State Athletic Commission, and they started using me as a judge. I didn't have any amateur experience, but before long, I had my first assignment as a referee in a four-round bout at the Felt Forum."

Two decades later, Neuman is widely respected within the boxing community and has been the third man in the ring for thirty-one world title fights involving champions like Mike Tyson, Meldrick Taylor, and Buddy McGirt. In addition, he's familiar with Saturday night's combatants, having refereed Golota's 1999 fight against Michael Grant and Byrd's 2002 victory over Evander Holyfield.

"A referee gets paid for his judgment and the physical ability to exercise that judgment," Neumann posits. "If you think like a fighter, you can anticipate and be there when something happens, so I have an edge. But refereeing isn't as easy as it might look. Sometimes, you have to play a tape back two or three times to determine if a head butt was intentional and look at several camera angles to know if a punch was low. In the ring, we only see it once. But one advantage to having been a fighter is that, if I give a warning for a foul and the fighter protests, I can tell him, 'Hey, I saw what you did. I was doing this before you were born.'"

So there you have it. Randy Neumann was a marginal high school student who became a dean's list scholar in college, a certified financial planner, and a world-ranked athlete in the toughest sport in the world. "My life is fairly straightforward now," he says. "What's important to me is my family and my work. I don't go to clubs. My best friend is a guy I've known since first grade. I have three sons and a daughter, who I'm very proud of. And I've done it the right way. There were no short-cuts."

And then Neumann adds, "You know, I never really saw myself as a fighter. I never expected to be a champion. Everything I achieved in boxing was beyond my expectations. It was a quixotic adventure from beginning to end."❏

Bill Cayton was a personal friend and a man who brought honor to boxing.

BILL CAYTON
1918-2003

In October of last year, Bill Cayton told me that he had inoperable cancer in both lungs. He was getting ready to undergo chemotherapy, but the prognosis was poor. "Realistically," he acknowledged, "I don't expect to be here much longer."

Bill wasn't maudlin. To the contrary, he declared, "I'm reconciled. I'm not afraid of dying. Very few people are as lucky as I've been. I've had a wonderful life."

Bill also gave me a bit of advice to live my own life by. "Always make people feel they're appreciated," he said. And to make his point, he told me what he called "the lamb-chop story."

"When I married Doris," Bill explained, "she had no idea how to cook, and that made her feel very insecure. The first time we had dinner at home as husband and wife, Doris made lamb chops. They weren't very good, but I told her, 'These are wonderful! You were pulling my leg. You're a gourmet cook. Who taught you to cook this brilliantly?' And over time," Bill reminisced, "with proper encouragement, Doris became a very good cook."

Then Bill's voice wavered a bit. "I miss Doris terribly," he said. "We were married for fifty-eight years, and it was a fifty-eight-year honeymoon. There was never a second when I wasn't totally in love with her."

That was Bill at his best. He inspired love from his family and loyalty from those who worked for him. He was a brilliant businessman too. Over the years, he guided Mike Tyson, Wilfredo Benitez and Edwin Rosario to championships and generated an incredible amount of money for other fighters. But more important from a professional point of view, he amassed the greatest sports film collection ever assembled, and the heart of that collection was boxing.

Not long ago, Bill reflected back on his career in the sweet science. Here, in his own words, is a list of his ten most satisfying achievements in chronological order:

(1) Purchasing film rights to the July 4, 1919, bout between Jack Dempsey and Jess Willard. That was the film that took me away from a career set entirely in advertising and put me in the fight-film business.

(2) Receiving a "best documentary" Academy-Award nomination for my production of *Jack Johnson*.

(3) Working with Muhammad Ali during his exile from boxing and producing *A/K/A Cassius Clay*.

(4) Negotiating with Mike Trainer on behalf of Wilfredo Benitez for a fight in 1979 against Sugar Ray Leonard. Wilfredo lost, but he was paid the then-staggering sum of $1,200,000 plus $200,000 in training expenses. Also, Wilfredo's 1981 knock out of Maurice Hope to win the WBC junior-middleweight title. That gave him three championships in three different weight divisions at a time when three championships really meant something.

(5) Mike Tyson knocking out Trevor Berbick on November 22, 1986. That seemed to confirm our view that Mike was destined for greatness.

(6) Negotiating what was then an unprecedented $26,500,000 multi-fight deal for Tyson with HBO.

(7) Edwin Rosario knocking out Anthony Jones in 1989 to win the WBA lightweight title. That was the culmination of Edwin's comeback twenty months after he was knocked out by Julio Cesar Chavez and written off by most people as a shot fighter.

(8) Landing Tommy Morrison a starring role as Tommy Gunn in *Rocky V*. I loved playing the game.

(9) Licensing my fight film collection to Classic Sports and, later, selling it to ESPN for a sum that confirmed its value.

(10) The loyalty and support of the people who knew me best and worked with me on a daily basis.

Bill's film collection made him a rich man. But of greater significance, his persistence and determination over a fifty-year period preserved boxing's heritage. Most of the films that he acquired were on nitrate stock, which was the only film used for motion pictures prior to 1947. Nitrate film is highly combustible and given to disintegration. Bill transfered his early fight-film footage to acetate stock. In later years, it was transfered to videotape. Without his intervention, the images on those films would have been lost forever.

Over the past few years, Bill and I talked on the telephone almost every Sunday morning. Either I'd call him or he'd call me, and we'd review what had happened in boxing the previous week. Bill always wanted to know what was going on. He loved the excitement and the action.

This past Saturday, I was in Las Vegas for the fight between Evander Holyfield and James Toney when Bill's daughter, Trish, telephoned and told me that Bill had died. Later in the day, I was sitting with Evander in his suite, and he told me a story that bears repeating.

As most people in boxing know, there were times when Bill and Don King were bitter adversaries. Two years ago, King was trying to arrange a fight in China between Evander Holyfield and John Ruiz; so he went to Beijing with both fighters.

King has a certain modus operandi when he's in a foreign country. In Puerto Rico, he goes around waving a Puerto Rican flag, shouting, "Viva Puerto Rico." In Mexico, he waves a Mexican flag and shouts, "Viva Mexico."

Once King arrived Beijing, he asked his translator how to say "I love China and the Chinese people" in Chinese. The translator told him and they went over it together several times to make sure that Don had his pronunciation down correctly. But as Evander tells it, gremlins got into the translation.

So King went around Beijing waving Chinese and American flags. Wherever he went, he'd shout out his phrase, and people would laugh, cheer, and applaud. But what Don didn't know was that he was going around Beijing, waving his flags with his hair up in the air and that wonderful trademark smile on his face, shouting out in Chinese, "I love watermelon."

Evander recounted that scene for me, and the first thought that flashed through my mind was, "God, I wish I could call Bill. He'd love that story." And it made me realize how much those of us who cared about Bill will miss him.

Dying is no great accomplishment. Everyone does it. It's the way a person lives that counts.

Bill lived his life the way he wanted to and enjoyed his life to the fullest. I suspect that he's is up in heaven now, managing Joe Louis, haggling with God over the details of a multi-fight contract. Most likely, Doris is tugging gently at his sleeve, saying, "Bill, don't push too hard. You're dealing with God." And Bill is telling her, "I know it's God; but Joe Louis is the greatest boxer in heaven."

Meanwhile, down here on Earth, every time we look at Jack Dempsey, Joe Louis or Sugar Ray Robinson on television, we'll be reminded of how much we're indebted to Bill Cayton.❏

Pat English is part of boxing's legal elite.

PAT ENGLISH

"The first thing we do," wrote Shakespeare in *Henry VI, Part II*, "let us kill all the lawyers."

A lot of people in boxing have similar sentiments.

Lou DiBella formed DiBella Entertainment in May 2000. By the start of this year, he'd spent close to two million dollars on attorneys. Cedric Kushner has spent a similar sum in legal fees over the past few years. "It's reached a point," says Kushner, "where you're not considered a major player unless you're being sued and suing someone else at any given time. Don King's legal fees are astronomical. Mike Tyson's budget for lawyers goes through the roof."

Over the years, a handful of lawyers have carved out a niche for themselves in the sweet science. Judd Burstein is the litigator of the moment, although he suffered an arbitration loss last year in *DeGuardia v. Tarver*. Jim Thomas did wonders as the go-to guy for Evander Holyfield. Mike Heitner is known as the "best contract attorney" in the business. There are times when it seems as though Milt Chwasky has a piece of everything; a situation that led to a $1,175,000 jury verdict against him in favor of heavyweight champion Lennox Lewis for breach of fiduciary duty. Jimmy Binns has been inextricably linked with the WBA for years. Jeff Fried represents Dan Goossen. Don King turns to Charles Lomax on a regular basis and relies on Peter Fleming when he's in trouble. John Hornewer is a steady presence for myriad fighters. And then there's Pat English.

The 53-year old English was born and raised in New Jersey. His father was a turkey farmer and municipal health officer. English went to college at Drake University and law school at Rutgers. After graduation, he began work as an associate at the law firm of Lordi, Imperial & Dines. Three years later, Dines and English went off and established a two-man partnership that lasted until Dines died in October 2002. "He was my mentor," says English, who now practices law on his own.

English's introduction to boxing came in 1982. Main Events, which had been formed in 1978, was trying to position itself as the "good guy" alternative to Don King and Bob Arum. Its marquee fighters were Rocky

Lockridge, Johnny Bumphus and Tony Ayala. English was retained by company president Dan Duva (also an attorney) to litigate against the World Boxing Association. The lawsuit centered on an effort by Ayala (a Main Events fighter) to enforce his rights pursuant to WBA rules as the mandatory challenger for the 154-pound crown. English won the case, but it was a Pyrrhic victory. Ayala was sidetracked, first by injury and later by incarceration, and never fought for the title.

After the 1984 Olympics, Main Events signed Evander Holyfield, Pernell Whitaker, Mark Breland, Meldrick Taylor, and Tyrell Biggs. That boosted it to "big three" status. Duva remained his own general counsel, while English continued to handle litigation and some contract work.

Then, in 1995, Duva was diagnosed as having brain cancer. He set up a structure pursuant to which he remained chairman of the board and chief executive officer while his brother Dino took over as president. In 1996, he succumbed to the cancer and his wife Kathy succeeded him as chairman and CEO. Then Dino developed a serious substance abuse problem that interfered with his job performance. The "Duva Wars" followed.

Dan Duva had put the entire equity in Main Events in a spousal trust for the benefit of Kathy and their three children. In 1999, Dino and his sister Donna broke off from the promotional company and sued the trust, Kathy, and English (who was a trustee), claiming an equity interest in Main Events. Lou Duva (the father of Dan, Dino and Donna) filed a separate lawsuit that was dismissed. The primary lawsuit was settled on terms favorable to the trust after opening statements and the testimony of one witness at trial. "It's over now," says English. "And Main Events continues on the basis of the principles that Dan set up."

Kathy Duva is still chairman and CEO of Main Events. Carl Moretti is vice president and Glenn Jones is chief financial officer. English is general counsel and is paid on an hourly basis. He states flatly that, contrary to the belief of some, he has never had an equity position in the company.

English estimates that more than half of his legal work today is performed on behalf of Main Events. The rest of his practice is an ecclectic mix of commercial litigation. Among the cases he's proudest of is litigation brought against the IBF by Michael Moorer in the mid-1990s.

"Main Events alleged that Bob Lee was rigging the rankings for money," English says, explaining the lawsuit. "For years, everyone had been saying that the ratings organizations were corrupt, but there's a difference between saying something and proving it. Dan Duva authorized bringing the lawsuit knowing that it would help Michael get a title opportunity, but also knowing that the IBF would punish Main Events. And we were right on both counts. In the years after the lawsuit, before the government indicted Bob Lee, the IBF was not kind to us."

"As far as boxing is concerned," English continues, "there's an appalling disregard for contracts and the rights of others, and I don't limit that observation to the sanctioning organizations and other promoters. Not everyone in the business is like that. If a person like Jim Thomas gives me his word on something, I'll take it to the bank. But the problem is systemic."

English is far from universally beloved within the fistic community. "He's not Mr. Congeniality," observes one denizen of the boxing world. "In fact, he can be downright abrasive."

Don King has strong feelings toward English that boiled over at the press conference immediately following Rahman-Lewis II, when he accused the attorney of being a white slavemaster. Others see English as too combative and adversarial. "Pat comes at you straight but he comes at you too often," says a fellow lawyer. "And he's totally inflexible when he feels he's protecting his turf."

Another participant on the boxing merry-go-round complains, "Pat acts high and mighty when it suits his purposes, but he's not above leaking tidbits and disseminating misinformation when it's to his advantage." And a high-ranking television executive notes, "I think Pat cares about boxing, and I want to like him. But too often, under the guise of being a friend, he tries to manipulate you into doing something that he says is in your best interests when, clearly, it's not."

Still, the consensus is that no attorney is more fluent in the labrynith of boxing politics than English. He knows boxing; he knows litigation; he's loyal to his clients; and he's a formidable adversary. Meanwhile, English maintains that criticism of his style doesn't bother him. "I just do what I think is right and in the best interest of my client," he says. "Whatever happens after that happens."

Beyond the sweet science, English is something of an enigma. "Given the nature of the business and some of the people in it," he says, "I like people to know as little about me and my family as possible." But he acknowledges having myriad interests that include a passion for sailing and a love of history. He's proud of the fact that his 15-year-old daughter, Lauren, holds the national public high school record in the 100-meter backstroke and finished ninth in the recent Olympic trials. "And my son Andrew is a pretty good soccer player," he notes.

English also served as counsel to the Clifton Board of Education for a decade before becoming a member of the board of the Lincoln Park school system. Over the years, one of his causes with regard to public education has been the desire for accountability in spending. In New Jersey, many school districts pay millions of dollars to educate students in high schools located in neighboring districts. Yet they have little say as to how their tax dollars are spent. English took a case that challenged the set-up all the way to the United States Supreme Court on a pro bono basis. He lost, but says, "I'm still fighting the issue. When someone takes your money and spends it any way they want, that's taxation without representation."

Larry Merchant can attest to the sincerity of English's interest in public education. "When we were in South Africa for the first Lewis-Rahman fight," Merchant recalls, "Pat and I went to a school in Soweto because he wanted to see what the schools there were like."

Jim Lampley also has a Pat English story to tell regarding Lewis-Rahman I.

"At the time," Lampley remembers, "Pat was the point person for Main Events on matters involving Lennox Lewis. Lennox was knocked out around four-thirty in the morning. Our plane back to the United States left Johannesburg about five hours later. The plane took off. Pat took a yellow legal pad out of his attache case and started writing. And his pen never left the pad until we landed at JFK fourteen hours later. You remember the litigation that Lennox had to go through to force Rahman back into the ring for a rematch," Lampley continues. "I'm convinced that the legal work Pat did on that plane served as the foundation for everything that followed. And without that, Lennox might not have had the opportunity to become heavyweight champion of the world again."

"It's a nice story," English says when apprised of Lampley's evaluation. "But the truth is, I was writing an article on racial profiling for the *New Jersey Law Journal*."❏

Cathy Paolillo is one of the people behind the scenes who keep boxing alive.

THE TIMEKEEPER

Last month, Final Forum promoted a night of club fights at Jimmy's Bronx Cafe. One of those in attendance was a good-natured, 40-year-old mother of two from Long Island, who works as a postal clerk by day and was involved in every second of every fight.

Cathy Paolillo grew up on Long Island rooting for the New York Yankees and Islanders. Her husband, Tony, also works for the United States Postal Service.

"I started as a timekeeper in the late 1980s," Paolillo explained. "My husband wanted to be a ring judge and was told to get some experience by working amateur fights. So he went to the amateurs as a referee, timekeeper, and judge. At the time, there were a lot of amateur shows in New York, and it seemed like Tony worked every one of them. I figured, if I wanted to see my husband, I had to get involved. I didn't have the concentration to be a judge, so I decided to try my hand as a time-keeper."

A long training period followed. The first professional card that Paolillo worked was on Long Island in 1996. Since then, she has been the timekeeper for close to a hundred shows. The biggest card she worked was Felix Trinidad versus Bernard Hopkins at Madison Square Garden on September 29, 2001. She was also among the officials sched-uled to go to China for Evander Holyfield versus John Ruiz, but that happening never happened.

Statewide, there are seven licensed professional timekeepers in New York. Their duties are defined by statute as follows: "Sound the gong to begin and end each round by striking it vigorously with a metal hammer . . . Count for knockdowns at the rate of one stroke per second by vigorously striking the floor of the ring or a suitable wooden striking board with a substantially constructed hammer or mallet . . . Signal by striking the floor of the ring to indicate when ten seconds remain in a round . . . Signal by whistle when ten seconds remain before the beginning of a round . . . Except as above, the timekeeper shall give no signal or other information during a contest."

New York won't license a timekeeper who doesn't have amateur experience. Oddly, until recently, the New York State Athletic Commission licensed timekeepers but did not appoint them. The timekeeper was appointed by the promoter. And on top of that, the promoter paid the timekeeper whatever amount was agreed upon betweeen them. That drew some criticism.

"There are moments in boxing when the timekeeper is as important as the referee and judges," opined Marc Ratner (executive director of the Nevada State Athletic Commission). "And with any sport, when it comes to game operation, the regulatory body should be in control."

Larry Hazzard (Ratner's counterpart in New Jersey) concurred, adding, "There's no sense in trying to get around it. The conflict is obvious. Promoters have favorites, and a second here and a second there can make a big difference."

Then, in June 2003, Ron Scott Stevens (the newly-appointed chairman of the New York State Athletic Commission) announced that timekeepers would be appointed by the commission and paid at a fixed rate. "You assume honesty on the part of people," said Stevens. "But at the same time, you want to remove as many temptations as possible."

That's a good idea, as evidenced by the following.

Promoter-matchmaker Don Elbaum is a highly-principled individual. Whether Elbaum's principles are good or bad is a matter of interpretation. "I had a fighter named Lou Bizzarro," Elbaum remembers. "Good chin, no punch. In 1976, I got him a title fight against Roberto Duran in Erie, Pennsylvania. I tell people that I had a thirty-foot ring specially built for the fight; but the truth is, it was only twenty-eight feet inside."

"Anyway," Elbaum continued, "the timekeeper was Bernie Blacher. Bernie was a great guy and a dynamite friend of mine. Before the fight, I told him, 'Bernie; whatever you do, if my kid gets Duran hurt, keep the round going. And if Lou is hurt, please, ring the bell.' So the fight starts. Lou is running like crazy. He's going backwards faster than Roger Bannister ever went forward, and Duran can't catch him because the ring is as big as a parking lot. Finally, in the seventh or eighth round, Duran nails him. And the bell rings to end the round, which was maybe two minutes and ten seconds long. Then there's an extra fifteen seconds between rounds, which gives Lou a bit more time to recover. Next round; Duran nails him again. Ding! There's the bell. That round was maybe forty seconds short, and now there a ninety-second rest period between rounds. Round ten, it happens again. And all of a sudden, there's a huge commotion at ringside because some girl from the TV truck has come into the arena and is screaming at Bernie, 'Goddamn it! You're killing our commercials.' She actually fought Bernie for the hammer he was using to ring the bell. But God bless him, he didn't give it up. There were five short rounds and five long rest periods before Duran stopped Lou in the fourteenth round."

Boxing maven Johnny Bos keeps a close eye on the fistic scene. In 1985, Juan LaPorte journeyed to Northern Ireland to take on local hero Barry McGuigan. Midway through the bout, LaPorte had McGuigan in trouble. Bos swears that Mickey Duff (McGuigan's co-promoter) ran over, grabbed the timekeeper's hammer, and hit the bell. McGuigan recovered and won a decision.

It's also worth mentioning that Greg Page (who was a Don King favorite) stopped Gerrie Coetzee in South Africa on December 1, 1984, to win the WBA heavyweight title in a protracted eighth round.

Meanwhile, Jim Borzell, who was a timekeeper in New York for years, has his own recollections. "The job can be dangerous," Borzell noted. "If there's an unpopular decision, flying objects are a potential problem."

Borzell was on duty when Andrew Golota was disqualified in his 1996 bout against Riddick Bowe at Madison Square Garden. In the riot that followed, Borzell suffered an ugly gash on his left eyebrow. Cutman Lenny DeJesus closed the wound for him. No sutures were necessary.

"Another time," Borzell continued, "I was working a club show on Long Island. A guy got knocked through the ropes, rolled off the ring apron, and hit his head on my bell. The bell rang like I'd hit it with a hammer."

Paolillo had her own brush with celebrity status two years ago, when Hector Camacho, Jr. squared off against Jesse James Leija at Coney Island in New York. Those were the days when the commissioners of the New York State Athletic Commission were Mel Southard, Jerry Becker, and Marc Cornstein (known in boxing circles as Larry, Curly, and Moe).

Against Leija, Camacho suffered a cut from an accidental head butt in round five and quit moments after the bell sounded to start the sixth round. Then, after a protracted caucus by the officials in attendance, he was awarded a technical decision since he was ahead on the scorecards. This struck most observers as unfair, since it appeared to have been the power of Leija's punches rather than the cut that led to Hector's decision to abstain from further violence. And in any event, the ring doctor had said that Camacho was capable of continuing. Thus, eighteen days later, the Three Stooges issued an opinion reversing the decision. But rather than award a TKO victory to Leija, they declared the bout a technical draw on grounds that Paolillo had improperly rung the bell to start the sixth round.

At Jimmy's Bronx Cafe, as is her custom, Paolillo arrived for the fights an hour before the first bout. She was carrying a black Samsonite attache case that held the tools of her trade. A ringside bell, a hammer, two blocks of wood, a whistle, and two digital stopwatches.

The first bout of the evening was Gary Pierre Louis versus Michel Agard. Louis was 0 and 1 as a pro. Agard was making his professional debut. Ring announcer Joe Antonacci introduced the fighters, Paolillo hit the bell with her hammer, and the fight began.

"You develop a feel for the time," says Paolillo. "At the start of each round, I watch the fight. One minute in, I check the clock to make sure my instinct is right. Then, at the two-minute mark, I check again. Two minutes and forty seconds into a round, the fight becomes virtually non-existent for me. At that point, I'm only interested in the clock, except for knockdowns and keeping one eye on the referee to see if he calls time. At two-fifty, I give the ten-second warning. At three minutes, I hit the bell."

In round two at Jimmy's, Agard went down. Alternate referee Eddie Claudio began the count, while Paolillo held up fingers designating the seconds for referee Joe Santarpia. In round three, Santarpia called "time" after a low blow. Paolillo stopped the round clock and started her back-up watch to monitor the five minutes that, if necessary, would be given to the aggrieved fighter to recover. Louis won a four-round decision.

It's always a long night for the timekeeper. In a single ten-round fight, Paolillo will hit her bell with a hammer twenty times (once at the start and once at the end of each round); strike a block of wood with her hammer to designate the two-fifty mark of a round on ten occasions; and blow her whistle ten seconds before the start of a round nine times. There are knockdowns, breaks in the action for loose tape, lost mouth-pieces, and other interruptions. Paolillo must closely monitor every-thing for every bout on the card.

Very few people in the audience at a fight notice Paolillo, but the lack of recognition didn't bother her. "I do it because I love it," she says. "In fact, I'd rather not be noticed. Nobody notices the timekeeper unless we screw up." ❏

Holger Keifel provided the cover photograph for this book. But that's just one of many treasures his camera has recorded, as I noted in this article for Boxing Digest.

HOLGER KEIFEL

For the past year, readers of *Boxing Digest* have been treated to a series of images by renowned portrait photographer Holger Keifel.

Keifel began photographing the face of boxing in 2002. Since then, he has recorded two hundred subjects. Superstars like Evander Holyfield, Roy Jones, Bernard Hopkins, and Oscar De La Hoya are in his portfolio. But equally important, Keifel has worked his magic on trainers, cutmen, managers, promoters, and other members of boxing's supporting cast.

Keifel is friendly and gentle-mannered with an open smile and cheerful persona. He always wears black. He was born on September 8, 1962, in the small town of Ettenheim in Germany's Black Forest. For three years, he trained to be an electrician. Then, in 1986, he travelled around the world with an old Canon camera that belonged to his father and became interested in photography.

As Keifel remembers, "I said to myself, 'This is fun; to travel and take pictures. It would be great to sell them and travel again. I should go somewhere to learn the trade.'"

Thereafter, Keifel worked in several photo laboratories to learn development techniques and took a series of jobs as a photographer's assistant. In 1993, he moved to New York. Since then, his portraits have appeared in such diverse publications as *GQ, Der Spiegel, Stern*, and the *New York Times Magazine*.

The first photographs of boxers that Keifel shot were at a club card in New York. "I wanted to show what happens to a face during a fight," he explains. Then the boxing bug bit. "I like a series," Keifel says of his work. "Anybody can take one good picture, but a series tells a story."

Keifel has photographed boxing personalities at numerous weigh-ins, press conferences and fights. He works quickly, using a Mamiya RZ camera, shooting within the time allotted. "Often, these guys are not in the mood for a picture," he says. "Sometimes, I have less than a minute, but most of them are pretty good about it. A lot of fighters start with the traditional pose, putting their fists up. But I tell them, 'No, I'm not interested in that. I'm interested in your face.'"

Keifel's images are detailed and powerful, and reveal the scars, permanent bumps, and other signature marks of a fighter's trade. "The close-up is important to me," he says. "I don't fake things. I want a clear sharp honest document of a face. I don't add anything and I don't take anything away. For this series, I knew right away that the pictures had to be in black-and-white. There was no question; I didn't think for a second about color."

Keifel's favorite boxing portraits to date include subjects as diverse as Emile Griffith, Bouie Fisher, Tokunbo Olajide, and Rich Giachetti. He's particularly fond of Evander Holyfield's ear. As for the future, he says, "I'd love the opportunity to photograph Muhammad Ali and Joe Frazier. Don King would be great too. If I had Don King in a studio for an hour, that would be a picture for the ages."

Keifel's boxing photographs will be exhibited at the Butler Institute of American Art in Ohio from March 28 through May 30, 2004. Meanwhile, he is creating a body of work that, years from now, will constitute a treasure. And his photographs are starting to be appreciated within the boxing community.

At the kick-off press conference for Evander Holyfield versus James Toney, Keifel set his equipment up in a corner of the room and waited for his chance to photograph the fighters. As always, there were demands from major media. Finally, Toney headed toward Keifel but was stopped by a publicist.

"James," the publicist said. "Someone from *The New York Times* wants to interview you."

"I don't care," Toney responded. "This is that guy from *Boxing Digest*."❏

This article could just as easily have been titled "The Simpsons Meet Boxing."

SAM SIMON AND THE ALLURE OF BOXING

When Lamon Brewster steps into the ring on April 10, 2004, to face Wladimir Klitschko for the WBO heavyweight crown, a 48 year-old man named Sam Simon will be on the cusp of fulfilling a dream.

Simon was born and raised in Southern California. "Fourth generation," he says. He had what he calls a "privileged upbringing" and went to Beverly Hills High School, where he played football and wrestled. Then he attended Stanford, where he was a cartoonist for the school newspaper. That led to assignments from the *San Francisco Chronicle* and *San Francisco Examiner*. Next, he was hired as a story-board artist at Filmation Studios, where he worked on a number of projects including *Fat Albert*.

"I figured, as long as I was writing, I should write good shows," Simon remembers. "So I wrote a script on spec for *Taxi* and sent it in. They liked it; they made it; and all of a sudden, at age twenty-three, I was producing *Taxi*."

The entries on Simon's resume since then are the stuff of dreams. He has been a writer, director, producer and/or creative consultant for *Cheers, The Drew Carey Show, The George Carlin Show, It's Garry Shandling's Show, Barney Miller, Best of the West, Bless This House, Men Behaving Badly, Norm,* and *The Tracey Ullman Show.* The latter venture led to his greatest creative and commercial triumph.

Each episode of *Tracey Ullman* contained a one-minute animated segment. Simon and co-producer James L. Brooks thought that the animated characters were strong enough to support a half-hour series and, in 1989, they launched *The Simpsons.*

The Simpsons is now the longest-running animated series in the history of prime-time network television and has contributed handsomely to Simon's total of twelve Emmys.

Simon has been married twice; the first time to actress Jennifer Tilly ["We're still good friends"]. More recently, he wed a woman with whom he had a "long stormy on-again-off-again-on-again relationship." That marriage was annulled after three weeks.

161

"I wrote two jokes to cover my humiliation," Simon reports. "Number one: In this day and age, can any marriage that lasts three weeks really be called a failure? And number two: Oh, no! Where am I going to find another hot blonde gold-digger in this town? But I'd like to have a family," he adds wistfully. "Very few things are important to me, but that's one of them. I hope the race isn't fully run."

And then there's boxing.

"I used to go to fights with my grandfather," Simon remembers. "Then I got caught up in the hype for Ali-Frazier I, although I'll confess that I was a big Joe Frazier fan. Mike Tyson revived my interest when he was coming up through the ranks. But I didn't see a heavyweight championship fight in person until (CBS executive) Les Moonves took me to Buster Douglas against Evander Holyfield. That was electrifying to me. And around that time, I started training in a gym. Eventually, I had nine amateur fights at gym shows and won six of them. I loved the anonymity; the fact that no one was kissing my ass. It was all very refreshing and exciting."

Simon was on hand as an alternate for the first night of *Celebrity Boxing* on Fox television. "There was a chance of my fighting Joey Buttafucco but it didn't happen," he notes. Meanwhile, he had ventured into the world of high-stakes professional boxing as the manager of Lamon Brewster.

"When *The Simpsons* was sold into syndication, which was the pot of gold in my life, I was a fan of two sports: football and boxing," Simon explains. "I knew I couldn't own an NFL franchise, but I thought I might be able to manage a heavyweight champion. I knew Lamon from the Wild Card Gym in Los Angeles. I'd seen him fight, and the word around Southern California was that he was a prospect. Then Freddie Roach told me that Lamon was having managerial problems; so I put my lawyer on the case and became his manager."

Brewster's first fight in conjunction with Simon was a second-round stoppage of Mario Cawley on June 22, 1999. That brought his record to 21 and 0 with 19 knockouts. Victories over Quinn Navarre and Richard Mason followed. Then, on May 6, 2000, Lamon stepped up in class and lost a ten-round decision to Clifford Etienne on *KO Nation*. Five months later, he lost again, this time to Charles Shufford. Since then, he has won five fights in a row and risen to number one in the WBO rankings. His promoter for the last four fights has been Don King.

King's contract with Brewster was the product of seemingly endless negotiation. There were drafts and redrafts and scribbled notes in margins. At last, after a final six-hour session, King, Brewster and Simon came to terms. At that point, King produced a blank sheet of paper and told the members of Team Brewster, "Sign at the bottom and I'll have my attorneys type up exactly what we agreed to above your signatures."

That ploy didn't work and Simon is bemused when he talks about it all. But there are times when he seems a bit shaken by the business of boxing. "I think I'm a good person," he says. "An honorable person. And there are things that come up constantly in this business that bother me. Don has been great for Lamon's career. He has been tough with us but never crooked with us. As for some of the other people we've dealt with . . ." The rest of the thought goes unspoken.

Simon estimates that he is out-of-pocket several hundred thousand dollars as a consequence of managing Brewster. He has paid the fighter a salary of roughly $50,000 a year on top of his purses from fights. Meanwhile, his manager's share of each purse has been a modest ten-percent and Lamon lives rent-free in a house that Simon owns. Some of that money will be recouped from an arbitration award that Brewster secured recently against Bob Arum. A bit more will come from the $225,000 plus $60,000 in expenses that Lamon is being paid to fight Klitschko.

"Boxing isn't a source of revenue for me," says Simon. "But it's more than a hobby. I take my responsibilities very seriously and get very involved emotionally in Lamon's fights. The three days before a fight feel like they're an hour or two long for me. I love the rules meetings and press conferences and hanging out in the hotel lobby with the fighters. But on the night of a fight, once we get to the locker room, everything moves very slowly. I feel very tense in a way that nothing else, including my own wrestling matches and gym fights, ever made me feel. I'm aware that Lamon's career is on the line and he's risking his life every time he steps into the ring."

Brewster has never beaten a world-class fighter. And to protect his number-one WBO ranking, he has fought only once in the past fifteen months—a third-round knockout of a 309-pound punching bag named Joe Lenhart on the undercard of Roy Jones versus John Ruiz last March. Thus, the prevailing view among the boxing intelligentsia with regard to Klitschko-Brewster is that Klitschko will win big.

Still, Simon is optimistic. "Klitschko bails out under pressure," he says. "And the two things that Wladimir is known for, being 6-feet-7-inches tall and having a doctorate, are two things that are totally use-less in boxing. Lamon has never been stopped in a fight and he has never quit."

"The whole experience has been good for me," Simon says, putting his involvement with the sweet science in perspective. "And I think I've been good for Lamon. I hope, when we're done, he has a home of his own and enough money to live on for life. But whatever happens, I can honestly say that I've lived up to all of the promises I made to him. Lamon is going to be on HBO, fighting for a world title. What happens now is up to him."

And . . . oh, yes. The week after Klitschko-Brewster, Sam Simon will be directing the final episode of *The Drew Carey Show*.❏

Some boxing writers are more than chroniclers of the scene. They're part of it.

GEORGE KIMBALL

The term "boxing writer" is often a misnomer. There are people with press credentials who report on fights. Others write snippets. But there are few writers.

George Kimball is a man of letters. He was born on December 20, 1943, the oldest of seven children. His father was a career military officer, who retired as a colonel and maintained that he would have been a general were it not for the anti-war activities of his offspring. But that comes later in the saga.

"I grew up all over the world," Kimball recalls. "When I was young, I spent more time in Kentucky than anyplace else. But I was born in California. I lived in Texas and Taiwan. My freshman year of high school started in Maryland and ended in Germany."

Kimball's college years began on a ROTC scholarship at the University of Kansas. He and future Hall of Fame halfback Gale Sayers lived on the same dormitory floor as freshman.

And they were buddies; right?

Wrong.

"Gale was cold, moody, and glowering, "Kimball remembers. "Years later, we talked about it, and he told me that, when he was eighteen, he hadn't been around white people before. He didn't think he belonged in college. He wasn't unfriendly, just insecure."

Meanwhile, in Kimball's words, "The revolution was calling." Ergo, in 1965, he was expelled from the University of Kansas for picketing the local draft board while carrying a sign that read "fuck the draft." The same incident led to his arrest on a charge of committing an act of gross public indecency. "They treated it like a sex crime," he explains. Ultimately, he served two-and-a-half days in jail for the offense. One of his nights in incarceration was spent in a cell with two murderers.

Thus began a pattern, in Kimball's words, of, "Go to school, drop out; get a job, quit; get another job, go back to school, quit again. I never graduated from college," he acknowledges, "although over the years, I've taken courses at the University of Kansas, St. Mary's College,

Massachusetts Bay Community College, and the Iowa Writers Workshop; also extension courses at Harvard."

Kimball was arrested for anti-war activity a half-dozen times. But his most dramatic run-in with the law came in New York on a charge of assaulting a police officer. "That one was non-political," he notes. "The cop was refusing to help a woman who was ill; some words were exchanged and I slugged him. The cop was clearly in the wrong and the charges against me were dismissed, although I did get beaten up and spent a night in jail. In my younger days," Kimball admits, "I spent many nights in jail for drinking, partying, and possession of marijuana, but never more than a night or two at a time."

In 1970, Kimball embarked upon a new adventure: returning to Lawrence (home of the University of Kansas) to run for county sheriff. Douglas County was heavily Republican. The Democrats didn't even run a candidate for many local offices. A half-hour before the deadline to enter the primaries, Kimball showed up with the hundred-dollar filing fee, entered the Democratic primary, and ran unopposed, which meant that he got the Democratic nomination for sheriff by default.

"A lot of the campaign was high theatre and camp," Kimball reminisces. "The Republican incumbent was the same guy who had arrested me in 1965. He had a withered arm, so I distributed bumper stickers that read, 'Douglas County needs a two-fisted sheriff.' Abby Hoffman came for a campaign rally and offended some voters when he was photographed afterward at a rock concert blowing his nose into an American flag."

But on a more serious note, there was a lot of violence in Lawrence that summer. The black section of town erupted after a police officer shot a black teenager in the back of the head and killed him. Soon, there were riots, bombings, sniper assaults, and arson. A state of emergency was declared. The governor ordered the Kansas Highway Patrol into Lawrence.

And it all played out against the backdrop of the war in Vietnam, the invasion of Cambodia, and the killings at Kent State.

"I was a member of the Lawrence Liberation Front," Kimball says of that time. "And I was also defense chairman of the White Panthers Party, so I wasn't a particularly popular candidate with the establishment. I got blamed for a lot of things that I didn't do and a few that I did. The chairman of the state Democratic party endorsed my opponent, and I got something like thirteen percent of the vote."

"That was a long time ago," Kimball says, reflecting back on his run for public office. "I'm not the active political person I once was, although I'm still politically interested. And I have a strong sense of outrage toward the present administration. I wouldn't say that I roll out of bed each morning saying, 'Fuck George Bush.' But it's close to that."

Meanwhile, as Kimball was living as a counterculture activist, his life took a literary turn. After several hitchhiking trips to San Francisco and stints as a bartender and cab driver, he moved to New York and got a job at the Scott Meredith Literary Agency in 1965. He also immersed himself in the Lower East Side poetry scene and authored several articles for the *Village Voice*. Then, in 1967, Maurice Girodias (publisher of the Olympic Press in Paris) took an interest in his writing. Olympic was publishing English-language editions of erotic fiction like *Lady Chatterly's Lover*, which American publishers were loath to print. Thus it came to pass that *Only Skin Deep* by George Kimball (described by its author as "the erotic adventures of a high school girl in Kansas") was bequeathed to the world.

In 1968, Kimball authored a poem that appeared in *The Paris Review*. Thereafter, he published several volumes of poetry. "I wouldn't say that poetry was my first love," he muses. "But yeah, I guess you could say that. Eventually, though, I drifted away from poetry and found other ways to express myself."

One mode of expression was writing about sports.

In 1970, after living in New York and running unsuccessfully for Douglas County sheriff, Kimball moved to Massachusetts to pursue a career as a freelance writer. There, he reviewed music for *Rolling Stone* and books for *Playboy*. But his primary gig was writing a weekly sports column for a counterculture weekly called *The Phoenix*.

Kimball's career as a sportswriter had begun in Kentucky when he was in eighth grade and reported on junior high school football games for the *Murray Democrat*. Then, as a high school student in Maryland, he'd covered local sports as a stringer for all four Washington, D.C. daily newspapers. "But *The Phoenix* was the real turning point for me," he reminisces. "I was there for almost ten years. And I can honestly say that *The Phoenix* took me everywhere that I've gone to since."

Kimball left *The Phoenix* in late 1979 on the theory that it was time to do something else. Then, in February 1980, after freelancing several pieces for the *Boston Herald*, he went on staff as a columnist. That same year, Marvin Hagler (who was from the Boston area) won the world middleweight championship and Kimball prevailed upon the powers that be to let him write a weekly boxing column. By the time Hagler retired, seven years and many championship fights later, George was well-established as the *Herald's* boxing writer.

Over the years, Kimball has covered thirty Super Bowls, the World Series, the NBA Finals, all four golf majors, Wimbledon, the summer and winter Olympics, and countless other sports events. He's also the primary football columnist for the *Herald*. By his estimate, he spends twenty-five percent of his time on boxing. That includes covering big fights and local boxing stories in addition to writing a Sunday "boxing notes" column.

"When I first started writing boxing," Kimball says, "I knew virtually nothing about the business end of it. I'd enjoyed watching boxing on television, but that was the extent of my knowledge. I've now covered something like 330 world title fights. And I realize that understanding the business end of boxing is essential to understanding the rest of it."

"The best fight I've ever seen," Kimball continues, "was Leonard-Hearns I, although Ward-Gatti I is up there. Hagler-Leonard was memorable for many reasons, one of which was the fact that Marvin had no idea that the fight was slipping away from him. I scored it for Leonard by a point. And it still amazes me how fighters, good fighters, can go through their entire career and not understand how a fight is scored. Ray Leonard understood; Marvin didn't. He didn't realize that Leonard was winning rounds with flurries of punches and by going all out in the last thirty seconds of each round to impress the judges."

Kimball smokes at least two packs of cigarettes a day ["closer to three when I'm driving or playing golf"]. He hasn't had a drink in twelve years ["I just decided I'd had enough"]. And he hasn't smoked marijuana in more than a decade ["I came to the realization that it was making me sleepy and stupid"].

He has been married three times. The first two marriages were when he was young and lasted two years each. His third marriage, which ended in divorce in 2003, lasted twenty-one years and begat him a son and daughter. He plans to marry for the fourth (and final) time on April 3, 2004, in a ceremony presided over by the Reverend George Foreman. His bride to be, Marge Marash, is a New York City psychiatrist.

Thus, reflecting back on the habits of his youth, Kimball says philosophically, "Finally, after sixty years, I'm marrying someone who can write drug prescriptions for me. And it's too late."

ADDENDUM

The wedding took place at The Nuyorican Poets Cafe in Manhattan. The Reverend George Foreman, wearing a tuxedo, looked relaxed and fit. Long ago, he was a glowering presence, but now there's an aura of good will about him.

"The first marriage I performed was in New Jersey in 1978," Foreman reminisced shortly before the noon service. "I had an old friend who had become a lion and tiger trainer. He fell in love with the lady who cleaned the cages and decided he couldn't live without her, so I flew all the way from Texas to marry them. Since then, I've married hundreds of people all over the world. I even did a wedding once in the Astrodome with 52,000 people watching during haltime of a football game. I'll never forget that. A young man and woman who were engaged won a contest to be married by George Foreman. I asked the whole crowd to be quiet and they were respectful."

"I wish people would think more carefully before they get married," Foreman continued. "I know what it's like to fumble and mess up because I've been married five times, and I'm proud of the fact that I've been married now to the same woman for twenty years. Marriage is serious; it's hard work; it's not to be played with. A good marriage is for the rest of your life."

At the start of the ceremony, Foreman offered a brief prayer. Then, speaking in a preacher's cadence, he led the bride and groom through the language of the ages. There was one moment of levity when his voice hardened and he intoned, "If there's anyone here today who knows why these two should not be wed in holy matrimony, speak now or forever hold your peace."

No one spoke.

"I didn't think so," Foreman said.

Then the ceremony continued.

"With this ring, I declare my faith in you and in us . . . With this ring, I declare my intention to cherish you as I do today for all the days of our lives together."

And finally, "I declare thee man and wife. What God has joined together, let no man tear asunder."

So congratulations to George and Marge Kimball. They're a well-matched couple. And how many people can say to the world, "We were married by George Foreman."❏

I wrote about Al Gavin on numerous occasions, but this was the saddest.

AL GAVIN: IN MEMORIUM

"Don't expect loyalty in boxing," cornerman Al Gavin once said. "Just be good and they'll come to you."

Al Gavin was both loyal and good. Earlier this month, when he suffered a stroke, there was sadness throughout the boxing community. His death at age 70 spares him from further suffering.

In celebration of Oliver Wendell Holmes Jr.'s seventy-fifth birthday, Walter Lippmann wrote, "Each generation of the young depends upon those who have lived to illustrate what can be done with experience. That is why young men feel themselves very close to Justice Holmes. He never fails to show them what they wish men to be."

The same could be said of Al Gavin.❑

ROUND 3

ISSUES AND ANSWERS

This article opened some eyes in the boxing community.

SHELLY FINKEL'S PACKAGING FEE

The business of boxing is generally conducted behind closed doors. But on occasion, the veil of secrecy is lifted and some interesting truths are revealed.

This writer has taken a long hard look at the maze of contractual relationships regarding three fighters from the 2000 Olympics and a fourth who was too young to compete in the games. Francisco Bojado, Rocky Juarez, Jeff Lacy, and Juan Diaz turned pro in early 2001 under the promotional banner of Main Events. Many of their early fights were televised by Showtime.

The four boxers have been successful in the pro ranks, but the primary beneficiary of their careers to date appears to have been Shelly Finkel. Now Finkel has been named as a co-respondent in litigation between Bojado and Joe Hernandez (one of the fighter's former co-managers). Hernandez alleges that, unbeknownst to him, Finkel received at least $1,725,000 from Showtime in violation of a fiduciary duty that Finkel assumed when he too became Bojado's co-manager.

For twenty years, Shelly Finkel has been a survivor in the jungle that is professional boxing. The cornerstone of his career was his role as a manager and advisor to Evander Holyfield, Pernell Whitaker, Mark Breland, and Meldrick Taylor, the best of America's 1984 Olympic boxing team. In recent years, he has been prominent as the primary advisor to Mike Tyson.

Finkel is one of the most knowledgeable people in the world with regard to the business of boxing. He has the ability to relate to television executives, promoters, the media, and fighters. He also stirs passions (both pro and con) in the manner of Bill Clinton and George Bush.

Finkel's supporters say that he's trustworthy, tenacious, and tough. They point to his quiet personality and ability to get most jobs done.

Finkel's detractors say that he's hypocritical and shameless. They talk of "Shelly speak" ("carefully phrased truths that leave a misimpression") and "Ninety-Percent Finkel" ("Shelly tells you ninety percent of the truth, but not the last ten percent, which is what you need to know"). Don King has labeled Finkel "Bob Arum in sheep's clothing."

Given King's dislike for his rival promoter, it's unlikely that the remark was intended as a compliment.

Everyone agrees that Finkel is a tireless worker, persistent, and very smart.

On December 4, 2000, Finkel entered into a contract with 17-year-old Francisco Bojado to serve as the fighter's co-manager. Joe Hernandez and Al Marquez were also signatories to the contract as co-managers.

The contract (which was re-executed on May 11, 2001, when Bojado turned eighteen) bound the fighter to his co-managers for a period of five years from his first professional fight (which was on January 13, 2001). In addition, if Bojado were to become a world champion in any weight division under any world sanctioning body, the managers could extend the term of the contract to cover eight title defenses from the date that Bojado won his first championship bout. Bojado received a $75,000 signing bonus. Finkel, Hernandez, and Marquez were to each get ten percent of his purses.

On September 5, 2002, Bojado terminated Hernandez and Marquez as his co-managers while retaining Finkel. On February 24, 2003, Hernandez and Marquez initiated an arbitration proceeding against the fighter for breach of contract. Bojado subsequently settled with Marquez for $157,000. Then, as a consequence of documents produced during discovery, Hernandez amended his claim to add Finkel and Finkel's management company (Shelly Finkel Management) to the proceeding as co-respondents and charge them with breach of contract and fraud.

The Finkel-Hernandez-Bojado arbitration offers a fascinating insight into the complicated, and sometimes questionable, finances of big-time boxing. One network executive likens the case to the masking tape found on the lock of a door at Watergate three decades ago.

The events that led to the dispute began in early 2000, when Finkel met with Showtime executive vice president Mark Greenberg and senior vice president Roy Langbord. Senior vice president Jay Larkin and Showtime attorney Ken Hirschman later became involved. Overall, Finkel had a good relationship with the network. And because of his influence with Mike Tyson, Showtime wanted to keep Shelly happy to maintain the inside track on Iron Mike. "The idea behind the meetings," one Showtime participant later recalled, "was to recreate the 1984 Olympians. We wanted Showtime to get a star."

Ultimately, Showtime sent Finkel shopping with its checkbook at the Sydney Olympics. The original concept was for the network to pay Shelly a set amount of money to sign certain fighters and deliver a series of fights. Finkel would also designate an approved promoter (who he would pay out of a predetermined license fee given to him by

Showtime) to do the nuts and bolts work on the fights. Main Events and Top Rank were pre-approved as promoters.

The above understanding was reflected in a December 1, 2000 draft contract between Shelly Finkel Management and Showtime that provided:

(1) Showtime would pay Finkel $2,000,000 to be used as signing bonuses for management contracts for Rocky Juarez ($1,400,000) Jeff Lacy ($250,000), Juan Diaz ($150,000), Francisco Bojado ($100,000), Malik Scott ($50,000), and another fighter to be named later ($50,000).

(2) Finkel would provide the services of these six fighters to Showtime.

(3) Showtime would pay Finkel an additional $250,000 for expenses associated with securing the participation of the fighters under the Finkel-Showtime agreement.

(4) Over a four-year period, Finkel would, as a packager, deliver sixteen shows to Showtime for a total licence fee of $18,950,000. Each of these telecasts would showcase one or more of the designated fighters and involve at least one "headliner" bout (that is, a fight featuring "more established, seasoned, and publically recognized fighters"), or when the designated fighters reached that stage, a world championship bout involving one of them. There would be reductions in the license fees for losses suffered by the fighters.

Main Events had known that Finkel was working with Showtime and would receive some sort of packaging fee. It was not aware that the entire contract might run through Finkel and that Main Events could be reduced to the role of a promoter for hire. That realization came with a crash when Pat English (the attorney for Main Events) saw the December 1st draft contract, which had been preceded by a half-dozen similar drafts.

Main Events refused to go forward with Finkel and Showtime within the structure outlined in the December 1st draft. Also, there were concerns that Finkel would be acting both as manager and de facto promoter for the fighters. That would have constituted a violation of federal law, which states, "It is unlawful for a manager to have a direct or indirect financial interest in the promotion of a boxer."

Thus, the December 1, 2000 draft contract was never signed. Instead, Main Events negotiated contracts directly with Bojado, Juarez, Lacy, and Diaz. Willie Savannah was the primary representative for Diaz (who had been too young to make the Olympic team but was included in the group). Finkel was the lead negotiator for the other three fighters.

Meanwhile, Main Events was conducting parallel negotiations with Showtime on a licensing fee deal, but an omnibus contract proved elusive. Thus, the promoter and network decided to proceed on a show-by-show basis. Bojado, Juarez and Diaz had their first pro fights on a January 13, 2001 card featuring a championship match between Zab Judah and Reggie Green. Showtime's license fee for the title fight was separately negotiated. The license fee paid to Main Events for the three undercard bouts was $600,000.

Finally, in 2002, a comprehensive contract between Showtime and Main Events was signed. There was no contract between Main Events and Finkel. The only Main Events contracts were with Showtime and the fighters.

How did Finkel get reimbursed for his services? He had signed six fighters (Juarez, Bojado, Lacy, Diaz, Scott, and Dominick Guinn) with the "signing bonus" money he received from Showtime. Ultimately, only the first four of those fighters would be relevant to what followed.

Finkel was contractually entitled to a twenty percent co-managerial share of Juarez's purses and a ten percent share from Bojado, Lacy and Diaz. That money was compensation for guiding their careers and fulfilling a fiduciary duty to them. But instead of taking his managerial share, Finkel entered into a "packaging fee" deal with Showtime.

There was no reference to Finkel's packaging fee in the final contract between Showtime and Main Events. Nor does there appear to be any final document showing a direct contractual relationship between Shelly Finkel Management and Showtime with regard to the packaging fee. Finkel says that there was never any written contract between Showtime and himself, but rather an oral understanding.

The bottom line was; each time Juarez, Bojado, Lacy, or Diaz fought on Showtime, the network paid Finkel a packaging fee equal to twenty-five percent of the licensing fee that it paid to Main Events.

In other words, Bojado received a $10,000 purse for his pro debut on January 13, 2001. Finkel was entitled to ten percent of that purse. And he was also entitled to a percentage of the purses that Juarez and Diaz earned that night. But he didn't take his managerial share. Instead, he opted for a "packaging fee" of $150,000. That is, Showtime paid Finkel an amount equal to twenty-five percent of the $600,000 license fee that it paid to Main Events.

How much did Finkel make pursuant to this packaging fee arrangement?

In a written answer to interrogatories put to him in his arbitration proceeding against Joe Hernandez, Finkel acknowledged, "Respondent

[Shelly Finkel Management, Inc.] received the following payments from Showtime in connection with boxing cards on which Bojado was a participant [date of payment precedes the amount listed]:

January 17, 2001	$150,000
May 21, 2001	$150,000
September 4, 2001	$175,000
February 19, 2002	$175,000
October 21, 2002	$200,000
February 3, 2003	$275,000
October 24, 2003	$200,000

Finkel further acknowledged, "Respondent received the following payments from Showtime in connection with boxing cards on which Bojado was not a participant:

July 12, 2002	$157,500
July 18, 2002	$42,500
July 19, 2003	$200,000

That totals $1,725,000.

According to Finkel's interrogatory answers, he also received a $15,000 co-managerial fee in conjunction with Bojado's January 24, 2004 fight against Emmanuel Clottey on HBO. And all of this is in addition to the $2,200,000 that Showtime advanced Finkel to sign the fighters to boxer-manager contracts and for related "expenses."

Finkel maintains that his conduct was entirely proper. With regard to the current legal arbitration, he says that Bojado, Hernandez and Marquez all knew about the packaging fees and that Bojado gave him a waiver of fiduciary duty with regard to any possible conflict of interest. He concedes that taking a management fee on the fights for which he received a packaging fee would have been "double-dipping." But he says that no such impropriety occurred (although he acknowledges that, when it came time to make a deal for Bojado with HBO, he took his percentage as Bojado's co-manager). And he argues, "If I hadn't taken a packaging fee, the entire amount of that fee would have been retained by Showtime or paid to Main Events. None of it would have gone to the fighters. There's no merit to any of the claims against me. I got these kids the best deal that anyone could have gotten them at that time."

There's no doubt that Finkel created a significant opportunity for the fighters in question. He constructed the parameters of a deal with Showtime and then (before the TV package was finalized) brought the fighters into the fold. As far as Showtime was concerned, except for

Juarez, the boxers were fungible. Lacy was considered an ordinary fighter. Bojado and Diaz weren't even on the United States Olympic team (Bojado fought under the Mexican flag). Without Finkel's involvement, it's unlikely that the fighters would have made as much money as they did.

But (and this is a big "but") according to his interrogatory answers, when Finkel negotiated with Showtime, he represented to the network that he was Bojado's co-manager. And as a co-manager, he had a fiduciary duty to his fighter.

Jim Thomas is one of the most respected men in boxing. A partner in a large Atlanta law firm, he represented Evander Holyfield for years and has counseled numerous other fighters. Thomas declined a request by Finkel to testify as an expert witness on Finkel's behalf in the current arbitration proceeding.

"Without commenting on the specifics of the case," says Thomas, "I can give you my view regarding some general principles that should govern situations of this nature. A manager is supposed to work for the benefit of the fighter at all times. If you're a fighter's representative and have a fiduciary duty to the fighter, all available money should go to the fighter and then you take your share of that. You don't make your own deal on the side. You can't properly separate the fighters' financial interests from your own. The key here is fiduciary duty."

Also, while Finkel says that Bojado, Hernandez and Marquez all knew about the packaging fees and that Bojado gave him a waiver of fiduciary duty, he is non-commital on the issue of whether Bojado was advised by legal counsel prior to the waiver and whether Bojado, Hernandez and Marquez were advised of the packaging fee arrangement in writing.

Bojado seems like a nice young man, but one can assume that he's not a world-class economist. Did Finkel sit him down and say, "Francisco, you're only getting $10,000 for your first fight, so I'll waive my managerial fee. You don't have to pay me anything. I've worked it out so Showtime will take care of me." Or did he say, "Francisco, you're only getting $10,000 for this fight so, instead of taking my managerial cut from you and the other fighters, I'll opt for a packaging fee from Showtime that will be $150,000 for this card and ultimately will run well over a million dollars."

Finkel could have avoided this ambiguity by putting a clause in his managerial contract with Bojado clearly stating that he would receive a packaging fee from Showtime. Shelly certainly was aware then that he would be getting the fee, but no such clause was included in the contract. Moreover, there's a public policy issue as to whether a 17-year-old can waive a fiduciary duty that's owed to him.

Then there's Finkel's contention that, if he hadn't taken a packaging fee, the entire amount of that fee would have been retained by Showtime or paid to Main Events and that none of it would have filtered down to the fighters. That claim is questionable at best.

Showtime personnel say that, as a practical matter, they viewed the payments related to this deal as one license fee broken up into two checks, not as a licensing fee plus a packaging fee. Indeed, the attachments to checks sent to Finkel by Showtime bore notations such as "license fee" and "add'l lic fee." And while Main Events negotiated the highest license fee that it could for itself, it was handicapped by the fact that Showtime was holding back a portion of available funds to pay Finkel.

Most likely, if Finkel's twenty-five percent premium had gone to Main Events, some portion of it would have been added to the fighters' purses. The contracts that Main Events negotiated with the fighters were based in significant part on the amount of money that Main Events was receiving from Showtime. One can only begin to imagine Shelly Finkel sitting down at the bargaining table with representatives of Main Events.

"I'd like more money for my fighters," Shelly might have said.

"We'll be happy to give your fighters more money," he might have been told. "Put your million-dollar-plus packaging fee on the table, and we'll divide it equitably between Main Events and the fighters you represent."

There's no way to know how the Finkel-Hernandez-Bojado arbitration will play out. Hernandez is asking for enforcement of his managerial contract with Bojado and the "disgorgement" of all packaging fees paid to Finkel. Bojado, for the moment, seems more concerned with defending himself against Hernandez than with cross-claiming against Finkel. There are technical issues in the arbitration that might supercede questions regarding the propriety of Finkel's packaging fee arrangement. And litigation is capricious. If Finkel wins, it won't necessarily mean that what he did was right. And if he loses, it won't necessarily mean that his conduct was wrong.

What is clear, however, is that this is another example of the blurred line between promoters and managers and the role that the television networks play in boxing. It points to the need for full disclosure to fighters and government authorities regarding license fee payments and related expenditures. And it leads to questions regarding many more issues.

For example, Shelly Finkel is now the person most responsible for

Mike Tyson's career. In recent years, he has functioned as Tyson's de facto manager and (by power of designation) de facto promoter. Yet he is not required to be licensed in those capacities. Also, as one of the primary creditors in Tyson's bankruptcy proceeding, he had input into a settlement that envisions keeping Iron Mike in the ring until age forty-one.

Finkel says that there has been no conflict of interest with regard to Tyson. "I was not involved with Mike when he declared bankruptcy," he states. "I resigned from the creditors committeee when I started working again with Mike. I give no financial advice to Mike other than how much money he can make from a given fight. Other than that, I have nothing to do with Mike's finances or bankruptcy."

We shall see.❑

New revelations led to a follow-up article on Shelly Finkel's dealings with Showtime and others.

THE TANGLED WEB

On August 18th, I posted an article entitled *Shelly Finkel's Packaging Fee*. The article outlined the complex contractual relationship between Finkel, Showtime, Main Events, and a group of young fighters that led to Shelly receiving a "packaging fee" of $1,725,000 from Showtime. This fee was paid to Finkel in conjunction with appearances by the fighters on Showtime at the same time that Shelly was managing or co-managing the fighters and thus had a fiduciary duty to them.

The $1,725,000 figure came in part from information provided by Finkel under oath in an arbitration proceeding brought against him by Joe Hernandez (his co-manager in guiding the career of Francisco Bojado). In a written response to interrogatories posed in that litigation, Finkel listed ten payments on ten specific dates. There now appears to have been an eleventh packaging fee payment in the amount of $200,000 for a fight card that took place on April 27, 2002. That payment raises the packaging fee paid to Finkel by Showtime to $1,925,000.

Finkel's interrogatory answers also acknowledge that he received an additional $2,200,000 from Showtime as reimbursement for signing bonuses and expenses. The best available information is that $200,000 of this amount was for reimbursement of expenses incurred by Finkel in signing the fighters, although a Showtime executive involved with the deal now says that the expenses weren't fully documented for the network and might have been designed to "give a little something extra to Shelly." Hernandez also received $50,000 as an expense reimbursement. The remaining $2,000,000 is believed to have been intended by Showtime to fund signing bonuses for managerial contracts between the fighters and Finkel as follows: Rocky Juarez ($1,400,000), Jeff Lacy ($250,000), Juan Diaz ($150,000), Francisco Bojado ($100,000), Malik Scott ($50,000), and Dominick Guinn ($50,000).

It now appears that Finkel paid a signing bonus of $150,000 to Jeff Lacy (not $250,000); $100,000 to Juan Diaz (not $150,000); $75,000 to Francisco Bojado (not $100,000); and $20,000 to Dominick Guinn (not

$50,000). The amount of the signing bonuses paid to Rocky Juarez and Malik Scott is unclear at the present time.

Finkel has said that the numbers quoted above are incorrect; that the fighters received everything they were entitled to, and that no impropriety occurred. But he refuses to say what the correct numbers are and, when asked, responds, "Please quote my entire response in your article. All the moneys received by me from Showtime for the reimbursement of expenses and for signing bonuses of certain fighters, including certain 2000 U.S. Olympic boxers, were disbursed as per the contracts with these fighters and the agreement with Showtime."

So let's recap what happened here.

Some promoters spend hundreds of thousands of dollars of their own money developing fighters and then beg for television dates. Showtime gave Finkel $2,200,000 so he could sign fighters to managerial contracts and cover his expenses. It gave Finkel a series of television dates for his fighters and a $1,925,000 packaging fee. On top of that, it paid Main Events a substantial licensing fee for the fights. And it did all of this without having a formal written contract with Finkel. Isn't that strange, even for boxing?

"I know it's unusual that we gave Shelly $2,200,000 without a signed contract," says a Showtime executive who was involved in the transaction. "But that's the sort of relationship we had with Shelly."

Meanwhile, a high-ranking HBO executive says, "We learned a lot about the way Showtime does business when we did Lewis-Tyson two years ago. We got to look behind the curtain, so this doesn't surprise me."

In the days after *Shelly Finkel's Packaging Fee* was posted, I received numerous telephone calls offering information of interest. One caller pointed out that, in addition to his dealings with Showtime, Finkel has also enjoyed a profitable relationship with HBO.

TVKO was once the pay-per-view arm of HBO. In 1991, it planned on televising a pay-per-view card each month, with Top Rank and Main Events as the promoters. For about a year, TVKO paid Mike Malitz a consulting fee on each Top Rank show. Malitz worked for Top Rank and was an expert on the technical side of the pay-per-view business.

At the time, Finkel was actively involved in the management of a number of fighters who were under contract to Main Events and appeared on TVKO. Unlike Malitz (who worked for a promoter), Finkel had a fiduciary duty to his fighters. It has now been confirmed with present and former HBO executives that, each time Main Events promoted a TVKO show during that period, Finkel received a $25,000 consulting fee from TVKO.

But the most intriguing message received in response to *Shelly Finkel's Packaging Fee* consisted of five words: "Follow the money in Louisville."

"What?"

"You heard me. Follow the money in Louisville. Who paid Danny Williams [for his July 30, 2004 fight against Mike Tyson]? How did Williams get paid? How much did he get paid? How was the money divided?"

As most boxing fans know, Finkel has served as an advisor to Mike Tyson for nine fights beginning with Tyson versus Frans Botha in 1999. When Danny Williams knocked out Iron Mike, I watched the fight on television but didn't pay much attention to the business end of things. Then, on August 20th, an Associated Press report caught my eye.

The gist of the AP article was that Chris Webb and Straight Out Promotions (Webb's promotional company and the promoter of record for Tyson-Williams) are suing Frank Warren, Sports Network (Warren's promotional company, which promotes Danny Williams), and several other entities involved in Tyson-Williams. Webb claims that he has an interest in the promotion of future Danny Williams fights and is owed money from the sale of international rights to the July 30th bout.

Warren claims that Webb and Straight Out Promotions failed to fulfill their financial obligations prior to the fight. He further says that, as a result of this alleged breach of contract, he maintains exclusive rights to promote Williams's future fights.

I don't know where the equities lie in the dispute between Webb and Warren. But a sentence in the Associated Press article picqued my interest: "Minutes before the bout, the [Webb] suit says, a Sports Network official demanded that Straight-Out pay everything immediately—$125,000 for future promotional rights, plus $125,000 owed to Sports Network for Williams's participation in the fight and $100,000 for a brokering fee."

A $100,000 "brokering fee"?

Intrigued, I telephoned Michael Tigue, the attorney for Chris Webb. Tigue seems like a capable attorney who's getting a crash course in boxing ethics. He told me that Straight Out had a $350,000 contractual obligation to the Williams camp that was broken down as follows:

(1) $125,000 due to Sports Network for Williams to participate in the fight;

(2) $125,000 due to Sports Network for an option to co-promote future Williams fights; and

(3) A $100,000 "arrangement fee."

More specifically, Webb's complaint against Warren and Sports Network states, "Straight Out was to pay Sports Network an arrangement fee of $100,000 upon conclusion of the boxing match by wire transfer to a United States bank account to be designated by Sports Network."

This is confirmed by a June 24, 2004 letter agreement signed by Webb and Stephen Heath (the in-house solicitor for Sports Network), which states that the $100,000 "will be wired to Sports Network or, at its election, deposited in the U.S. account of Sports Network Inc." The letter, which was written by Heath, adds, "This sum is in addition to the provision of services fee set out in the separate agreement."

Tigue says that, ultimately, Sports Network demanded that the $350,000 be paid as follows:

(1) $100,000 to Danny Williams in the form of $50,000 in cash, a $20,000 check, and an Internal Revenue Service certificate guaranteeing that Straight Out will pay $30,000 in taxes owed by Williams on income he received from the fight.

(2) $150,000 to Sports Network. Warren says that this $150,000 will be generously shared with Williams.

(3) That leaves the $100,000 arrangement fee. Webb's complaint states that, on the night of the fight, Sports Network, "demanded that Straight Out issue a check in the amount of $100,000 made payable to Sterling McPherson of Sterling Productions in full satisfaction of the Arrangement Agreement . . . Straight Out then issued a check made payable to Sterling McPherson in the amount of $100,000."

Then came another twist. On August 2nd, Straight Out learned that Warren was disavowing its future promotional rights and stopped payment on the check.

Frank Warren confirms that he instructed Straight Out to make the $100,000 check payable to McPherson. "Sterling was my representative," he says. "He told me that the money would have to be paid for Danny Williams to have the opportunity to fight Mike Tyson. I can't say for certain where the money was to have gone after he received it."

No suggestion is made here that Frank Warren or any of his companies or anyone else did anything improper. But one does wonder why it was intended that $100,000 be paid to Sterling McPherson (a small promoter who has served as an American representative for Sports Network and an interface with the Tyson camp on Tyson-Williams). One also wonders what was supposed to happen to the $100,000 once McPherson got it.

McPherson's explanation in the first instance was as follows. "Sports Network called me and asked me to work out something with Shelly Finkel to make the fight. My job was offering Danny Williams to Shelly and getting him to accept Williams as an opponent. After Shelly accepted the fight, my job was done. Then it was up to Sports Network to work out their own deal and Danny's purse."

Later, McPherson elaborated upon his remarks, saying that Chris Webb wanted to substitute Williams for Kevin McBride because Webb thought he could get Williams for less money than McBride and foreign rights would be more valuable with Williams as the opponent. It's not completely clear who first asked McPherson to act as a go-between on the fight.

What about the $100,000?

"That's what Sports Network offered me," McPherson says. "I've heard the talk that the money was going back to Shelly Finkel, but that's untrue. I did a job, I got a check, and the check bounced. I'm owed $100,000, and all the other stuff means nothing to me. All this talk about a kickback muddies the waters. I delivered a service to Sports Network. I got Shelly Finkel to accept Danny Williams as an opponent. So now Sports Network owes me $100,000."

Finkel says that none of the $100,000 "arrangement fee" was intended for him. Secondsout is unaware of any evidence that contradicts him on this point. But the arrangement fee is illustrative of the strange manner in which large sums of money are distributed and redistributed in boxing. And given Finkel's packaging fee arrangement with Showtime, one can be forgiven for asking questions regarding his overall relationship with Tyson.

One person who has asked questions is Dan Goossen. Goossen was the CEO at America Presents when the now-defunct promotional company crafted a six-fight deal to become Mike Tyson's promoter of record. The first two fights pursuant to that contract were Tyson versus Frans Botha and Tyson against Orlin Norris.

"We were the promoter of record," says Goossen. "But virtually all of the negotiations ran through Finkel. Finkel was in control. It was Finkel who made most of the deals with the venues and suppliers and on foreign rights, and he kept most of the paperwork on those deals away from us. I never saw most of those contracts," Goossen continues. "That's one of the reasons I decided after Tyson-Norris to distance myself from future Tyson fights. I didn't have an understanding of what was going on behind-the-scenes. That made me uncomfortable, and I didn't feel it was in the best interests of Mike or myself for me to stay actively involved."

Goossen did not attend Tyson versus Julius Francis in London or

Tyson against Lou Savarese in Scotland. In his words, he "boycotted" those bouts. He was at Tyson-Golota in Michigan, but not as the promoter of record. By the time Tyson fought Brian Nielsen in Denmark, Goossen had left America Presents.

"It would be interesting," says Goossen, "if the Tyson-Finkel relationship were to be audited as aggressively as the relationship between Tyson and Don King."

Stephen Espinoza (who has served as Tyson's attorney) says that there was an extensive audit of Tyson's finances by the trustee in bankruptcy in Tyson's bankruptcy proceeding and that this audit satisfied the creditors committee in the proceeding. Of course, Finkel was on the creditors committee from its formation on August 22, 2003, through his resignation on May 4, 2004.

Finkel says that he produced thousands of pages of documents from his files in the bankruptcy proceeding and that his deposition was taken for several hours. The transcript of his deposition has been sealed and is not available to the public. But given its brevity, one might assume that it dealt mostly with Finkel's claims as a creditor; not with a thorough study of each and every deal he made regarding the nine fights on which he served Tyson as an advisor. Also, one wonders how much the attorney who took the deposition knew about the intricacies of the business of boxing.

Finkel vigorously defends his conduct as Tyson's advisor. "Every day of my life since I've been involved with Mike, people have taken shots at me," he says. "I've been accused of all sorts of things, and the accusations are totally false."

Why does Finkel stay with Tyson given the headaches involved?

"One, I enjoy it. Two, it gives me a lot of strength in the business. Three, Mike winning the heavyweight title back under me would be an incredible thrill. And four, I like Mike. I like him a lot and I care about him a lot."

What about the financial rewards?

"My present contract with Mike began with the Williams fight," Finkel answers. "It calls for me to receive a small percentage of what Mike gets on each fight. For the fights before that when I was with Mike, I got a flat fee on each fight. Beyond that fee, I got nothing, zero, from anyone in any way, shape, or manner or in any capacity in connection with Mike. And I took less from Mike than I was entitled to because Mike needed money. That's why I'm a creditor."

"I know who I am," Finkel says, summing up. "I do what I feel is right. I live with myself. I sleep well at night. I know that I've done nothing wrong."

It's possible that Shelly Finkel has been a model of financial propriety in his dealings with Mike Tyson. But the truth is, it's easier to cross ethical boundaries in the business of boxing than in any other sport. The way the business works and the culture that has taken root afford ample opportunity for misconduct.

And more significantly, the tangled web of contractual relationships involving Finkel, Showtime and others demonstrates the inadequate nature of current (and proposed) regulations for the governance of professional boxing. Whether there is wrongdoing or not, fighters will always be at risk of exploitation unless ironclad mechanisms are put in place to allow all participants and government regulators to follow every dollar generated by every fight.❑

For most Americans, TV "reality" shows are simple entertainment. But one of those shows had the potential to impact heavily upon boxing.

THE CONTENDER

Somewhere in America, there's an unknown fighter who, a year from now, may well be more famous than any of today's heavyweight champions. In a matter of months, he will be the beneficiary of a massive promotional campaign backed by some of the most powerful economic interests in the world. His face will be on the cover of major magazines, and his first "title" fight will be watched by more Americans than have ever seen a fight before.

Reality-TV isn't new. It dates to television's early days, when contestants vied for audience sympathy on *Strike It Rich* and *Queen For a Day*. But in recent years, shows like *Survivor* and *The Apprentice* have become both commercially successful and cultural phenomena. Meanwhile, in a very real sense, all sports telecasting is reality programming. Enter *The Contender*.

Physical combat between human beings is one of the most intense experiences imaginable. The premise behind *The Contender* is that if one assembles, in a small setting, sixteen young men who will be called upon to engage in physical combat against one another, emotions will surface and viewers who watch will be entertained. But beyond that, *The Contender* has the potential to restructure the business of boxing. So pay attention. The sweet science may well be on the verge of significant change.

The Contender has three primary producers: reality-show guru Mark Burnett, who's best known for having created *Survivor* and *The Apprentice*; movie executive Jeffrey Katzenberg; and Sylvester Stallone. Lisa Hennessy and Bruce Beresford-Redman are the co-executive producers. Hennessy is Burnett's point person on the business end, while Beresford-Redman serves in a similar capacity on the creative side. Show business veteran Jeff Wald is also a producer, and Sugar Ray Leonard is an equity participant. Journalistic ethics require the notation that I've been hired by *The Contender* as a consultant.

At present, *The Contender* is canvassing the country for sixteen young fighters who will be the heart of the show. Staffers are visiting thirteen cities for auditions pursuant to the following casting-call procedure.

Fighters will arrive at a designated location, fill out some paperwork, and undergo a preliminary medical examination. Then Frank Stallone and Prentiss Byrd will take over. Stallone is a longtime boxing fan and Sylvester's brother. Byrd was affiliated with the legendary Kronk Gym from 1977 through 1992 and has worked with fighters like Thomas Hearns, Leon Spinks, Aaron Pryor, and Michael Moorer. "I'm not a trainer," says Byrd. "I'm more of a manager-handler type of guy."

Byrd and Stallone will evaluate each applicant's credentials, watch them shadow box, and look on as they hit the speed and heavy bags. Approximately twenty-five percent of the applicants will be rejected out of hand as unfit to spar. The rest will be put in the ring for a round or two with a fighter of comparable experience and weight. At that point, if an applicant still appears to be qualified, he'll be passed on for a more comprehensive interview with casting director Michelle McNulty regarding background and character. All of this activity will be taped and transpire in a single day.

Beresford-Redman expects that, by the time auditions are over, the producers will have auditioned roughly 3,000 fighters. Then the production team will go back to Los Angeles, analyze the talent pool by weight class, skill, and character, and evaluate options. Eventually, one weight class will be selected and the most qualified candidates will be flown to Los Angeles in July for a week of further interviews, background checks, and sparring. The final sixteen fighters will be chosen from this group. It's possible that certain applicants will be given an opportunity to move up or down in weight to fit within the chosen class.

"My job," says Beresford-Redman, "is to deliver the sixteen best candidates in terms of skill and character. We want interesting personal dramas, but none of us is forgetting that this starts with fighters. Ultimately, we'll need sixteen guys who are close in skill. We can't have one guy of championship caliber and fifteen amateurs. Our goal is for sixteen guys who give us good drama and fifteen competitive fights."

In other words, the producers are looking for fighters with personality, who are upbeat like Shane Mosley, manic like Vinny Pazienza, out there every moment like Arturo Gatti, or a glowering presence like Mike Tyson. But Beresford-Redman puts the quest in perspective when he says, "We can never lose sight of the fact that you can get good character out of boxing, but you don't necessarily get good boxing out of character."

From August 16th through September 26th, the fighters will live in a facility being built now at an undisclosed location in Southern California. During that time, they will train and fight in a gym at the same site while a production team of more than 200 people monitors their every more. "Girlfriends and families who visit will be part of the show," says Beresford-Redman. "During those forty days, the young men who are chosen won't have much privacy."

Sylvester Stallone and Sugar Ray Leonard will be present much of the time, although they won't sleep on site.

"Ray will be the flesh-and-blood champion," Stallone says, elaborating upon their respective roles. "He'll be conversing with the guys on things like fighting technique and how to deal with the pressures of combat. On the night before a fight, he'll be able to say to them, 'Look, I went through the same thing. I felt the same fear, and this is how I dealt with it.'"

"I'll be more of a personal mentor," Stallone continues. "The guys will be talking with me in a way that reveals their personal feelings away from the ring, their likes and dislikes, their hopes and aspirations, their feelings of self-worth and self-doubt. Things that will help the audience identify with them as people rather than simply as two men in the ring wearing different color trunks punching each other. People are used to seeing fighters expressing themselves physically. This will be an opportunity for people to see fighters express themselves in a meaningful way verbally too."

Prentiss Byrd will also be on site. "Most people don't understand what it takes to be a professional fighter," Byrd notes. "They think that some guy who wins a fight in a bar can get in the ring and fight. But that's not boxing; that's toughman contests. That's like thinking someone who looks good dancing in a nightclub can go on stage without any training and be a ballet dancer. *The Contender* will give people more understanding and more respect for what it takes to be a professional fighter."

The centerpiece of the show will be an elimination tournament. For dramatic purposes, the fighters will be divided into two teams; although as the tournament progresses, team members are likely to fight one another. Each team will have a head trainer.

The first fifteen episodes will air on tape beginning in January 2005. The first episode will introduce the fighters. The dramatic conclusion of each succeeding episode will be a fight that is presented in a style more like a feature film than a regularly-televised boxing match.

The first fourteen fights will be waged on a closed set at roughly three-day intervals. The final fight will be telecast live in late April or early May.

The referees and judges for the first three rounds of the tournament will be regular officials licensed by the California State Athletic Commission.

"It's professional boxing with professional rules," says Beresford-

Redman. "Each of the fighters will have to turn pro, and we're working with the California commission to find a way to adhere to their rules and at the same time recognize the exigencies of a TV show."

The promoter of record will be a corporation formed for that purpose and affiliated with Mark Burnett Productions. Prentiss Byrd is the matchmaker of record. Second-round match-ups will be determined after the first-round bouts have been fought. It's likely that the final episode will also have a live consolation bout between two "fan favorites" chosen by viewers.

Each of the sixteen fighters will receive one hundred dollars a day during the forty-day shoot. In addition, the winner of each first-round match gets $1,000 and the loser $500. Second round payments are $2,500 and $1,000. The semi-final winners receive $3,500 each and the losers $2,000. The big payoff is in the finals. The loser gets $50,000. The winner will take home $1,000,000.

If *The Contender* is successful, NBC will follow with other weight classes in succeeding seasons.

Is there a danger that, after living together, these guys will become friends and their fights will be the equivalent of sparring sessions?

"Unlikely," says Redman. "Remember, this is an elimination tournament with the winner getting one million dollars. These guys will fight."

The Contender will face both criticism and problems. For starters, it's a time-honored axiom that there are no secrets in boxing, and it will be difficult to maintain secrecy with regard to early-round fight results.

"That's a concern," Lisa Hennessy acknowledges. "Everyone involved with the show will sign a non-disclosure agreement. We'll have a closed set, and eliminated contestants will stay on site. What more can we do? The final show will be live. For that one, there will be no secrets to keep."

A more pointed criticism is that, in reality, TV reality shows aren't real. "Real" people don't get married the way they get married on *The Bachelor*. And in boxing, reality isn't sixteen guys living in the same training facility, hanging around with Sylvester Stallone. Former Time Warner Sports president Seth Abraham, the man most responsible for building HBO's boxing franchise, makes that point and observes, "We developed story lines for HBO Boxing. And in a sense, we treated *HBO Championship Boxing* as an ongoing mini-series; but this is different. HBO told the stories as it found them. We didn't artificially create them."

Again, Hennessy puts the matter in perspective. "This is a reality show," she says, "not a documentary. A reality show takes people and puts them in situations they wouldn't normally be in and shows how they react. That's what was done on *Survivor* and *The Apprentice*, and that's what we're doing with *The Contender*."

Then there's the observation that, in boxing, one doesn't build a "contender" in sixteen weeks. At best, you create a television personality. Thus, the criticism, "*The Contender* will be like a made-for-television home-run-hitting contest with the fences set 150 feet from home plate. This will be more like watching Butterbean than Bernard Hopkins and Roy Jones Jr."

Here, Mark Burnett himself responds. "Many current champions are far from being the best fighter in their weight division," he posits. "So if our fighters aren't the best fighters in the world, in that respect it's no different from the way things are now. People love watching college sports in the United States even though they know that the weakest professional team would clobber the strongest college ones. Arturo Gatti and Micky Ward are the model for us. They weren't the best fighters in the world; but they were well-matched, they had dramatic personal stories, and they put on great fights."

Hardcore boxing fans can like *The Contender* or not. But one thing is certain. For the first time in decades, many Americans will be paying attention to boxing as a consequence of *The Contender*.

In 1976, millions of Americans set aside several nights to watch a handful of amateur boxers like Leon and Michael Spinks, Howard Davis, and Ray Leonard compete for Olympic medals in Montreal. That, coupled with the release of *Rocky*, led to renewed interest in boxing.

"The 1976 Olympics told a story," says Leonard. "People knew more about me as a person than they did as a boxer. They knew I had a son named Ray Jr. They knew I had a girlfriend named Juanita. And the same thing was true of the other guys on the team. Howard Davis's mother had just died. Leon Spinks was the fighting marine. People turned on their television sets because they cared about us as people, not because they were fans who never missed a fight."

Survivor and *The Apprentice* each averaged roughly 20,000,000 viewers per show. More than 40,000,000 viewers tuned in at some point during the final episodes.

Thus, HBO Sports president Ross Greenburg says, "I'm encouraged that NBC, Mark Burnett, and Jeffrey Katzenberg believe that boxing can work its way into mainstream America because, if that happens, it's good for boxing. We've lost the average sports fan and have been struggling for years to get him back. This could help."

And Jay Larkin of Showtime, declares, "At first, I didn't like the idea of a reality-TV boxing series. Boxing isn't wrestling, and it's not about who's going to win a date with a hot stripper. I take the sport and its inherent risks very seriously and was concerned that something like this might trivialize the sport. But I'm all in favor of anything that treats boxing with respect and puts it before a mainstream national audience. Boxing has been relegated to a backseat in the sporting world because of its absence from network television, and this is a terrific opportunity to put boxing back in the public consciousness."

But there's another aspect to *The Contender* that also bears watching. It's possible that the fighters who emerge from the show, like the winners of *American Idol,* will have such great stature with the American public that it will lead to a reconfiguration of the balance of power in boxing. The show's equity partners (Mark Burnett, Jeffrey Katzenberg, Sylvester Stallone, Ray Leonard, and Jeff Wald) are well aware of this fact. And they plan to be an integral part of the process.

"We're still working on the post-tournament business formula," says Burnett. "But we plan to stay in the boxing business through a promotional entity. That's the business model. There's a bonafide business element for me and my partners that will continue on after the show. Our fighters will be treated fairly," Burnett continues. "We'll do right by them as they continue their professional careers. They'll have a pension plan and medical coverage. If they get management, the manager will be limited to fifteen percent of a fighter's purse; not one-third. I assure you, our boxers will not wind up poor. But yes, we intend to continue to profit as a business from their future fights because, without our massive investment, no one would know who they are."

Jeff Wald elaborates on that notion. Wald has produced myriad television shows and at various times managed Sylvester Stallone, Roseanne Barr, James Brolin, Miles Davis, Marvin Gaye, Donna Summer, George Carlin, and Flip Wilson. He was once friendly with Don King, but the two had a bitter falling out. Wald and Irving Azoff promoted George Foreman versus Lou Savarese and Foreman against Shannon Briggs. In January 1998, Wald became a financial adviser to Mike Tyson. "When Mike showed me what passed for financial statements," he recalls, "the eight thousand dollars a week he was being charged for towels in training camp sort of stood out."

Wald is not afraid to ruffle feathers, which is good because he ruffles them a lot. "Boxing is a sport that's ruled by predators with no rules except what's in their own self-interest," he states. "There's an unholy alliance between the powers that be. What they do to fighters is no better than what was done to sharecroppers in the rural south or to workers who had to shop in the company store."

"It's all about access," Wald continues. "And the other key is marketing. Boxing today is in the same shape that the NBA was in before David Stern became commissioner. People look back now and say that the NBA changed course because Magic Johnson and Larry Bird came into the league, but that's nonsense. Jerry West and Oscar Robertson and Bill Russell and Wilt Chamberlain were there long before Magic and Larry, but there wasn't any commercial explosion. It was marketing that did it. David Stern took a sport that was looked down upon by corporate America as an urban ghetto sport, got the club owners together, and, with the help of Nike, turned NBA basketball into a cultural phenomenon."

"Ultimately, we want to do for boxing what David Stern did for the NBA," Wald says, elaborating upon his hypothesis. "Virtually all of the Fortune 500 CEOs have said 'no' to boxing. They don't want their companies identified with the sport. So we're reinventing the business—not the sport, the business—to make it more legitimate. *The Contender* will bring boxing back to prime time television with Fortune 500 sponsors on a permanent basis."

Not everyone is pleased with the scope of those plans.

"The one thing I'd advise," says Ross Greenburg, "is that the people behind *The Contender* not come out with bravado and try to create a boxing franchise. Do a reality show and enjoy that success. Don't think you're going to recreate or restructure the sport of boxing. That's up to John McCain in Washington."

But the creators of *The Contender* take a different view.

"You can't run a sport the way boxing is run today," says Mark Burnett. "The schedule alone tells you that something is wrong. Can you imagine the two conference champions not playing one another in the NBA finals? Or the Lakers are supposed to play the Celtics during the regular season, but the Celtics don't feel like playing so the game is called off. One of the problems with professional boxing is that fans get interested in two guys who are fighting and then they have to wait six months to see either one of them fight again. And on top of that, winners don't always fight winners. To the contrary, they often avoid them on purpose or are forced into meaningless matches against mandatory challengers."

"I saw Winky Wright fight Shane Mosley," Burnett continues. "Winky Wright is a great fighter, but I guarantee you that I can go to a hundred malls and no one will know who Winky Wright is. It's bad for a sport when no one knows who its champions are. We plan on changing that."

Sylvester Stallone is in accord. "The universal respect that people once had for boxing is gone," he says, "and that's very sad. The people who run the sport don't care about anyone but themselves. The world sanctioning organizations make up the rules as they go along. Boxing is in such a bad way that some of the promoters are more famous than the fighters. The winner of our tournament won't be on a par with the great fighters of today," Stallone acknowledges. "But he will be 'The People's Champion.' That's a start, and people will be rooting for him as his career goes on."

Jeffrey Katzenberg puts it all in perspective. Katzenberg is one of the most storied entrepreneurs in the entertainment industry. After successful tenures as the president of Paramount and chairman of Walt Disney Studios, he joined with Steven Spielberg and David Geffen to found DreamWorks SKG. When Katzenberg speaks, he has to be taken very seriously.

"We hope to completely change the structure of boxing," Katzenberg states. "Boxing has lost a lot of its popularity, but *The Contender* can be the foundation for a Renaissance in the sport. We're going to build an organization that operates in an open and transparent way. There will be an independent commissioner, strong rules and guidelines, and a boxers' bill of rights that protects fighters and ensures that they're the ones who reap the rewards for their talent."

But the question remains: "Will Team Contender be able to succeed outside the protective cocoon of a television reality show?"

No less a personage than Don King has declared, "You can't do anything without public opinion. Public opinion is everything in boxing."

In the short run at least, *The Contender* is likely to have public opinion on its side. But beyond that, things are murky.

"I don't think this will change the structure of boxing," says Shelly Finkel, one of boxing's most knowledgeable managers. "The winner, no matter how good he is, will still be a few years away from a title shot. Just like Ray Leonard, Roy Jones, and the other big names who came out of the Olympics, he'll still have to work within the system. And one thing more," Finkel adds. "People talk about network television being the launching pad for boxing's biggest stars. Muhammad Ali, Ray Leonard, Oscar De La Hoya, Mike Tyson; you know the names. But let's not forget, those guys were also great fighters."

Thus, the prevailing view among boxing's intelligentsia is that, after *The Contender* has aired, it's more likely that the sport will take over the show than it is the show will take over the sport. Indeed, one can argue that an equally-compelling reality show involving *The Contender* would be the one that occurs off-camera.

"Right now, everything is on the drawing board where it looks nice and clean," says HBO Sports vice president Mark Taffet. "But wait until Mark Burnett and Jeffrey Katzenberg get a taste of what professional boxing is really like. This isn't fantasyland. There are a million pitfalls that these guys will face. Injuries, bad decisions, complying with the Ali Act, dealing with state athletic commissions, and all the other problems that promoters in boxing deal with every day."

Also, boxing is a dangerous sport. At some point, *The Contender* will become more than a game, and reality in its truest sense will intervene.❏

In mid-2004, I had occasion to revisit The Contender.

THE CONTRACT

Don King has done a lot of things in his life, but his latest venture is truly special.

King is in the process of signing up fighters for a new fight series on network television. In the process, he has spread a considerable amount of money around the boxing industry with special incentives for one or more individuals currently affiliated with the California State Athletic Commission.

King intends to sign sixteen fighters, who are being told that they will compete in a tournament with a purse of $1,000,000 going to the winner of the final fight. The contract that each fighter is being asked to sign includes the following provisions:

(1) King can, under certain circumstances, claim promotional rights to the fighter for up to five years, during which time King shall have the sole and exclusive right to secure, arrange, and promote all bouts requiring the fighter's services as a professional boxer.

(2) During the term of the contract, the fighter must fight at least twice a year at a site and on a date designated by King against opponents chosen by King in King's sole and absolute discretion.

(3) King can lie to the fighter about "any and all topics of every kind and nature whatsover." More specifically, the contract states that, among other things, King may lie to the fighter about "the other [fighters] in the series . . . any purse . . . the conditions applicable to any purse . . . and the choices and decisions [the fighter] may be required to make that may affect [his] ability to compete for any purse."

(4) The fighter must waive his right to challenge any decision rendered against him in the tournament, including his right to challenge a decision under the rules and regulations of the California State Athletic Commission.

(5) King, in his sole discretion, may abandon the project at any time. If he does so, the fighter will be allowed to keep the money earned for fights he has already participated in. For example, the winner of each first-round fight will receive $1,000 and the loser will receive $500. But King is under no obligation to actually hold the final fight for which the

winner is supposed to receive $1,000,000.

(6) Even if the fighter wins all of his preliminary fights, King can still choose two other fighters to compete for the $1,000,000 prize.

(7) If the fighter loses a fight, King may terminate his services.

(8) If the fighter is unable to fight or retires from boxing before fulfilling all of his obligations under the contract, he cannot engage in any other form of athletic competition without King's permission.

(9) King can require the fighter to participate in forms of unarmed combat other than boxing such as mixed martial arts competition and professional wrestling.

(10) The fighter must live and train at training facility provided by King. He may bring a maximum of two pieces of luggage to training camp and may not bring a cell phone, pager, computer, credit card, cash, or any other form of currency. King may search the fighter's person and room whenever he chooses to make sure that the fighter has not brought prohibited items with him.

(11) At any time, King may advise the fighter that he has decided to require the fighter to engage in conduct that involves new "risks." If the fighter refuses to accept these risks, he forfeits his right to fight for future purses.

(12) The fighter assumes all risk of personal injury or death. Neither he nor his estate can sue King, King's employees, King's licensees, King's successors in interest, or King's assignees for negligence, even if their negligence was the direct cause of the fighter's injury or death.

(13) King has the right to obtain life insurance on the fighter or insurance against the failure of the fighter to participate in a bout with King as the beneficiary. However, King is under no obligation to provide insurance for the fighter. In fact, the contract states that the fighter is "solely responsible for maintaining health insurance to cover any bodily injury . . . as well as any insurance to cover any short-term or long-term disability from injury."

(14) King will provide the fighter with a "reasonable supply of food." However, at King's discretion, "in some circumstances," such food must be "earned" by the fighter.

(15) King may record the fighter on video and audio-tape at any time with or without the fighter's knowledge. This includes "actions in bedrooms and bathrooms" when the fighter is "partially clothed or naked."

(16) King gets the sole and exclusive rights to the fighter's life story in perpetuity. This includes, among other things, motion picture rights, theatrical stage presentations, and books. In exploiting these rights, King may reveal information that the fighter believes is "false, misleading, disparaging, defamatory, embarrassing, or of an otherwise

unfavorable nature."

(17) King may assign any or all of his rights under the contract to any other person or business entity. In the event of such assignment, King will have no further obligation to the fighter.

(18) If any person or corporation sues King, his employees, his licensees, his successors in interest, or his assignees, and that suit is based on a claim that conflicts with representations made by the fighter in his contract with King, then the fighter must pay all of King's expenses (including reasonable attorney's fees) in defending against the lawsuit. For example, if someone claiming to have a promotional or managerial contract with the fighter pops out of the woodwork and sues King, the fighter will be responsible for the expense of defending King against the lawsuit whether or not the claim is valid.

(19) King will establish and maintain a pension plan for the benefit of the fighter. However, King, in his sole discretion, will determine how much money is contributed to the plan.

(20) King can require the winner of the tournament to move to any location in the United States that King chooses. The fighter will be solely responsible for any and all expenses associated with relocation and moving.

(21) The fighter may not give an interview to any member of the media without King's prior authorization.

Typical Don King. Right?

WRONG ! ! !

The above has nothing to do with Don King. The promoter is Tournament of Champions LLC, which is the promotional arm of NBC's boxing reality show, *The Contender*.

Substitute "The Contender" for "King" and you'll have some of the contract provisions that *The Contender* is requiring fighters to sign.

The people who run *The Contender* might be well-intentioned, but there's enormous potential for abuse in these contracts. If Don King signed fighters to contracts like this, he'd be vilified in the media and government regulators would be all over him.

One of the equity participants in *The Contender* said this past week-end that the show would revise some of the provisions in its contracts. He also restated the commitment of the producers to treat fighters fairly and clean up boxing. If that's the case, *The Contender* should rethink its demand that fighters sign contracts that, in a worst-case scenario, will be economically unfair and strip them of their dignity.

Anyone who wants to take the lead as a model of probity in boxing should have model contracts for fighters.❏

I thought the following article would make waves. But the most disturbing thing about Marco Antonio Barrera's brain surgery was that, after it was revealed, almost no one in boxing seemed to care.

SHAME ON BOXING

Sources in Mexico say that Marco Antonio Barrera underwent brain surgery in 1997 and has been fighting with a metal plate in his head ever since.

The surgery, known as a craniotomy, took place after Barrera's second bout against Junior Jones and was related to a congenital defect—not the fight itself. Barrera's skull was opened, an abnormal vein was removed, and a metal plate to protect the area was affixed with screws inside his skull. Barrera has fought fifteen times since then and established himself as one of the best fighters in boxing. His most notable bouts have been a loss to Erik Morales in 2000, a win over Naseem Hamed in 2001, and a victory over Morales in their 2002 rematch. All three of these bouts took place in Nevada.

The first Barrera-Morales fight was promoted by Top Rank. Hamed-Barrera was promoted by Let's Get It On Promotions in association with Prince Promotions. The Barrera-Morales rematch was promoted by Top Rank in asssociation with Forum Boxing. Barrera is now promoted by Golden Boy Promotions. He is slated to enter the ring against Manny Pacquaio in San Antonio on November 15, 2003. That bout is to be televised by HBO.

On September 12, 2002, the New York State Athletic Commission announced that MRIs to perform brain scans would be required bi-annually as part of an examination for fighters who box in New York. Nevada followed suit with similar legislation several months ago.

The choice of San Antonio as the site for Barrera-Pacquaio is believed by some to have been motivated in part by the fact that Texas does not have an MRI requirement. However, Barrera's attorney, Stephen Espinoza, disputes that notion, stating, "San Antonio wasn't chosen to evade any restrictions. Texas is an incredible fight state, especially for Mexican fighters."

"There was a surgery in 1997," Espinoza acknowledges. "The surgery was performed in Mexico City by one of the top neurosurgeons in the world. Marco has consulted with several experts on a consistent basis since then and has had numerous MRIs and other examinations including two MRIs in this calendar year alone. All of the medical opinions that Marco has received from the time of the surgery through today have concluded that the surgery does not present any risks for Marco beyond the risks that are faced by any boxer."

Espinosa states that the surgery does not place Barrera at any competitive advantage or disadvantage and that the Texas State Athletic Commission was made aware of the situation in a timely manner. He also says that, immediately after the surgery, Barrera gave his medical records to the appropriate representatives on the understanding that the information in them would be communicated as necessary to the proper parties.

Passage of the MRI requirement in Nevada was spearheaded by Dr. Flip Homansky and Dr. Margaret Goodman. On May 19th of this year, Bruce Trampler of Top Rank sent a letter to the Nevada State Athletic Commission vigorously opposing the mandatory testing program. Promoter Gary Shaw also argued against mandatory MRI testing and canceled a series of fight cards in Nevada after the requirement was put in place.

Subsequent to Shane Mosley winning a controversial unanimous decision over Oscar De La Hoya on September 13th, Bob Arum accused Dr. Homansky of conspiring to improperly influence the outcome of the fight.

On October 4th, Dr. Goodman called a halt to the bout between Joel Casamayor and Diego Corrales when Corrales suffered dangerous cuts inside his mouth and did not have a proper mouthpiece. Shaw (who promotes both Corrales and Shane Mosley) then spoke with Marc Ratner (executive director of the Nevada State Athletic Commission) and said that Mosley would not fight in Nevada in the future if Dr. Goodman were assigned to his bout. Mosley himself later said that he had no problem with Dr. Goodman's work.

There is no indication that anyone at the Nevada State Athletic Commission was aware of Barrera's surgery at the time he fought in Nevada.

Ratner addressed the issue of Barrera's surgery yesterday in a telephone call with this writer. "We were made aware of certain information regarding the situation several weeks ago," said Ratner. "I have talked with [Golden Boy CEO] Richard Schaefer and my understanding is that Golden Boy has passed this information on to the commission in Texas."

During the dark days of Watergate, Senator Howard Baker frequently asked, "What did the President know, and when did he know it?"

A lot of people in boxing should be asking now, "Who knows what and when did they know it?"

I don't know if Marco Antonio Barrera should be fighting or not. One can argue that, since his surgery, he has passed the toughest tests of all: twenty-four rounds with Erik Morales and twelve rounds with Naseem Hamed. Barrera's future is an issue to be decided by qualified medical personnel in honest consultation with regulatory officials and Mr. Barrera himself.

I do know that there should be national standards for medical testing and a federal boxing commission.

There should also be an outpouring of revulsion from the media, from ring doctors, from the boxing community as a whole and, most importantly, from fighters over the way this matter has been handled.❑

People sometimes lose sight of the fact that today's fighters, like everyone else, have views on social and political issues. The following article was written three months before the 2004 presidential election.

HEAVYWEIGHT CHAMPIONS AND THE WAR IN IRAQ

This is the political season and the United States is at war in Iraq. Those realities have become inextricably intertwined.

Meanwhile, boxing's standard bearers have long held mixed views and reacted in different ways when called to serve in the United States military.

Jack Dempsey was indicted, and tried for conspiring to evade the draft during World War I. After a seven-day trial, he was acquitted; but the allegation that he was a draft-dodger haunted Dempsey throughout his ring career.

Gene Tunney, who defeated Dempsey in two historic fights, enlisted in the Marines at the start of Word War I.

Joe Louis donated several purses to the Navy Relief Fund and enlisted in the Army one month after Pearl Harbor.

Muhammad Ali has been largely silent during the current dialogue regarding the war in Iraq. But he refused induction into the United States Army during the war in Vietnam and was precluded from boxing for three-and-a-half years. He was also criminally convicted and sentenced to five years in prison, although ultimately his conviction was overturned by the United States Supreme Court.

That brings us to today's heavyweight champions. Vitali Klitschko holds the WBC crown. John Ruiz wears the WBA belt. Chris Byrd is the IBF champ. Lamon Brewster is on top at the WBO. And then there's Lennox Lewis, the last man to have been recognized as the undisputed heavyweight champion of the world.

The physical courage of these men is beyond question. They're warriors in the truest sense. Thus, it's interesting to hear their thoughts on the war in Iraq.

VITALI KLITSCHKO
"I'm very interested in politics. I spend a lot of time reading about

political things. Wladimir and I are are both very active with UNESCO [the United Nations Educational, Scientific and Cultural Organization]. We have traveled around the world and seen children without parents living on the streets; children without hope, just trying to survive one more day."

"On the war in Iraq, I am entirely negative about it. We come from a military family. Our father and grandfather were career military officers. I am a captain in the Ukrainian Army Reserve and a professional fighter. But I am against aggression. In every war, people lose their homes; children lose their parents; young men have their bodies torn apart. Sometimes a war has to be fought, but people are dying in Iraq for no good reason. I am against the war. I have no sympathy for Saddam Hussein, but what America is doing now in Iraq is wrong. War is never a good answer. I hope it ends as soon as possible before too many more people die."

JOHN RUIZ

"I'm worried about this country. We're drifting backward. What's going on in politics today isn't good. We're losing jobs; people who want to work can't get jobs. And at the same time, the big companies are sending jobs overseas and getting ridiculous tax breaks. Teachers supply wisdom and knowledge to our children, but our teachers are underpaid. Rich people keep getting richer. And the way things are going, I'm not even sure Social Security will be around when I retire.

"The most painful thing to me is the way our veterans are being treated. These are guys who risk their lives for our freedom. Then they come home. A lot of them have problems from the war. And instead of the government taking care of them, they're left out in the cold. There are veterans coming back from Iraq who are living homeless on the streets. That's heartbreaking to me.

"When the war started, the government told us that it was a noble war to fight terrorism. But even if that was true, President Bush didn't have a master plan to deal with the situation. I'm not sure he even told us the truth about why we were going to war in Iraq. And now our troops are dying every day. America needs a change in leadership now."

CHRIS BYRD

"I'm not that interested in politics. I'm registered and I vote. But my thing is, whatever Scripture says, I'm with it. If a candidate is in favor of abortion, I won't vote for him. I'm against teaching evolution in the schools. I'll vote for Bush in November because he's the closest of the candidates to Scripture. As far as Iraq is concerned, I think Bush is on a bit of a power trip. I don't know if we should have gone in there or not. But we're in so far now that we can't just pull out."

LAMON BREWSTER

"At first, I thought the war in Iraq was justified. I understood the need to protect ourselves and respond to the World Trade Center bombing. But now, it seems like that's not what this whole mess in Iraq is about. I think Bush knew there were no weapons of mass destruction in Iraq. He was just sitting up at night, trying to find a reason that would justify in peoples' minds going to war. Oil was the real reason Bush went in. Hey, I'd give my life for this country if the cause was just. But I don't think people should be dying just so the oil companies can make bigger profits.

"And we got a bigger war going on in this country right now. We pay for the government, but Bush and the government aren't working for us. You got mothers living on the street with their children. People can't get decent health care. Kids can't get an education. But unless you're making a million dollars a year, Bush doesn't care about you. People say, 'Things are bad, but I'm just one person. What can I do?' Well, what you can do is vote and persuade one other person to vote, who persuades another person to vote and on and on. If the people vote, we can regain control of our country."

LENNOX LEWIS

"You don't want people coming over to your country and blowing up the place. Obviously, you have to protect against that. But this war isn't about defending America. It's about oil.

"America and England have this air of superiority. What we're doing in Iraq reminds me of when white Christians went to Africa and said, 'You people are living like heathens. You don't know what's good for you and, whether you like it or not, we're going to show you.'

"There are times when you can't have peace without war, but I don't think this is one of them. The government is trying to create an atmosphere where people believe we have to be there, but we don't. Rumsfeld is a liar, and Bush is a puppet.

"I haven't said more publicly about the war because I'm of the opinion that what I say about world politics doesn't matter. I don't have the background in that area to be credible. If I say the war in Iraq is bad, the government will simply find another athlete who says, 'No, it's good.' But I believe that what the United States is doing over there will effect the world negatively for a long time."

●●●

Nothing that any of these champions said was meant to question the courage or decency of American soldiers and other coalition troops serving in Iraq. Nor is there anything "anti-American" about their sentiments. John Ruiz, Chris Byrd, and Lamon Brewster are American citizens, while Vitali Klitschko and Lennox Lewis have chosen to live in the United States.

In judging their thoughts, one should remember the words of Mark Twain: "True patriotism, the only rational patriotism, is loyalty to the nation all the time, loyalty to the government when it deserves it."

One should also keep in mind that, just as there's nothing courageous about a manager sending a fighter into the ring, there's nothing courageous about middle-aged men sending young men overseas to kill and die in battle.❏

The business of boxing is a chess game that goes on and on.

THE BATTLE OVER "WHO'S A PROMOTER?"

Oscar De La Hoya versus Shane Mosley was the second most important fight in boxing last week. And although it ended in controversy [with a decision in Mosley's favor], the bout was an economic success with HBO and Bob Arum joining forces to sell out the MGM Grand Arena and engender close to a million pay-per-view buys. However, an even higher-stakes battle raged behind the scenes in Washington, D.C., where lobbyists seeking to influence legislation that would create a federal boxing commission have been at odds over the definition of the word "promoter." Ironically, the chief adversaries in this battle have been HBO and Bob Arum. Now there are reports that, in the tumultuous wake of De La Hoya versus Mosley, HBO and Arum have reached a compromise.

The television networks don't want to be classified as promoters because it would (1) be bad for their image; (2) subject them to the financial disclosure requirements of the Professional Boxing Safety Act; and (3) propel them into the murky area of legal liability to fighters and others. By contrast, Arum (with a little help from his friends) has lobbied long and hard for legislation that would label the networks as "promoters" unless they significantly alter the way they do business.

Senator Harry Reid, whose support is crucial to passage of the legislation, has backed the Arum position. Meanwhile, AOL Time Warner lobbyists have told persons involved in the legislative process that HBO supports the overall purpose of the bill but will work against the legislation if passage would result in HBO being classified and regulated as a "promoter."

The long-standing practice within the boxing industry of contract affirmations has been a key component of the debate. When HBO and Showtime sign a contract with a promoter for a major bout or for the long-term services of a fighter, they ask each fighter involved to sign a one-page affirmation stating that he is familiar with the contract and will abide by it. Thus, when HBO and Top Rank signed a contract giving HBO exclusive television rights to Oscar De La Hoya's fights, Oscar signed a ratification of that contract. Then, two years ago, the Golden

Boy broke with Arum. Subsequently, they reunited. But in the interim, HBO claimed rights directly from De La Hoya pursuant to the one-page contract ratification that Oscar had signed. And before De La Hoya reconciled with Top Rank, he fought twice on HBO with Jerry Perenchio as his promoter. Arum would prefer that nothing like that happen again.

To date, Harry Reid has championed the Arum position. He has supported proposals that allow for ratifications of contracts, but only to the extent that a ratification confirms the promoter's right to provide the services of the fighter. If the ratification is construed as giving rights directly to a television network, then that network would be a promoter. Reid has reportedly also sought language in the legislation that would have the effect of restricting the manner in which the networks do business in other ways as well.

Meanwhile, having watched De La Hoya versus Mosley with Senator John McCain at his side, HBO Sports president Ross Greenburg later told Flip Homansky of the Nevada State Athletic Commission, "We [AOL Time Warner] will not allow legislation that we think is unfair."

McCain, who has spearheaded the reform movement, has been caught in the middle. He has the votes necessary to get the proposed boxing reform legislation out of committee, but lacks the votes required for passage on the Senate floor. Thus, he has had to find compromise language that is both consistent with the policy purposes of the proposed legislation and acceptable to those whose votes are necessary to win passage in Congress. One option he considered was deferring the task of defining "promoter" by placing it within the rule-making authority of the proposed federal boxing commission. But that solution was unacceptable to the warring parties.

As noted previously in this space, HBO and Showtime are involved in virtually every aspect of a big fight. The networks put up the money, dictate match-ups, organize press events, and have the final say over various crucial elements such as fight date and site. Anyone who thinks that Prize Fight Boxing (as opposed to HBO and Showtime) was the true promoter of Lennox Lewis versus Mike Tyson also thinks that Santa Claus puts all those presents beneath the tree for children to open on Christmas morning.

Within the boxing industry, HBO is particularly powerful by virtue of its checkbook. That was confirmed by Ross Greenburg when he testified before Congress on February 5, 2003, and declared, "We are the bank, and a powerful one at that . . . Here is one big pocketbook that is willing to stand up and speak out . . . We are a bank. We are powerful."

During the course of his testimony, Greenburg maintained that HBO is not a promoter and likened its televising fights to other networks televising sports such as tennis and golf. But when Mike Weir won the Masters at Augusta this year, the first words out of his mouth weren't, "Thank you, CBS, for giving me the opportunity to participate in this tournament." NBC doesn't dictate which players compete at Wimbledon. Yet when HBO has an exclusive contract with a world champion like Lennox Lewis, Roy Jones, or Oscar De La Hoya, it can shut fighters other than "mandatory" challengers out of fighting for the title by simply refusing to accept them as an opponent.

Indeed, Don King complained that, after Ricardo Mayorga beat Vernon Forrest, HBO told him that the only Mayorga fight it would accept was a Mayorga-Forrest rematch. "What HBO said to me," King wailed, "was, if you want Mayorga to be on HBO, then you have to fight our guy." One can imagine King continuing his discourse with the complaint, "When a poverty-stricken Nicaraguan wins the title in the ring, HBO tries to take it away from him. It's not fair."

Much of what King says about the sweet science should be taken with a grain of salt; particularly when his own interests are involved. But King is on the mark when he suggests that HBO has enormous power to influence the course of boxing. That suggestion has also been made in Congress.

During the question-and-answer portion of the February 5th Congressional hearing, Senator Byron Dorgan asked Greenburg why HBO wasn't taking a more proactive role to help clean up boxing in light of misdeeds like the IBF ratings scandal. "Why," Dorgan demanded, "are not the largest beneficiaries from a revenue standpoint, including the networks and HBO; why are they not pushing very hard to say, 'Look, let us clean this up. We put the prestige and the energy of our organization behind it?'"

In relevant part, Greenburg answered, "We have absolutely no involvement with any of these sanctioning organizations to know what is going on behind the scenes between the promoters and the sanctioning organizations." But as HBO commentator Larry Merchant has said, "In the real world, that separation doesn't exist." And more to the point; if the powers that be at HBO don't have a pretty good idea of what goes on behind closed doors, they should. Everybody else in boxing does.

HBO also contends that it doesn't choose opponents except to the extent of trying to avoid mismatches and that it doesn't tell promoters that they have to make a certain match. But the fighters themselves tell a different story. Recalling the negotiations that led up to his June 21, 2003, encounter with Vitali Klitschko, Lennox Lewis declared, "After Kirk Johnson got hurt, HBO told me it was Klitschko or nobody. We offered them alternatives like Joe Mesi, Lamon Brewster and Jameel McCline, and they said no to all of them even though those guys were the same level opponent as Kirk Johnson. All the discussions regarding the opponent were with HBO; not Gary Shaw, who was my promoter. HBO gave me a choice. Take the harder fight for more money or go home empty-handed. HBO made that fight."

Vitali Klitschko's August 26, 2003, conference call with the media is equally instructive. During the question-and-answer session, a reporter asked, "You are going to be fighting on December 6th. When will we know your opponent?" Klitschko answered, "I am not ready to give a name for December 6th. HBO will decide my opponent, and I hope they find me an interesting opponent."

Now comes word that HBO and Arum are pulling in their horns a bit. Under their reported compromise agreement, HBO will get most of what it wants. The network's previously-existing contracts with fighters will be "grandfathered in" under the legislation, so HBO's relationships with fighters already under contract won't be affected. And the proposed compromise language will have only minor limiting effects on the conduct of television networks in the future. Arum appears to have won several smaller victories including restrictions on fighters promoting themselves.

Meanwhile, there's sad irony in the pronouncements that emanated from HBO and Arum after the decision in De La Hoya versus Mosley last Saturday night. HBO's commentators condemned the judges in that fight as inept or worse. Arum was so angry with the decision that he denounced boxing as "the garbage can of sports" and threatened to abandon the sweet science at the end of the year.

But it's HBO and Arum who have done more than anyone else in recent weeks to block the proposed legislation that offers the best hope of cleaning up boxing. And as long as they continue to flex their political muscle, boxing can expect more avoidable deaths in the ring and more financial exploitation of fighters. One expects that type of conduct from Arum, but HBO is a different story.

HBO has been good for boxing, and it has been fairer to fighters than most promoters. For a long time, the network has been seen as part of the solution to what ails boxing. It would be a shame if HBO were to become part of the problem.❏

For a long time, ESPN was an important factor in keeping boxing alive. But in recent years, there have been problems.

IS A SCANDAL BREWING AT ESPN?

In 1998, when ESPN inaugurated *ESPN2 Friday Night Fights*, the network promised viewers an experience reminiscent of *Gillette Friday Night Fights* from the 1950s. Now the public might be getting a rerun of ABC's scandal-ridden 1977 United States Boxing Championships.

ESPN is aware that issues have been raised regarding its boxing programming. Earlier this summer, it launched an internal probe. ESPN personnel and others from the boxing industry have been questioned. Meanwhile, on September 2, 2003, the network suffered another setback when it televised a fight card from the Mountaineer Race Track and Gaming Resort in Chester, West Virginia.

The September 2nd card featured 6-foot-9-inch 278-pound Tye Fields versus Sherman "Tank" Williams. Fields entered the ring with a record of 28 wins, 1 loss, and 27 knockouts. Twenty-three of those knockouts came in the first round. Prior to Williams, Fields had never fought a quality opponent. He is widely regarded as a mediocre pugilist. Only two of Fields's fights had gone past two rounds.

Williams, a veteran of Cedric Kushner's "Heavyweight Explosion" cards, sported a 23-7-1 record against more serious competition, including a ten-round draw with Jameel McCline.

On the day of the fight, online betting odds are said to have shifted significantly in Fields's favor. That afternoon, Bob Yalen, who oversees boxing for ESPN, received a telephone call from an industry acquaintance who he talks with several times a week. The acquaintance asked a single question.

"Have you heard the rumors that your fight is fixed?"

Yalen said "no" and promised to call the site to check into the allegation. The performance by Sherman Williams that night did nothing to dispel the notion of a fix.

People of good will can interpret what they see differently. But to a lot of observers, it looked as though Williams was aiming to miss. Over the course of twelve rounds, he consistently threw punches in the wrong place at the wrong time and landed only 53 blows. Possibly, he was intimidated by the fact that a big muscular southpaw was standing in front of him. But remember, this is a guy who, three years ago, didn't have a size problem with Jameel McCline.

Williams looked like a man who didn't want to win the fight. And during the fight, telephone wires started humming.

"Turn on the TV. They're showing a fixed fight on ESPN."

Emanuel Steward was in Fields's corner by virtue of the fact that the fighter had trained for a month at the Kronk Gym.

"I think Williams wanted to win," says Steward. "He just couldn't. He gave up because he understood early in the fight that he was a beaten fighter. It wasn't much different in principle from Mike Tyson understanding from the second round on that he was going to lose to Lennox Lewis."

Ron Scott Stevens, who worked for Cedric Kushner Promotions and is now chairman of the New York State Athletic Commission, also sounds a cautionary note regarding conclusions that might be reached. "I made a lot of fights for Sherman when I was with CKP," says Stevens. "He's a good guy, but you never know which Sherman is going to show up. There are times when he fights and times when he doesn't. He didn't fight against Derrick Banks or Taurus Sykes either [both ten-round losses], and no one ever suggested that those fights were fixed."

But usually, when a fighter doesn't give much of an effort, it's in a fight that he doesn't think he can win. And Eric Bottjer, who served as CKP's matchmaker for years, observes, "I don't care who you send to Emanuel Steward. If he can't fight, he won't learn how in four weeks. I can't think of a single heavyweight we've promoted in the past five years who wouldn't have beaten Tye Fields."

And Henry Foster, Williams's manager, was extremely disturbed by what he saw. "I was as surprised as anybody," Foster acknowledged several days after the bout. "I'm totally shocked by the way the fight went. I came there expecting Sherman to win by knockout, and I felt that his effort was non-existent. I'm not going to make any excuses for Sherman's performance. There was no evidence of any desire on his part to be a champion. As the fight went on, I got more and more depressed. Sherman has lost fights before that he should have won. He's had a couple of bad fights in the past when he just couldn't fire, and this might have been one of them. After the fight, I asked him one question: 'Do you think you lost to a better fighter?' And he told me, 'Absolutely not.' Sherman is not a wealthy guy. I know he's behind on his bills. I've heard the rumors, but I don't want to give credence to them."

No one should blame Tye Fields for any of this. By all accounts, he's a decent hardworking young man who's doing the best he can in a very tough business. Wes Wolfe, who trained Fields for thirteen months, says, "Tye is the hardest-working fighter I've ever had; a real good kid; never gives anyone any problems. The whole thing stinks, but it's not his fault."

But one has to take a long hard look at the way ESPN2 handled the situation. Here, the thoughts of Showtime boxing czar Jay Larkin are instructive. "If someone who I respected called me on the day of a fight with the rumor of a fix," says Larkin, "I'd call the local state athletic commission; I'd call the promoter; and I'd call our announcers to put them all on alert."

That's what happened on July 29, 1997, when rumors circulated that journeyman Bert Cooper had agreed to take a dive against the much-hyped Richie Melito in a bout at Madison Square Garden. Properly advised, New York State Athletic Commission officials visited Cooper in his dressing room shortly before the fight and transmitted a stern warning. Whatever Cooper's previous plans might have been, he knocked Melito out with a body shot in the first round.

No one is suggesting that ESPN fixed a fight or knowingly televised a fixed fight. But no matter how one looks at the situation, ESPN dropped the ball. Yalen says that, after receiving the warning, he telephoned his coordinating producer and "told him to keep an eye on the situation." But that's not how the telecast looked.

Televising a fight is a team effort. ESPN blow-by-blow commentator Joe Tessitore and "expert" commentator Scott LeDoux should have been told of the rumors beforehand. Instead of lavishly praising Fields, they should at some point have called Williams's effort into question. But instead, LeDoux babbled on about how great Fields looked, likening him to Lennox Lewis. And five days after the fight, Yalen still hadn't reported the pre-fight call he received to the West Virginia State Athletic Commission.

There are a lot of questions to be answered regarding Tye Fields versus Sherman Williams. The authorities responsible for enforcing the law should ask them under oath. Meanwhile, Fields versus Williams arises at a time when ESPN's boxing programming is already under fire.

ESPN and ESPN2 televise close to seventy fights a year, including forty-eight on Friday nights. There's not a lot of money to be made on ESPN dates. But the network is crucial to moving young fighters; it's a place where careers are molded; and ESPN fights can make or break a promoter. In other words, decisions at ESPN can alter the balance of power in the boxing industry.

Bob Yalen controls the budget for ESPN boxing and has final responsibility for quality control over fights. When *ESPN2 Friday Night Fights* were in their infancy, he and Russell Peltz shared authority as to which dates would go to which promoters. A year later, Peltz was stripped of his power and Yalen assumed full control over key decisions. Peltz's role has been reduced to that of an on-site trouble-shooter for *ESPN2 Friday Night Fights*. He has no connection to the Tuesday offerings.

The boxing community was told that ESPN fights would be open to the competitive market. Each promoter would be encouraged to make its best offer. ESPN would then buy the best that was offered, and the public would see competitive bouts featuring a new generation of young fighters who were on their way to becoming superstars.

But it hasn't evolved that way. And within the boxing community, a number of people are upset by what they perceive as a tilted playing field. More specifically, they're asking:

(1) Why does ESPN give so many dates to promoters without specific match-ups attached?

(2) Why does ESPN give dates to promoters who don't have any fighters under contract?

(3) Why does ESPN allow the dates it gives to certain promoters to be sold to other promoters?

(4) Why has ESPN given so many dates to Sugar Ray Leonard Boxing?

(5) Why has ESPN frozen out so many promoters? For example, Main Events hasn't had a Friday night date since March 2, 2001.

(6) Why has ESPN turned down certain fighters as "boring" and then accepted the same fighter when offered by a favored promoter?

(7) Why has ESPN turned down certain fights and then accepted the identical fight when offered by a favored promoter?

(8) Why does ESPN give dates to promoters who change fights at the last minute as a matter of course?

(9) Why does ESPN put so much emphasis on buying bogus alphabet-soup title fights?

These questions are being asked against a backdrop of persistent rumors regarding the motivation for the choices that Yalen has made. And the rumors are ugly.

Yalen is entitled to his own philosophy of programming. Also, it should be noted that, over the past two decades, virtually every television executive who buys fights has been accused of misconduct by one disgruntled seller or another. Often, the accusations are simply untrue. Some very honest people have been wrongly accused on the rumor circuit.

Yalen says, "I can't please everybody. Unless a promoter gets all the dates he wants, he won't be happy. There's a lot of things people talk about that they just don't know."

Still, the bottom line is that ESPN is in a position of power. When it comes to buying fights, supply is far greater than demand. On the level at which ESPN does business, it can pick and choose.

Moreover, fans who turn on ESPN are entitled to see competitive bouts of importance. That hasn't happened enough lately; viewers resent it; and as a result, ratings have plummeted.

The first sixty *ESPN2 Friday Night Fights* shows did an average rating of .864. The most recent sixty shows for which ratings were made available [through June 20, 2003] did a .542 rating. In other words, ratings were 59.8 percent higher five years ago than they are now.

Here, the relationship between ESPN and Sugar Ray Leonard Boxing is instructive. SRL has been a frequent provider of programming to ESPN. Among other things, starting September 5, 2003, it has been guaranteed the first Friday of each month for a full year. In and of itself, that's not unusual. Top Rank has a huge block of dates from Telefutura. Golden Boy Promotions has a generous allocation from HBO Latino, as does Goossen-Tutor from Fox.

But critics of the ESPN-SRL relationship claim that an unholy alliance exists between Yalen and Sugar Ray Leonard's matchmaker, Ron Katz. They ask why Vassiliy Jirov hasn't been able to get a date on ESPN since he left SRL. They're troubled by fundraising material for Sugar Ray Leonard Boxing that lists ESPN as a "strategic partner." And they take issue with Yalen's claim that ESPN's largesse to SRL is justified because SRL's shows get higher ratings than the competition.

Eleven of the last sixty *ESPN2 Friday Night Fights* shows for which data was made available were promoted by Sugar Ray Leonard Boxing. Those eleven telecasts averaged a .515 rating. The non-Leonard shows did better, averaging .548.

In sum, there's concern within the boxing community that something is wrong at ESPN. Some promoters get dates without any set fights while others are required to lock in a full card. Promoters who have been the backbone of boxing for years can't get dates while others of lesser pedigree are treated well. And clearly there's not enough quality control.

ESPN wouldn't allow match-ups like those featured on *ESPN2 Friday Night Fights* in other sports. Viewers don't turn on ESPN for its marquee college football game of the week and see Towson versus Morgan State. And some critics see a direct link between ESPN's current practices and the Tye Fields versus Sherman Williams fiasco. Their view is that questionable business dealings at ESPN have created an environment where more of the same can be expected. In other words, if a network creates an environment in which anything goes, it shouldn't be surprised when anything goes.❏

This was the start of a painful ongoing saga.

THE RUMORS ABOUT JOE MESI

Joe Mesi is believed to have suffered a subdural hematoma (bleeding on the surface of his brain) in his March 13, 2004, fight in Las Vegas against Vassiliy Jirov. Mesi was comfortably ahead in the fight after eight rounds, but was knocked down once in the ninth and twice in the tenth. All three judges scored the bout 94-93 in Mesi's favor.

The final stanza against Jirov was hell for Mesi, who wobbled around the ring and barely survived. Now there are rumors that he was close to not surviving at all.

After the fight, Mesi complained of a headache. Later in the month, he went to neurologist in Buffalo, who ordered various tests including an MRI. There are reports that the neurologist discovered a small blood clot that was the result of a recent subdural hematoma. Mesi's condition did not require surgery. Over time, the blood will be reabsorbed by the brain in the manner of a bruise. But if the rumors are true and Mesi-Jirov had been scheduled for twelve rounds, the tear in Mesi's brain could have been exacerbated and he might have died in the ring.

"It's all nonsense," said Jack Mesi, who serves as his son's manager. "I've heard the rumors and I don't know what they're talking about. How can someone make up stories like this? There's utterly no truth to them. It's just ridiculous. Joe had an MRI, and there was nothing more serious than a concussion."

After Mesi-Jirov, Mesi was suspended by the Nevada State Athletic Commission because of the knockdowns he suffered. That's common practice. Suspensions of this nature are usually lifted within thirty to sixty days.

"I've received a letter from the Nevada commission," Jack Mesi acknowledged. "They want to see Joe's doctors' reports and other documents regarding Joe's post-fight condition. When Joe's doctor says he's fine, we'll send a response to Nevada with all of the necessary back-up. The proof will be in the test results. They'll show that Joe is fine."

Mesi's suspension will not be lifted by the Nevada State Athletic Commission until the appropriate documentation is received and evaluated. Nevada has a policy that no one who has had bleeding in the brain from a fight-related injury can fight again.

Last month, there were rumors that Mesi was planning to defer his scheduled August HBO date to the fall and fight a "bring-your-own opponent" on an Indian reservation in Ontario this summer. Indian reservations, unless they are members of the Association of Boxing Commissions, are not required to recognize suspensions by other jurisdictions.

Now negotiations are underway for a fight between Mesi and Mike Tyson to be held in December at Madison Square Garden. "I'm eighty percent sure that it's going to happen," Tyson adviser Shelly Finkel said yesterday. "The Mesi people have not in any way indicated during negotiations that there is a medical problem." Then Finkel added, "I'm told that Mesi might take an interim off-television fight this summer."

New York, like other members of the ABC, is required to honor medical suspensions by other jurisdictions. Moreover, if Nevada lifts Mesi's suspension, it's likely that the New York State Athletic Commission would order tests of its own before allowing Mesi to fight in the Empire State.

Recently, Dr. Barry Jordan (medical director of the New York State Athletic Commission) was asked to comment generally on allowing fighters who have suffered bleeding in the brain to be allowed into the ring again. "If there's evidence of past injury to the brain," said Jordan, "our policy is to not let a fighter fight. I can't think of any exceptions. Morally, I would be obligated to put a fighter with a past brain injury on permanent suspension."

Morever, if Mesi in fact suffered a subdural hematoma, the thought of his sparring in the gym is troubling. Again, speaking generally, Dr. Jordan declared, "After the type of injury you're describing, there's no fixed timeline for exercise. You start with mild exercise and work your way up slowly. But when it comes to contact, whether it's football or sparring in the gym, there's always an increased risk of bleeding."

Mesi's situation is different from the case of Marco Antonio Barrera. Last year, it was revealed that Barrera underwent brain surgery in 1997 and had been fighting since then with small metal implants in his head. The surgery was related to a congenital defect. Barrera's skull was opened, an abnormal vein was removed, and a metal plate to protect the area was affixed with screws inside his skull. By contrast, the blood clot reportedly found in Mesi's brain is presumed to have been the result of uncontrolled bleeding from a fight-related injury rather than a congenital abnormality.

Mesi's situation underscores the need for the mandatory MRI testing of fighters. At present, Nevada and New York are the only two states that require such testing.◻

Subsequent to this article being published, the Mesi camp conceded that Joe Mesi had, in fact, suffered a subdural hematoma in his fight against Vassiliy Jirov.

MORE ON JOE MESI

On April 22, 2004, this writer recounted reports that Joe Mesi suffered a subdural hematoma (bleeding on the surface of his brain) after his March 13th victory in Las Vegas over Vassiliy Jirov. Following the fight, Mesi complained of a headache. Later in the month, he went to a neurologist in Buffalo, who ordered various tests including an MRI.

"It's all nonsense," Jack Mesi (Joe's father and manager) said at the time. "I've heard the rumors and I don't know what they're talking about. How can someone make up stories like this? There's utterly no truth to them. It's just ridiculous."

After Mesi-Jirov, Mesi was suspended by the Nevada State Athletic Commission because of the knockdowns he suffered. On March 19th, John Bailey (chairman of the NSAC) sent a letter to Mesi informing the boxer that his suspension would not be lifted until he underwent a new MRI of the brain and forwarded to the commission the results of that MRI and all other medical evaluations performed on him subsequent to the Jirov fight.

Nevada has a policy that no one who has suffered from bleeding in the brain can fight again. In addition, Section 467.017(3) of the Nevada Administrative Code states, "The commission will not issue or renew a license to engage in unarmed combat to an applicant who has suffered a cerebral hemorrhage."

All states and Native American reservations that are members of the Association of Boxing Commissions are required to honor medical suspensions by other jurisdictions.

On May 11, 2004, an attorney named Stuart Campbell from Tulsa, Oklahoma (the home base of Mesi's promoter Tony Holden), sent a letter to the NSAC. The letter referenced "rumors and false accusations" being made in the media and said that Mesi had scheduled an appointment with one of the top neurosurgeons in the country. It then promised to provide the commission with information regarding Mesi's status so that he could be cleared to continue his career.

In early June, Campbell sent a second letter to the Nevada State Athletic Commission stating that Mesi was ready to come to Nevada and undergo MRI testing by a neurologist of the NSAC's choosing. And on June 14th, Mesi told the Associated Press, "My health is great. I'm just looking forward to progressing my career. We're hoping to make an announcement in the next week or so."

Meanwhile, the Mesi camp has yet to forward to the NSAC the documents requested by John Bailey on March 19th. And its offer to have the fighter undergo a new MRI appears to be an attempt to circumvent the fact that Joe Mesi had at least five MRIs subsequent to the Jirov fight. More specifically, this writer has been told the following:

A March 17, 2004, MRI revealed a left parietal subdural hematoma (a hemorrhage pressing on the left side of Mesi's brain).

A March 25, 2004, MRI appears to have been misread in that there was an internal belief that the problem had been resolved.

An April 8, 2004, MRI is believed to have shown two additional subdural hematomas that had gone undetected in the initial readings. In other words, Joe Mesi may have suffered not one but THREE subdural hematomas.

An April 27, 2004, MRI showed that the two hematomas discovered on April 8th were still present.

A May 27, 2004, MRI was normal.

All of the MRIs were conducted at the same imaging facility. They were read by two different radiologists.

Mesi's lawyers might still make the argument that a fighter who has suffered a subdural hematoma is no more at risk in the ring than any other fighter. Or they could claim that, even if Mesi is denied a license to fight in Nevada, his suspension should be lifted to allow him to fight in another state. But that's not their present position. At the moment, they're denying that there was a subdural hematoma.

Here, the thoughts of Dr. Neil Martin (chief of neurosurgery at the UCLA Medical Center) are instructive. "Although medical studies are limited on boxers," Dr. Martin stated, "the proof is right in front of you. If a fighter bled once in his brain, he has proved he is susceptible and can bleed again. You don't need years of research to prove it. The risks are too high to keep fighting."

Meanwhile, Nevada's chief deputy attorney general Keith Kizer (who represents the NSAC) said, "Whatever the facts might be, we're not going to pass the buck to another state. A fighter can't be taken off suspension until he's fit to fight." And without prejudging the case, Kizer added, "If it turns out that a great athlete like Joe Mesi can't continue his career, it would be a shame, but nothing like the tragedy of Joe Mesi or any other fighter dying in the ring."

Mesi's situation highlights the unacceptable variation in boxing medical regulations from state to state. Some jurisdictions require extensive testing before a boxer is allowed to enter the ring. But in other states, a warm body seems to suffice. For example, if the same set of facts had unfolded following a fight in Utah, then, most likely, Mesi would not be on medical suspension today and would be free to fight.

There has been talk that Mesi might seek a fight outside of the United States and beyond the jurisdiction of the Association of Boxing Commissions. Were such a fight to happen, the ABC could permanently suspend any promoter, manager, trainer, or other licensee who was involved with it.

Last year, before his son fought at Madison Square Garden, Jack Mesi was asked if he was concerned that Joe might get hurt in the ring. In response, Jack answered, "I cross my fingers every time because there are no guarantees in boxing."

Joe Mesi is lucky he's alive today. If he's allowed to fight again by the powers that be in boxing, it will fuel arguments that the sport should be banned.❑

In early 2004, a rumbling of potentially seismic proportions shook the landscape of professional boxing.

THE TIP OF THE ICEBERG

On Tuesday, January 6th, a dozen FBI agents raided the offices of Top Rank, Bob Arum's promotional company, in Las Vegas. The raid was conducted pursuant to a sealed search warrant. The agents seized computers, boxing contracts, medical records, and financial documents.

Jim Stern, a spokesman for the FBI, confirmed that the raid was carried out as part of a two-year investigation conducted in conjunction with the New York City Police Department.

The key man in the investigation was a New York police detective who posed as a fringe mobster trying to sell stolen goods in Las Vegas. "Big Frankie" teamed with an FBI agent who served as his driver. Over time, he was embraced by various members of the Las Vegas fight community and brought into their confidence.

As the investigation progressed, telephones were tapped pursuant to search warrants. Suspects "flipped" and wore wires. It's amazing that the operation was kept under wraps for as long as it was.

Forget about reports that Oscar De La Hoya versus Shane Mosley was fixed. The De La Hoya fight that has aroused the most suspicion was Oscar against Yory Boy Campas on May 3, 2003. Campas lasted just long enough to beat the "over-under" line.

Rumors are also swirling with regard to the following:

(1) Allegations that employees of Top Rank fixed fights by enticing fighters to take dives. The 2001 rematch between Jorge Paez and Verdell Smith and the 2002 bout between Joey Torres and Perry Williams are high on the list.
(2) The illegal transportation of Mexican fighters into the United States; tax fraud with regard to their purses; and skimming re. same.
(3) The submission of fraudulent medical documents.
(4) The corruption of ring judges.

The Top Rank personnel whose names have been most commonly

bandied about during the past week are Bob Arum, Todd duBoef (Arum's son-in-law), Bruce Trampler, Sean Gibbons, Pete Susens, and Cameron Dunkin. Others outside of Top Rank such as Robert Mittleman have been prominently mentioned.

The investigation might also involve Top Rank's dealings with Telefutura and ESPN. That, in turn, could spiral into a major investigation of Telefutura's entire boxing program and ESPN2 *Friday Night Fights*. If the FBI is looking at fixed fights, it might check out Tye Fields versus Sherman Williams. The world sanctioning organizations could come in for renewed scrutiny, as might the involvement of Top Rank personnel in the death of Bradley Rone.

If, as has been reported, the telephones at Top Rank were tapped for two years . . . Wow! Who knows what was said in conversations with executives of television networks, casinos, and state athletic commissions?

Top Rank issued a statement on Friday, January 9th that declared, "Upon Mr. Arum's return to Las Vegas, he stated that Top Rank has done nothing wrong. Top Rank does not know the scope of the government's investigation. Top Rank is lawfully cooperating with that investigation. Top Rank will not comment on or respond to the rumors, speculations, and unverified allegations appearing in the media. Top Rank will continue to focus on its business of promoting its boxers and fights and appreciates all the support it has received from the boxing industry."

Meanwhile, Joe Hawk of the *Las Vegas Review-Journal* (which has been supportive of Arum over the years) wrote this week, "There is deliciously sweet irony in seeing a whiney boxing promoter, who just four months earlier threw accusatory stones at regulators in his home state, suddenly having his glass house searched and stripped by FBI agents."

If a small portion of the rumors presently circulating are proven true, the fate of Top Rank could make the *Titanic* look like a successful ocean voyage.

But Top Rank is a case study; that's all. Whatever its employees have done, they aren't the only ones.

It has been said that this week's developments are bad for boxing; that they will deter potential corporate sponsors and constitute another black eye for the sport.

But black eyes are the least of boxing's problems. The industry suffers from a pervasive cancer that requires chemotherapy, radiation and surgery.

It's not enough to just cut off a tentacle. Now is the time to go for the whole octopus. That means it's crucial for someone who knows all aspects of the sport and business of boxing to read the transcripts of wiretap evidence on behalf of the government. And that someone should be a person who is unafraid to rock the boat.

Meanwhile, one biproduct of this week's revelations might be to breathe new life into the proposed federal boxing commission. Senator Harry Reid of Nevada has been a major stumbling block to passage of the legislation. But it's unlikely that Mr. Reid wants to be known at the moment as "the senator from Top Rank." Also, the scandal emphasizes the need for a federal commission by demonstrating that too many state athletic commissions acquiesce in what they know to be improper conduct.

Stay tuned. What we're watching now isn't "the worst thing that could happen to boxing." It might be the best.❏

After news of the FBI probe into boxing broke, things continued to worsen.

THE DOWNWARD SPIRAL

The current FBI probe into boxing has broadened to include a manslaughter investigation into the death of Bradley Rone. Rone died in the ring following a first-round stoppage of his July 18, 2003, fight against Billy Zumbrun in Cedar City, Utah.

The probe, designated Operation Match Book, has been underway since 2002. On October 31st of that year, an undercover New York City police detective using the alias "Frank Manzione" applied for a Las Vegas business license for a company called YGJ & Co. Working with the FBI, "Big Frankie" infiltrated the underbelly of the Las Vegas fight community. Court-ordered wiretaps culminating in a January 6th raid on the offices of Top Rank followed.

Investigators are now focussing on allegations that false medical records were created and filed with the Utah State Athletic Commission as part of the licensing process for Rone and in conjunction with his pre-fight physical. One of boxing's dirty little secrets is that false medical records have become a cottage industry. Manslaughter is a state criminal offense, not a federal one.

Amidst the turmoil, Top Rank is continuing the veneer of business as usual. But boxing is reeling. There are rumblings out of Nevada that the Nevada State Athletic Commission is bowing to Top Rank in the selection of ring officials. Don King has been barred once again from promoting in Atlantic City. And Lennox Lewis's retirement leaves boxing without a standard bearer in its flagship division.

Lewis has made a graceful exit, which is rare in boxing. But there's a problem. Historically, a new heavyweight champion gains credibility by beating his predecessor. Now, whatever comes next, that won't happen. The WBC heavyweight title will be fought over by Vitali Klitschko and 38-year-old Corrie Sanders. Should Klitschko win, he'll rise to the top of most heavyweight rankings. But he still won't have a true championship victory to his credit.

Meanwhile, boxing's most bankable stars remain Oscar De La Hoya and Mike Tyson, neither of whom holds a title. Given the fact that four heavyweight belts are up for grabs, Tyson may fight soon for one of them. But Iron Mike is hardly the poster boy that the sport needs at the moment.

In other words, boxing has problems. And its downward spiral is accentuated by current happenings at HBO, Showtime, and ESPN.

Carlo Rotella wrote recently, "From ringside, you can see the signs of television's dominance of boxing. Bouts begin when the networks' schedule requires them to begin. Announcers, producers and technicians have a roped-off section of ringside to themselves. Camera operators with shoulder mounts stand outside the ropes on the ring apron, trailing cables behind them as they follow the action, interfering with the crowd's view of the fighters."

But if HBO, Showtime and ESPN dominate boxing, in recent years they have also supported it. Now that support might be wavering.

On September 8, 2003, Secondsout.com posted an article entitled *Is A Scandal Brewing At ESPN?* The very next night, ESPN2 televised what might have been its worst fight card ever. Earlier in the year, Jeremy Williams overwhelmed Andre Purlett. But against all apparent logic, ESPN turned down Williams versus Gerald Nobles in favor of Purlette versus Saul Montana and matched that fight with Audley Harrison versus TBA. Then Montana fell out and, four days before the fight, ESPN2 put together Purlett against Lionel Butler and Audley Harrison versus Quinn Navarre. Butler and Navarre were two of the deadest 36-year-old opponents ever seen in televised co-features. Butler had been knocked out six times and disqualified on three occasions. Navarre had been stopped eight times, including second-round losses at the hands of Ed Donaldson and Rodney McSwain.

If someone wants to make a case for the abolition of boxing, ESPN2's September 9th card would be a prime exhibit. Navarre never had a chin and was counted out the first time that Harrison hit him with a solid shot, which was 33 seconds into round three. Butler had fought ten days earlier and came in at 282 pounds. Purlett stopped him in two rounds. Viewers were also subjected to a shoving match between two women with a combined age of seventy-six and a combined weight of almost four hundred pounds. The most disgusting fight of the evening was a brutal beating administered to Thomas Grissom by Hicklet Lau. Lau had a record of 17-10-2. Grissom was 2 and 17. That's not a typographical error. To repeat, Grissom was 2 and 17.

Did the ongoing FBI probe change things for the better at ESPN?

Apparently not. On Friday, January 16, 2004, one week after news of the probe broke, Matt Vanda was given an outrageous split-decision victory over Sam Garr in a ten-round junior-middleweight bout that was promoted by Sugar Ray Leonard as the main event on ESPN2's *Friday Night Fights*. Garr dominated the bout, landing 254 punches to 144 for Vanda. ESPN commentator Teddy Atlas scored all ten rounds to Garr.

This fiasco came on the heels of ESPN announcing that it will no longer pay a rights fee for fights. Instead, it's offering a plan that calls for promoters to sell a minimum of $240,000 in sponsorships in exchange for four television dates. The promoter would receive twenty percent of the advertising revenue. This means that a promoter meeting the minimum sales level would receive $48,000 spread over four shows ($2,000 less than ESPN used to pay for one show). ESPN would keep the rest. Sugar Ray Leonard is the exception. His company will continue to receive a monthly license fee through the end of 2004 because of a pre-existing contract.

ESPN2 says that it intends to televise forty boxing cards in 2004, but none during the months of October, November and December. Given the absence of license fees, the quality of these fights is expected to be mediocre.

Showtime has scheduled *Showtime Championship Boxing* for the first Saturday of each month and hopes to supplement it with eighteen *ShoBox* and three pay-per-view cards. But the network is struggling and suffered a significant blow when Kosta Tszyu and James Toney were forced to pull out of what had been an attractive doubleheader slated for February 7th.

That, of course, leaves HBO, the most powerful force in boxing. HBO bankrolls most of the sport's superstars and, to a great degree, defines how the sweet science is presented to the public. It still televises some of the best fights in boxing. But in recent months, there have been strange happenings at the cable giant.

On August 16, 2003, HBO was scheduled to televise a championship doubleheader. The opener was slated to be undefeated WBO junior-bantamweight champion Fernando Montiel against former titleholder Mark "Too Sharp" Johnson. That was to have been followed by Derrick Gainer versus Juan Manuel Marquez in a featherweight title-unification bout. One week before the planned bouts, Gainer suffered a torn pectoral muscle. As a substitute, promoter Lou DiBella suggested a heavyweight match-up between Juan Carlos Gomez and Erik Kirkland. Gomez, a former WBC cruiserweight champion, was undefeated in 36 bouts with 31 knockouts. Kirkland was 17-1 with 13 KOs. HBO said no. Next, DiBella offered two more heavyweights: Samuel Peter (14-0 with 13 knockouts) against Attila Levin (27-1 with 21 KOs). HBO said no again.

Then HBO accepted light-punching Marcos Licona as an opponent for Marquez in a ten-round non-title bout. Licona had lost two of his previous four fights and won only twice in the preceding thirty months. He arrived at the weigh-in weak and dehydrated with an icepack pressed against the back of his neck and tipped the scales at 133 pounds, six pounds over the contract weight. Marquez was a well-conditioned 127. The Mohegan Sun boxing commission then ruled that the fight could not proceed because the fighters were separated by too much weight and Marquez objected to the weight differential. The solution? Licona gave Marquez $30,000 out of his $85,000 purse. Marquez then drank two bottles of water, put on his sweatpants, and weighed in at 132.

Marquez versus Licona, when it took place the following night, had the intensity of a sparring session. In the first round, the crowd started booing. In round two, there were shouts of "Boring! Boring!" Licona quit on his stool after round nine. At the time, all three judges had the bout scored 90-80 in favor of Marquez.

HBO lowered its standards to make Marquez-Licona. The reason? Marquez is promoted by Bob Arum. And a lot of people believe that HBO's fight schedule is now dictated in part by a screw up.

Last year, HBO aired a twelve-part series entitled *Legendary Nights* highlighting its thirty years of boxing. Unfortunately, it forgot to license relevant fight footage before the programs were put together. The two main beneficiaries of this snafu were Main Events and Top Rank.

Pat English, the attorney for Main Events, acknowledges, "HBO made the documentaries without getting the rights. We were in the same situation as Arum. We decided to ask for what we would have asked for if we hadn't had HBO over a barrel. We didn't get dates as such, but there was a license fee and also some promotional considerations."

Arum wasn't as kind as Main Events. Thus, in the forseeable future, fight fans might be watching some match-ups on HBO that the network would not normally telecast. Or as one HBO insider put it, "Once the mix-up happened, there were ways to remedy the situation other than raping the core product of HBO Sports. But instead of dealing directly with the situation and paying a straight license fee for the footage, HBO entered into a deal that lets Arum put on crap with bring-your-own opponents."

That view was born out by the Top Rank fights that HBO televised on January 31, 2004. They constituted one of the worst *Boxing After Dark* cards ever. In the opener, IBF bantamweight title-holder Rafael Marquez faced off against Pete Frissina. Then WBO welterweight champion Antonio Margarito took on Hercules Kyvelos. Everyone in boxing with the possible exception of senior management at HBO knew going in that both fights were mismatches. True to form, both bouts ended with second-round knockouts. It was left to Larry Merchant (bless him) to tell viewers afterward, "These weren't serious fights. We're used to seeing competitive fights. This was junk."

HBO might try its hand at damage control by claiming that it was using the January 31st card to build Margarito and Marquez for the future. But in the past, when the network built stars like Arturo Gatti and Marco Antonio Barrera on *Boxing After Dark*, it did so through competitive fights. The only good thing to be said honestly about HBO's January 31st telecast came later from Jim Lampley, who declared, "My grandmother always told me, 'If you can't be interesting, be brief.' So I suppose we should be thankful that both fights together were shorter than Bernard Hopkins against Morrade Hakkar."

But there's a more important issue to be addressed than particular fights on a given night. Ratings for boxing are dropping at HBO. And the two men at the top of the HBO organizational chart—chairman Chris Albrecht and chief operating officer Bill Nelson—reportedly aren't as fond of boxing as their predecessors. Thus, there are two schools of thought with regard to the future.

"I'm optimistic," says Larry Merchant. "But the truth is, I'm a pathological Pollyanna."

And then there's the always-quotable Lou DiBella, who expresses the view, "Boxing has always been a filthy business. What concerns me now is that it's a filthy dying business."❑

If boxing is to flourish, its economic model must change.

THE FUTURE OF BOXING AND THE INTERNET

The major media has largely abandoned boxing. Twenty years ago, virtually every big-city newspaper had a writer whose primary responsibility was to cover boxing. Now some newspapers haven't staffed a fight since Lewis-Tyson. Many newspapers don't even print the results of championship fights anymore.

As the major media has marginalized the sweet science, the Internet has stepped into the void. Boxing's power brokers would like to see coverage of their fights in *The New York Times* or *Sports Illustrated*. But they can't get it, so they go to the Internet.

"Boxing," says Jay Larkin of Showtime, "is on life support, and the Internet is the IV-line that's keeping it alive."

It has been said that boxing is such a chaotic mess that it belongs on the Internet. Be that as it may, it's clear that no other sport is as interwoven with the Internet as boxing. The medium has become critical to the sport's ability to hold onto its current fan base and attract the next generation of boxing enthusiasts.

The primary role of the Internet in boxing today is as an information medium. It's the most important vehicle for fans to collect data and also the primary means of communication within the boxing industry. The first thing that many people in boxing do when they settle down to work in the morning is go online to one or more websites. The Internet has become boxing's equivalent of *Variety* and *Backstage*.

Overall, boxing is covered well on the Internet. Promoters, sanctioning organizations, television networks, even fighters, have their own websites. But the key components of Internet boxing coverage are the many independent sites. There's an immediacy to their reporting. Links to the mainstream press allow fans to read virtually every print article about the sport on the day it's published. And most important, virtually every big story about boxing in the past few years has broken on the Internet and been covered more comprehensively on the Internet than in the mainstream press.

Boxrec.com is an invaluable resource when it comes to verifying the records of fighters and their past opponents. Boxingtalk and

Cyberboxingzone are two more of many sites that have carved out a niche. But in recent years, four websites have separated themselves from the pack.

Internet statistics are unreliable due to technological variations (e.g. some sites measure pop-up ads as hits) and puffery (i.e. exaggeration and outright lies). However, everyone agrees that Fightnews.com is the most heavily-trafficked boxing website. There's little depth to its reporting, but the site serves as a useful ticker for each day's events.

TotalAction is the creation of Charles Jay, who has been involved with boxing for two decades as a writer, promoter, matchmaker, and booking agent. "The concept behind TotalAction," says Jay, "is to provide a sports and gaming portal with a lot of links." The Fight Page at TotalAction does just that. It's the best boxing links page on the Internet. Also, in May 2002, Jay began crafting a series of investigative articles under the heading *Operation Clean-Up*. Seven months later, *Operation Clean-Up* #2 followed. These articles offer a comprehensive look at many of the problems that ail boxing today.

Maxboxing went online in March 2001. Its principals are Gary Randall, Doug Fisher, Tom Gerbasi, and Steve Kim. The site offers features written by a staff of twenty. But as Randall notes, "The bells and whistles of Maxboxing are our videos. Ninety percent of our users have DSLs or cable modems, and we give them what they want."

Secondsout has extensive feature writing and particularly strong European coverage. It's the creation of English businessman Robert Waterman, who says of his venture, "I was more of a fan than in the boxing business. And I was disenchanted with the quality of information that was available about boxing, so I decided to set up a website."

Secondsout was launched on July 11, 2000. "We had very good traffic in Britain from the start," Waterman remembers. "But our penetration in the United States was weak. So to improve our demographics, we acquired Boxingpress.com, which was eventually folded into Secondsout."

Secondsout now runs first in the United Kingdom and second to Fightnews in the rest of Europe in terms of visitor traffic. Maxboxing runs second in the United States. Meanwhile, since starting the website, Waterman has begun to promote and manage fighters and has a multi-fight contract with the BBC. But his agreement with the Secondsout editorial board stipulates that he has no editorial control and can only intervene to alter the content of an article if there are legal considerations such as the fear of libel.

The current FBI probe of boxing is a defining time for boxing coverage on the Internet. The mainstream press has largely ignored, and sometimes misreported, the burgeoning scandal. That means there's a huge opportunity for Internet boxing writers. But with opportunity comes responsibility, and that highlights a major problem.

There's little quality control on the Internet. Newspapers have editors; television has producers. All major media have fact-checking procedures that, in theory, ensure accuracy and fairness. But there are virtually no checks and balances with regard to Internet writing. People can put whatever they want online.

Thus, the Internet today features some of the best and the some of the worst commentary imaginable on boxing. The quality of online coverage varies from careful fact-based ethical reporting to reckless uninformed irresponsible tirades fueled by personal bias.

By and large, Internet writers care about their work. They take their jobs very seriously. But just because someone is a diehard fan doesn't mean that he or she has the skill, training, and ethics to be a good writer. And some boxing websites seem to live by the creed, "Punish your enemies; reward your friends; get it out first and forget about the other side."

Also, there's another problem associated with boxing websites. Economics.

Boxing is the only major sport in the world where anyone can just walk in and be a player. Do you want to be a promoter? A manager? A trainer? A fighter? No problem.

It's the same with starting an Internet boxing website. The barriers to entry are negligible. In some cases, a site can be established for less than a thousand dollars. That means there's a glut of websites on the market competing for the same scarce dollars.

A question often asked of boxing website entrepreneurs is, "Where does your revenue come from?" Often, the answer is, "There is no revenue."

Five years ago, most people thought that the way to make money from a boxing website was through advertising. But virtually no one believes that now; and at present, no one is getting rich by running a boxing website. The advertising simply isn't there. Nor has the Internet proven effective in selling fight tickets or boxing-related merchandise. Often, the cost of servers (especially broadband capacity) outstrips revenue. And that's not even factoring in the cost of whatever staff exists.

In October 2001, Maxboxing activated a membership program that costs subscribers five dollars a month. Best estimates are that the site now has 4,000 members. But because of the nature of its content, Maxboxing has higher fixed costs than its competitors.

Thus, the most significant economic attribute of the Internet is its potential to become a platform for pay-per-view boxing. It's possible that, in the not-too-distant future, the Internet will become part of the fabric of boxing in the same way that cable television is now.

The first significant fight to be televised on pay-per-view was Buster Douglas versus Evander Holyfield on October 25, 1990. That fight was distributed to public venues via closed-circuit and to private homes via pay-per-view. Then, on April 19, 1991, HBO launched TVKO with Holyfield versus George Foreman. At the time, 16,500,000 homes in the United States were addressable by pay-per-view.

Holyfield-Foreman got people's attention. From a fan's perspective, championship fights could now be viewed in the comfort of one's home with a clear picture and audio that could be heard. Multiple viewers were able to enjoy the show for the price of one. And most significantly from the industry's point of view, Holyfield-Foreman engendered 1,400,000 pay-per-view buys, which translated into $53,000,000 in revenue. "That night," says Mark Taffet of HBO, "was the night the pay-per-view business was born."

There are now 50,000,000 homes in the United States that can be accessed by pay-per-view. 30,000,000 of these are addressable by cable and 20,000,000 by satellite television.

When pay-per-view sales first became a significant factor in the boxing industry, HBO, Showtime, and other distributors (such as promoters) would negotiate separate deals with each cable system operator to determine a suggested retail price, cooperative advertising, and the division of revenue for each fight. Then, over time, two entities emerged as clearing houses through which pay-per-view telecasts were distributed to cable system operators. One of these clearing houses was Viewers Choice, which transmitted the signal for fights and negotiated a package deal on a fight-by-fight basis on behalf of the cable system operators it represented. The other was Request Television, which simply transmitted the signal and let the distributor negotiate terms directly with each individual cable system operator. Ultimately, Viewers Choice and Request merged to form In Demand. In Demand is the conduit through which virtually all cable-TV pay-per-view telecasts now flow to cable system operators.

Meanwhile, over the years, local cable system operators have merged to form communications giants. Three major multi-system operators now control 22,000,000 of the 30,000,000 homes addressable by cable for pay-per-view telecasts in the United States. They are Comcast (12,000,000 homes), Time Warner Cable (6,000,000), and Cox Communications (4,000,000). Cablevision is a distant fourth with 2,000,000 homes.

Cablevision is the only major cable system that does not book pay-per-view telecasts through In Demand. All totalled, In Demand serves ninety percent of the addressable pay-per-view homes in the United States. More than coincidentally, In Demand is owned by Comcast, TimeWarner, and Cox Communications.

Direct-TV and Echo Star transmit pay-per-view content via satellite and are analogous to the cable companies, not In Demand.

In Demand represents its own interests and, to a lesser degree, the interests of the cable system operators. When a distributor negotiates with In Demand, it negotiates (1) satellite time for the event in question; (2) a suggested minimum retail price; and (3) the marketing support to be provided by cable system operators. But the most significant part of the negotiation is how the suggested retail price will be divided among In Demand, the distributor, and cable system operators.

As a general rule, where pay-per-view fights are concerned, the cable system operator receives fifty percent of gross revenue from pay-per-view sales. In Demand gets ten percent, and the program provider gets forty percent. That's subject to negotiation. The bigger a fight, the more leverage the distributor has. Every cable system operator wanted Lennox Lewis versus Mike Tyson. "Latin Fury" is a tougher sell. But if a program provider tries to cut In Demand's share too much, In Demand counters with other terms that the provider can't live with.

In most areas of the United States today, cable television is a regulated monopoly. The primacy of In Demand has implications that go far beyond boxing and raises the spectre of serious antitrust violations at the heart of how the cable-television industry operates today.

"In Demand is an illegal monopoly," says Don King. "Everybody in the business knows that."

He might be right. And if boxing promoters are looking for a common cause, they might look more closely at how In Demand controls their access to the public. It should also be noted that In Demand raises issues of vertical as well as horizontal monopolization. For example, HBO Pay-Per-View (which is part of Time Warner) bankrolls and distributes fights. The fights are sold to cable system operators through In Demand (which is owned in significant part by Time Warner). Then the fights are seen by much of the country on Time Warner Cable.

And . . . oh, yes. In Demand insists upon the restriction of Internet transmissions in virtually every pay-per-view contract that it negotiates with HBO and Showtime. That, in turn, limits the financial incentive that might otherwise exist for third parties to develop the technology and marketing programs necessary to sell boxing over the Internet.

The Internet has the potential to significantly change the business of boxing. The sweet science has long been on the cutting edge of techno-logical innovation. It was the first sport to capture the imagination of the American people on radio. Interest in newsreel footage, television, closed-circuit television, and pay-per-view followed. The transmission of fights on the Internet might be next.

In ten years, it will be common technology for people to watch Internet transmissions on their television sets through high-speed modems with the same picture quality as they enjoy now on regular television.

At present there are roughly 100,000,000 households in the United States. Only half of them are addressable by pay-per-view. The Internet has the potential to reach the other 50,000,000. Moreover, cable televi-sion companies are regional, no matter how large their region might be. The Internet is global. More than any other communications medium, it constitutes a truly worldwide market.

There are significant technological hurdles to surmount before pay-per-view boxing on the Internet becomes a profitable reality. But the Internet has revolutionized facets of American life ranging from the sex industry to politics.

In the past, boxing promoters have often been responsible for tech-nological advances in marketing their sport. And Internet boxing is of great potential interest to promoters. It would cut production costs. It would break the stranglehold on pay-per-view transmissions currently enjoyed by In Demand, Direct-TV, and Echo Star. And most signifi-cantly, it would eliminate the need for local cable-system operators. That means there would be no need to pay the cable companies fifty cents on every dollar of pay-per-view revenue.

No wonder Comcast, Time Warner, and Cox seem adverse to Internet boxing.

If pay-per-view boxing on the Internet becomes a reality, HBO, Showtime, ESPN, and other big players can be expected to dominate. But there will always be niche players. Virtually any promoter would be able to disseminate a pay-per-view show. That, in turn, could help small promoters break even or make a small profit on local cards. And some of the better-known boxing websites might be acquired at a handsome profit for their owner-investors.

In other words, the Internet has the potential to help boxing survive and prosper. To make money from the sweet science, one should go where the fans are. And right now, that's on the Internet.❑

ROUND 4

CURIOSITIES

*I won't say that I have a better chance of beating Lennox Lewis
in the ring than across a chess board. But it's close.*

CHESS WITH THE CHAMP

I felt like Al Malcolm, Noel Quarless, or one of those other anonymous club fighters who fought Lennox Lewis early in his career must
have felt as they were led out of the dressing room to slaughter.

I was about to play chess with Lennox Lewis.

When I was young, I'd played chess with friends. I wasn't bad, but I
wasn't particularly good either. And more to the point, I hadn't played
in twenty-five years. That meant there was considerable ring rust on my
game, and now I was staring across the board at a regular.

Lennox sat in an armchair, looking very cerebral and relaxed. He was
wearing jeans, a dark-blue sweatshirt and running shoes, and appeared
to be slightly over his fighting weight. This is a good time in his life. His
future is financially secure and he's planning both marriage and fatherhood.

The site of our encounter was a spacious office suite in midtown
Manhattan that serves as Lennox's workplace when he's in New York.
Lennox's personal office has a desk, sofa, several chairs, and a small
round table just the right size and height for a chess board.

"I learned to play chess in Canada, in public school when I was fifteen years old," Lennox told me. "Over time, my game improved
because of boxing. I had a trainer in the amateurs named Adrian
Teodorescu. He took me on trips to boxing tournaments and we'd play
chess to pass the time. Adrian was quite good. Now I play as often as I
can."

But only against people.

"I don't like playing against computers," Lennox continued. "You
can't distract a computer and a computer doesn't make mistakes. A lot
of this game is psychological, and it's impossible to get inside a computer's head."

Last year, Lewis played more than a hundred games of chess. "Many
of them were in training camp," he reminisced "With side bets for push-
ups against friends who felt that their skills were superior to mine."

"I honestly don't like him playing chess," Lennox's trainer, Emanuel

237

Steward, had said at the time. "I see him sitting there for ten minutes, thinking four moves ahead before he makes one. And he actually does the same thing in the ring; he thinks too much."

"I disagree with Emanuel," Lennox said prior to our own game. "The thought processes of chess are similar to boxing. You look at an opponent and what he does and then you devise a strategy to beat him."

"Chess has been here for a thousand years." Lennox continued. "It's a game for thinkers and there's a lot of strategy involved. Chess shows the power of the mind; it opens different doors in the mind; and without it, I might not use that part of my mind. Those things appeal to me. It's one of the reasons I'm teaching my fiancee how to play chess. She's just starting to learn now how the pieces move."

"How good are you?" I queried.

"Not bad. I haven't taken it seriously to the point of trying to become ranked. I use it purely for recreation. But I don't just play chess; I'm a chess player."

The first few moves of our competition were a feeling out process as Lennox satisfied himself that he wasn't sitting across the board from a ringer. In chess, as in boxing, one mistake can turn the competition around in a hurry. Lose a key exchange early and it's like fighting with blood dripping into your eye for the entire night.

Six moves into our game, Lennox took one of my knights at the cost of a mere pawn. The exchange reminded me of how Muhammad Ali used to go into a clinch early in a fight to test his oppponent's physical strength. When Ali fought Jean-Pierre Coopman in 1976, they clinched in the first minute and Muhammad came out of the clinch laughing. Then, after the first round, he leaned over the ring ropes and shouted down at a network television executive, "You guys are in trouble. Ain't no way you're gonna get all your commercials in."

The tone for Lewis versus Hauser was now set. Lennox attacking; me on the defensive, throwing an occasional punch, trying to land something but expecting to be knocked out.

I moved my queen to the middle of the board in the hope of establishing an offensive.

"Interesting," Lennox commented.

Then I brought my remaining knight into play.

"Not bad," Lennox noted.

And then something marvelous happened. The chess board began to look more even to me.

"Nice move," Lennox complimented. "Very good . . ."

We traded pawns twice, and I exchanged a rook for a Lennox Lewis bishop and knight. Now I felt like a club fighter who thinks that maybe he has a chance to beat the champion after all.

"Who do you think Wladimir Klitschko should fight after Lamon Brewster?" Lennox queried.

"You're trying to distract me."

Whack!

My queen went down.

Then Lennox started reading a newspaper between moves, which is the equivalent of a fighter eating Chinese food between rounds.

The outcome was no longer in doubt.

There are no decisions in chess, only knockouts and draws. This one had all the makings of a knockout. If our chess game had been a fight, the referee would have stepped in and stopped it at that point.

Lennox's queen was in my face like a poleaxing jab. Next, the heavy right hands started landing. In truth, I was obliterated. But like a fighter, I went out on my shield.

Forty minutes after we'd begun, Lennox leaned forward in his chair and smiled. "Checkmate," he said.❑

In early summer 2004, shortly after the birth of his son, Lennox Lewis and I engaged in an intensely personal dialogue regarding Lennox's childhood and how it shaped his view of fatherhood.

LENNOX LEWIS AND THE ROAD TO FATHERHOOD

Lennox Lewis is a father. Landon Lewis was born on June 15, 2004, and weighed in at eight-pounds-two-ounces.

Lennox is an English and Canadian citizen. Landon was born in the United States and is an American citizen.

The birth of his first child signals the start of the next stage in the former champion's life. A hard life has turned into a dream world.

The saga of Lennox Lewis begins with his mother. Violet Lewis (her maiden name) was born on May 10, 1938, on the island of Jamaica. Her father was a laborer. Her mother worked occasionally as a household domestic. Violet was one of twelve children. When she was young, she lived with her Aunt Gee. Then Gee married, and Violet was sent to live with another aunt. "I can't recall ever living at home with my brothers and sisters," she told Lennox's biographer, Ken Gorman, in 1992. "I hardly knew my mum and dad."

In 1956, Violet moved to London, where Aunt Gee had relocated with her husband. She lived briefly with Gee, then in a succession of rented rooms in tenement houses, and found work as a nurse's aid. On April 27, 1962, her first child (Dennis Stephen) was born. The father was Rupert Daries, a Jamaican who was working as a swimming instructor in London. Soon after the birth, Violet returned to work on a night shift at the hospital.

"Rupert was good to us," she later acknowledged. "I liked him as a brother, but I didn't love him. You think, if you don't love him at first, if you live together, you may grow to love him. But it never happened like that."

Then Carlton Brooks, another Jamaican living in London, entered her life. "We met at a party," Violet told Gorman. "I was madly in love with him, though we never lived together. It turned out that he was married, but I didn't know [Brooks had a wife and family in Jamaica]. He never told me he was married. He strung me along. Then, when I told him I was pregnant with Lennox, he said, 'I'm sorry, Vi. I'm married and I can't marry you.' It was a great shock for me. He was the only man I really really cared for. I would have married him. It made me very sad."

As a single mother who already had one child, Violet contemplated terminating her pregnancy. She even scheduled an appointment for an abortion, but couldn't bring herself to go through with the procedure. On September 2, 1965, in the East End section of London, her second son, Lennox Claudius Lewis, was born.

"I have fond memories of being young," Lennox says today. "I was generally a happy child. My earliest memory from childhood is of a rocking-horse that I used to sit on for hours at a time."

But those pleasant hours became fewer and further in between. When Lennox was four, Violet uprooted their home. She was still deeply depressed over the loss of Carlton and decided to start her life over somewhere else. Thus, she sent Dennis to live with his father (who had since married), left Lennox with Aunt Gee, and moved to Chicago in the hope of setting up a home in the United States for Lennox and herself. But she didn't have a proper visa, couldn't get regular work, and returned to England a year later. Meanwhile, Lennox had begun acting out in school and was expelled after getting into a series of fights and badly slashing his own arm by punching his hand through a window in the door to the principal's office.

"I was six years old," Lennox says of the incident. "I had a temper to begin with. And I was angry that I was in trouble and they were talking about expelling me and I didn't know why."

Next, Violet moved to Ontario with Lennox but, after six months, sent him back to England. She was still mired in depression; the school fees and rent were more than she could afford; and there was barely enough money to feed herself, let alone a growing boy.

Thus began a five-year separation between mother and son. Lennox stayed with Aunt Gee at first and then in two boarding schools that it was hoped would curb his behavior. "I was never in trouble with the law," he notes. "The boarding schools were run by the state and were for kids who were hard to manage and were having trouble at home."

Meanwhile, Violet took a job on an assembly line in a factory in Kitchener, Ontario. "I cried every day for those five years," she recalls. "They used to call me 'weeping willow.'" And Lennox looks back on their separation with the thought, "There was anxiety. I felt like I was out there by myself and I missed my mother."

Finally, in 1977 when Lennox was twelve years old, Violet sent for him. They hadn't seen each other in five years. She later said of their reunion, "I knew it was him as soon as I saw him at the airport. He was big, but he'd always been big. I'd watched him growing in the photographs he'd sent me. I kissed him and kissed him. You know what boys are like at twelve. He didn't want people to see me kissing him, but I hugged him and kissed him anyway."

"When we reunited, there was such a noise," Lennox remembers. "Loud happiness. 'Oh, my baby! My baby!' She gave me a kiss that went on for so long that I didn't think it was ever going to stop. I was a bit embarrassed, but I was also very happy to see her and the feeling that came over me was indescribable. There's something about being around your mother. A mother gives off a special kind of love. Right away, my energy became stronger."

Soon after arriving in Canada, Lennox started boxing. "And at the same time," he says, "I began to understand my circumstances and my anger better because the people I was around made an effort to understand me and they understood conflict. Arnie Boehm [Lennox's amateur boxing coach] became a father figure to me. He took me in hand and gave me guidance. Kids need that; kids want that."

Lennox's subsequent success in the ring has been well-catalogued. An Olympic gold medal . . . Undisputed heavyweight champion of the world . . . "My object was to be the best as long as I was in boxing," he says. "But it took a long time for me to gain acceptance as a champion. The Brits were saying, 'You're not our champion. Frank Bruno is our champion. He's a lovely guy.' The Canadians were mad at me because I left Canada, so they were saying, 'Oh, well, he was never any good anyway.' And the Americans all said, 'British heavyweights are horizontal heavyweights. Only an American can be the best.' But the belief I had in myself kept me going. And I put a lot of things I wanted to do in life on hold so I could stay focussed on boxing."

One of those deferred experiences was fatherhood.

"I vowed a long time ago," Lennox says, "that I would never be one of those fathers with a whole bunch of kids all over the place. When Landon was born, some of my friends told me, 'You're a man now.' But having a child doesn't make you a man. Being a good father makes you a man."

That thought has particular resonance where Lennox's own natural father is concerned.

"I saw Carlton from time to time when I was a child," Lennox recalls. "Sometimes he'd come by and take me to school, but there wasn't much more. The last time I saw him was in 1983. I was in England. He came to visit and said he'd like to have more contact with me. It was awkward for both of us. He's made efforts to contact me since then, but it's the same old story. I've seen a number of athletes go through it. You become famous, and then the father says, 'That's my son,' and wants back into your life. And my thing is, 'Where were you before I became famous?'"

As for his own son, Lennox says, "I don't want Landon to be a fighter. But if it's his choice, I'd allow it. My wish is that he be a lawyer or a doctor, but he can be whatever he wants to be."

"I'm looking forward to the responsibilities of fatherhood," Lennox says of his new role. "Landon comes into the world completely vulnerable with no ability to make choices. I'm one of the two people most responsible for shaping his life, and I'm looking forward to protecting him and making the early decisions that guide him. I want to teach Landon how to give. I want to give him a base so he knows the difference between right and wrong because values are the key to life. I won't be there for him forever and I won't be able to control him for long. But I want to give him the foundation to make his own choices. I ask myself all the time, 'If I were to die tomorrow, what would I want my child to know?'"

Meanwhile, Lennox notes, "I'm up at all hours. I'm changing diapers. It's a learning experience. I didn't realize that one baby could go through so many diapers in twenty-four hours. But every day brings something new. Landon is starting to recognize me now. If he's crying, as soon as I hold him, he calms down. And if a stranger holds him, he makes a fuss. He kicked his leg the other day and smiled for the first time. I want to be there for each moment of growth."

"I want everything for my son that I missed out on and wanted to do when I was young," Lennox continues. "The best education. A stable home. When I was growing up in Kitchener, we didn't have a lot of money but I had a picture on the wall in my bedroom of a house on top of a hill with three cars in the driveway. That was what I wanted out of life, although later I decided that I wanted a lot of land around the house too. I want to teach my son that everything is attainable if you're willing to sacrifice to reach your goal. But I also want him to understand the human condition. I want him to know about soup kitchens and homeless shelters and to have a social conscience. America and England are wealthy countries, but they have millions of children who are hungry, living in filthy homes, wearing filthy clothes with garbage all over the floor. You see pictures of them, and their mother is standing there smoking a cigarette. You can be poor and, at the same time, be poor and clean. And if you have enough money for cigarettes, you should be able to feed your children properly."

Violet Chang, Lennox's fiancee and the mother of his child, is Jamaican but grew up in the United States. They met when Lennox was on vacation in Jamaica four years ago.

"We're made for each other," Lennox says. "When you meet the right girl, you know. She's down to earth; there's no stress; it's not about diamonds and pearls. Our plan is to get married next year."

Why not now?

"It just feels like next year will be the right time," Lennox answers, "In essence, we're married already. We live like a married couple, and a marriage certificate won't change that. Look at J-Lo [Jennifer Lopez]. She's been through three marriages in the time my fiancee and I have been together. I plan on being married once; that's all. And there will be more children when the time is right."

Meanwhile, Lennox continues to guard his privacy, as he has done throughout his life.

"Privacy is important to me," he explains. "I know that some athletes' lives are open books, but I don't think the world has the right to know everything about me. My boxing life was always open. That's enough. I have no interest in my personal life becoming an ongoing soap opera or some kind of TV reality show. Halle Berry goes on *Oprah* and airs all her problems and tells the world she'll never get married again. Why? If you have problems, take them to a marriage counselor. Also," Lennox adds, "the other people in my life, my family and friends, have the right to their own private lives. Some of them might not want to pick up a newspaper and see their name or picture. They shouldn't be forced to give up their privacy just because I'm famous and they're with me."

There remains, of course, the question of Lennox's fistic future. In his retirement speech, delivered on February 6, 2004, he told the world, "I've been offered millions of dollars to fight again, which is all the more tempting because I believe that there are more championship-quality fights in me. In many ways, continuing to fight would be the easiest course of action."

Since then, Lennox has been offered in excess of $20,000,000 against a percentage of pay-per-view receipts to fight a rematch against Vitali Klitschko, whom he defeated in June 2003. And while he remains financially secure, he acknowledges, "In some ways, it's harder to keep money than it is to make it."

Lennox is still physically imposing. What kind of shape is he in today?

"Not bad," he answers.

How much does he weigh?

"I never had to make weight as a heavyweight, so why start weighing myself now?"

So will Lennox fight again?

"I told the world when I retired that I was no longer able to devote the same energy and desire to boxing that I felt from the start of my career," he says. "People don't understand how much it takes out of you to prepare properly for a fight. They'll never know what I went through physically and emotionally to get ready for Tyson and the second Rahman fight. I realized last year that I no longer had the passion to prepare for a fight the way I once did. And without that passion, I shouldn't enter the ring again."

Also, there's perhaps the most significant passage in Lennox's farewell speech. "I am particularly pleased to be stepping down while still the reigning lineal heavyweight champion," he told the world. "Only two other men, Gene Tunney and Rocky Marciano, have retired as champion and stayed retired. I promise you, I will be the third."

Thus, Lennox says firmly, "The money is tempting, but I'm not coming back. I'm fine with retirement. I haven't thought seriously about fighting again. There are things in life that are more important than money. That's one of the messages I hope to transmit to my son; and the best way to transmit it is by example. Boxing was good to me. But for every beginning, there's an end and another beginning. There's life after boxing."

And what will that life entail beyond marriage and fatherhood?

"Anything can happen," Lennox says in closing. "But I'm a positive person. I believe in treating people fairly; I believe in hard work; and I believe in love. I think good things will keep happening for me if I continue to live right."

Meanwhile, Lennox's mother still lives in Canada, but commutes regularly to the United States to visit her grandson. "Lennox is all grown up now," Violet Lewis says.

And her son says in return, "I hope that someday, when my son is a man, he feels as much love for me as I feel for my mum."❑

The eightieth anniversary of Rocky Mariciano's birth was one of those touchstones that called for acknowledgement.

A BIRTHDAY GREETING FOR ROCKY MARCIANO

Hello, Rocky. Big day coming up. On September 1st, you'll be eighty years old. A lot has happened since that small plane you were on crashed in 1969. You were forty-six years old then; too young to die. But we've kept you alive in our hearts, and the birthday celebrations will be starting soon.

So let's note for the record that you were born in Brockton, Massachusetts, the son of a shoe-factory worker, in 1923. Twenty-nine years later, you knocked out Jersey Joe Walcott to become heavyweight champion of the world. The punch you ended it with that night is one of the most devastating blows in boxing lore. You defended your title six times. "What could be better," you once asked, "than walking down any street in any city and knowing you're the heavyweight champion of the world?"

Then, after forty-nine victories in forty-nine fights, you did something that no one has done before or since. You retired, and stayed retired, as undefeated heavyweight champion of the world.

People say that, to be great, a fighter has to be an honest workman. And you were. You trained hard. Charlie Goldman, your trainer, described you with the declaration, "I gotta guy who's short, stoop-shouldered, and balding with two left feet. They all look better than he does as far as the moves are concerned, but they don't look so good on the canvas. God, how he can punch."

That was the ticket. Even though you were small for a heavyweight, you beat men down. In the ring, you moved forward with a will of iron, arms pounding, throwing punches from every angle, anxious to make contact with any part of your opponent's body to see which of you could give and take more pain.

Ed Fitzgerald, one of the leading sportswriters of your day, wrote, "Rocky is not in there to outpoint anybody with an exhibition of boxing skill. He is in there to kill or be killed. He is a primitive fighter who stalks his prey until he can belt him with that frightening right-hand crusher. He is one of the easiest fighters in the ring to hit. You can, as with an enraged grizzly bear, slow him down and make him shake his head if you hit him hard enough to wound him, but you can't make him back up. Slowly, relentlessy, ruthlessly, he moves in on you. Sooner or later, he clubs you down."

Budd Schulberg put it nicely when he wrote, "Marciano is the master of no defense, who moves in swinging punches like all the club fighters of all time."

But you were great when you had to be great. After a man fought you, it was said, he was never the same.

A man has to be a bit crazy to be a fighter, and you qualified. Jim Murray once opined that you lived life as if it were the fifteenth round and you were behind on points. There was an endless stream of women. Early in your career, your manager Al Weill said, "Rocky is a poor Italian boy from a poor Italian family, and he appreciates the buck more than almost anybody. He's only got two halfway decent purses so far, and it was like a tiger tasting blood." After boxing, most of your business ventures involved cash. Word is, you even did a bit of loansharking and were on friendly social terms with the mob.

Then there's the matter of black and white. Looking at all the WBA, WBC and IBF titleholders since you retired, there have been thirty-four claimants to the heavyweight crown. Only two, Ingemar Johansson and Gerrie Coetzee, were white. John Ruiz is Hispanic. These three will never be mistaken for you or Jack Dempsey. Johannson lost in his first title defense. Coetzee and Ruiz were shortlived paper champions during the reigns of Larry Holmes and Lennox Lewis.

In other words, you were the last white heavyweight who would have been favored over any other fighter in the world. I'm not saying that's the way people should think; and in an ideal world, they wouldn't think that way. But let's be honest; in boxing, as in the rest of society, color is an issue.

Despite all the praise that was showered upon you, there were critics. Some opponents complained that, too often, your rough brawling style degenerated to dirty. And the great fighters you beat were getting on in years when you fought them. Joe Louis was thirty-seven. Jersey Joe Walcott was thirty-eight. Ezzard Charles was thirty-three with the wear and tear of a hundred fights on him. Archie Moore was forty-one and had answered the bell for round one almost two hundred times.

Still, a half-century after your retirement from boxing, your unblemished record stands. In other sports, magic numbers come and go. Look at baseball . . . 60 . . . 714 . . . 2,130 . . . 4,191 . . . They're all gone. It's the way of the world. Standards for immortality change. But in the sweet science, the magic number remains "49".

I don't know how you'll celebrate your birthday. Rumor has it that you're planning to fight Jack Dempsey in a fifteen-round "Birthday Bash." What a fight that will be! I'd love to see it; although, all things considered, I'm happy to be alive and down here on Earth. Send me a videotape if you can.

Regards,
Thomas Hauser☐

Marilyn Cole Lownes and I collaborated on this article for The Observer Sports Monthly.

BOXING BLING-BLING

In January 2000, while in London to fight Julius Francis, Mike Tyson entered Graff Diamonds on Old Bond Street and embarked on a spending spree that could have changed the face of boxing, not to mention the face of boxing promoter Frank Warren. Tyson and Warren visited Graff together, and Iron Mike decided it would be nice to have a diamond-studded bracelet and two pocket watches, one of which was a pornographic automaton depicting a man and woman in the act of fornication. The store asked who would be paying the $800,000 bill. Warren said, "Not me." And Tyson announced, "Don't worry, I'll get Showtime to pay for it."

Showtime thought that was a bad idea. Thus, several days later, Tyson was told by his advisor, Shelly Finkel, that he had to give the jewelry back or face charges that it was stolen. Tyson gave the jewelry to Finkel and, in a fit of rage, stomped out of his hotel, took a limousine to the airport; and announced he was going home. At that point, Finkel and Warren agreed to get the bracelet for Tyson and arrange for payment later in order to keep the fight alive. Properly placated, Tyson returned from the airport and went directly to the final pre-fight press conference, at which he wore the bracelet and ostentatiously twisted his wrist back and forth in front of his chin during most of the commentary.

After disposing of Francis in two rounds, Tyson went back to the United States. He returned to London in June 2000 prior to fighting Lou Savarese and thought it would be nice to revisit his favorite jewelry store. However, the good people at Graff told him that he was persona non grata because the store had yet to receive payment for his prior acquisition. Tyson left the store in a fit. Later in the day, he summoned Warren to his hotel suite. It was not a friendly chat. The next day, Warren appeared at a press conference sporting considerable make-up on one side of his face beneath a bloodshot eye. A generous financial settlement in Warren's favor in the neighborhood of $3,000,000 followed.

All for bling-bling.

In 1999, a 17-year-old-rapper from New Orleans named B.G. (Baby Gangsta) penned the lyric, "Can see my earring from a mile, bling-bling." B.G. didn't know it at the time, but he had just coined a term that would cross over from the ghetto into mainstream culture and onto the pages of fashion magazines on both sides of the Atlantic. "I just wish that I'd trademarked it," Mr. Gangsta said later, "so I'd never have to work again."

The wearing of bling-bling is both a fashion statement and a display of power. The sartorial rules are simple. Bigger and flashier are better.

"When you're successful now, you buy jewelry," says veteran trainer Emanuel Steward. "It's a jewelry generation."

In boxing, the most prestigious bling-bling is also the flashiest. The world championship belts that fighters sweat and bleed for resemble giant cigar bands. Generally, they are made of leather, decorated with large mirrored ornaments, and lavishly studded with gobs of fake rubies and diamonds.

Veteran HBO boxing commentator Larry Merchant recalls, "Aside from the belts, the first time I saw bling-bling around the fight game was when Muhammad Ali came back from exile to fight Jerry Quarry in Atlanta in 1970. It seemed like the entire black elite of America was there and also a large number of underworld thugs. They were hanging around with gold dripping off them. You couldn't miss it."

Then, in the mid-1970s, Don King came on the scene.

There are days when King resembles a shining apparition, draped in bling-bling that seems to reflect off everything from the top of his hair down to his black patent-leather shoes. A typical Don King press conference finds the tuxedo-clad promoter clutching an American flag in a hand graced by a 9-carat solitaire diamond set in a white gold ring. Next, one's eyes fall upon a diamond-studded platinum Rolex heavy enough to cause tendonitis. Or King might opt for his white gold "championship" ring with 10 carats of miscellaneous diamonds and his Harry Winston watch with 30 carats of diamonds on the bracelet.

King also owns assorted diamond-studded crucifixes and a two-inch-wide diamond bracelet with the initials "DK" set in rubies. And then there are his two famous crown-logo necklaces, the larger of which has a 4-carat diamond centerpiece and 36-inch necklace with bullet links fashioned from diamonds and white gold.

In sum, Don KIng wears more bling-bling than most movie stars on Oscar night. The difference is that King owns his jewels. He doesn't borrow them for show.

"I have an array of jewels," King acknowledges with pride. "But without question, my favorites are the crown necklaces, which were designed by my wonderful wife Henrietta. I love them because they're beautiful and because they're the symbol of kings and the symbol of my achievement and success. Jewelers come to me in droves," King says, continuing his electric, slightly manic patter. "They're always bringing me sacks filled with baubles and doo-dads, showing me their wares."

Many of King's jewels come from a man named Mordechai Yerushalmi, known to his customers simply as "Mordechai."

Mordechai's showroom is located on the wrong side of the tracks in a drab industrial section of downtown Las Vegas. Rooms in a nearby motel rent for thirty dollars a night. A block away, Cheetah's Topless Bar sells draught beer for a dollar.

Mordechai's showroom has a low polystyrene-tile ceiling. Autographed photos of show business luminaries like Tom Cruise, Joan Collins, Sharon Stone, and Sammy Davis Jr. line the walls. A boxing glove bears the legend, "Mordechai, From Mike Tyson, I need good deals."

The jewelry on display is unpretentious. The contents of one case are partially obscured by a large yellow-and-black sign that declares, "75% off all merchandise; this case only."

Mordechai, wearing a short-sleeved shirt and slacks, is equally unpretentious. Born in Israel, 58 years old, he came to Las Vegas in 1973 and now owns shops at Mandalay Bay, Caesars, The Paris, The Venetian, and the Hard Rock Hotel.

"When the fighters come into my store," Mordechai says, "they want one thing. Diamonds; big diamonds, lots of diamonds. They call it 'ice.' They come in with a Rolex or some other piece and say to me, 'Ice it.'"

Mordechai's premier boxing client at the moment is 135-pound world champion "Pretty Boy" Floyd Mayweather Jr. It's no accident that the first thing one sees upon entering the showroom is a large poster of the 27-year-old Mayweather wearing bejeweled boxing gloves on either hand.

Mayweather is the new poster child for boxing bling-bling. On the road, an assistant carries the jewels that Floyd isn't wearing in an unobtrusive black leather attache case. If one asks to see what's inside and Mayweather is in the mood, the contents are revealed. Like a pirate reaching into a treasure chest, he brandishes myriad gold chains, pendants, watches, bracelets, and rings; most of them gold and platinum with large-carat diamonds embedded within. Clearly, "Pretty Boy" likes pretty things.

Mayweather's prize piece is a "Ferrari horse" fashioned by Mordechai. It has blocks of black, white, and yellow diamonds; more than 600 of them totalling 120 carats in an invisible setting. The horse took more than three months to make and cost Mayweather $180,000.

"I'm the master," says Mayweather. "I know all about jewelry. People say I'm cocky and arrogant, but I say I'm confident and slick. And my lifestyle is flashy and flamboyant. There's never too many diamonds."

Like Mayweather, 140-pound world champion Zab Judah is regarded by his peers in the sweet science as "ghetto-fabulous." When Zab smiles, he reveals a rim of thirteen glittering diamonds weighing eight carats that cover four of his front teeth.

"The stones are permanently attached," explains Judah. "My mouth-piece fits right over them and they fit my personality."

Zab was captivated by bling-bling as an adolescent and recalls an incident from his days as an amateur boxer. "I had a diamond earring," he says. "I felt it come off during a fight, so I started dancing around the ring during the middle of the round, looking down to see if I could find it on the canvas; but I never found it."

Judah owns necklaces, watches, bracelets, and rings; but his signature bling-bling is in his teeth. How does his smile compare with Don King's jewelry?

"No comparison," Zab answers. "My diamonds are better. I'm the only one in America with this."

And then, of course, there's the aforementioned Mike Tyson, whose love of "ice" contributed to his financial meltdown. Tyson spent millions of dollars each year on jewelry, as evidenced by papers filed in his current bankruptcy proceeding.

Tyson bought matching diamond-coated Piaget Galaxy watches from Mordechai for $800,000 and spent roughly $900,000 for a platinum "dog-tag" with "Tyson" spelt out in diamonds. On December 22, 2002, Iron Mike walked into Mordechai's showroom and left with a gold chain lined with 80 carats in diamonds worth $180,000. On his way out of the store, he told the owner, "Hey, Mordechai, you know I'm good for it."

"Knowing him for so long, I gave him the merchandise and knew he'd pay," Mordechai said later. "He had open credit with me. Compared to all the purchases he made with me over the years, it was very little."

When Tyson filed for bankruptcy protection from his creditors in August 2003, he listed the $180,000 as one of his debts.

Not all fighters are partial to bling-bling. Some opt for a more reserved look. "I have some nice jewelry, two sets of matching necklaces and bracelets," says former heavyweight champion Lennox Lewis. "And two watches: a Vacheron for its antiquity and a gold-and-silver Rolex for status. But where appearance is concerned, my thing is my suits."

As for his colleagues' motivation for wearing bling-bling, Lennox hypothesizes, "People wear it for different reasons. Some people like the jewels for what they are, but there are ulterior motives too. Don King wears it because it's part of his message. If he's seen to have millions, it makes you think that he can make millions for you too. Mike Tyson, I'm not a psychiatrist, but I have to think that, as a child, Mike never had toys to play with and now he's trying to fill some kind of void. With Mike, it's all for the moment. 'I want this one and this one and that one.' But whatever he buys, as soon as he has it, he stops caring about it and it's gone."

"For Floyd Mayweather," Lewis continues, "it's part of the image he's chosen for himself. It's his way of answering the question, 'How do I let people know that I've got all this money?' That's true of a lot of these guys. It's about status and showing people that you're making a lot of money. In that respect, it's no different from the private plane, the big house, the Bentley. It might not be as useful as those things, but the advantage to it is that you can take it everywhere with you to show off. They aren't wearing it for themselves. They're after a reaction from other people."

Lennox seems to be right on point.

Don King acknowledges, "If I wear diamonds, I get the ear of those within the system who are less fortunate than I am and who want to get to the top like I did. It's like the bait going on the hook for the fish. Young pugilists see the glitter and sparkle, and it draws them to me like a moth to a flame."

Meanwhile, Steve Lott (Mike Tyson's former roommate and assistant manager) recalls a time when, apart from a gold tooth, Iron Mike's only bling-bling was a gold necklace. "But Mike buys now to fill an emptiness inside," Lott posits. "He'll buy something and wear it for a week. Then the thrill is gone and he gives it away and forgets who he gave it to a day after he gave it to them."

Floyd Mayweather, on the other hand, covets his jewelery and adheres to the view, "If you've got it, flaunt it." He has been financially successful and wants people to know it. Thus, Mayweather's uncle and trainer, former world champion Roger Mayweather, reasons, "When you're young, you want to carry your success with you. No one would think twice if Floyd drove a nice car. But you can only drive one car at a time and you can wear all your jewelry together."

Showy materialism wasn't invented by boxers and urban rap artists. It has been ingrained in virtually every society. Gaudy jewelry might offend some people's sense of style. But former heavyweight champion and grilling-machine entrepreneur George Foreman is philosophical about today's craze for bling-bling.

"Old guys fall in love with their stuff and can't see the beauty of what young guys are doing," says Foreman. "You can't just take a picture from 1945 and have things look the same today."

But there are reasons that go beyond style to be concerned about the penchant of some fighters for bling-bling.

"I'm troubled when young men spend crazy amounts of money on overpriced gaudy shit that they don't insure," declares boxing promoter Lou Di Bella. "If you're making big money, first put enough of it away so you don't have to worry about money to live on for the rest of your life. Then, once your financial future is secure, you can go out and blow money on jewelry if that's what you want."

Sam Simon (who created *The Simpsons* and now manages WBO heavyweight champion Lamon Brewster) is in accord. "There's a culture that bites these guys in the ass," says Simon. "They're supposed to spend all their money on jewelry and cars and give stuff to their friends. And I feel bad about it because these guys have short careers. Even for the ones who make it to the top, the big money doesn't last long. And the idea they have that they can get money for their stuff if something goes wrong is nonsense. As a general rule, when these guys fall on hard times and try to sell whatever jewelry they bought that hasn't been given away or stolen from them, it brings in pennies on the dollar."

Unfortunately, that's true. Very few fighters adhere to the buying practices of Don King, who states, "I'm reluctant to treat dollars with reckless abandon, particularly when they're mine. You see, the Queen of England inherited her jewels, but I worked for mine. I wasn't born with a silver spoon in my mouth. So when faced with temptation, my number-one rule is, 'Keep common sense.' Too often, they give you something that's big and shiny and you think it's worth a lot and it's worth nothing."

Still, the lure of bling-bling remains strong and seems to be seeping down to the next generation.

"It's style man," enthuses Paulie Malignaggi, a promising junior-welterweight from New York with a 17-0 record to go with assorted rings, earrings, necklaces, and watches. "As a fighter, I represent something flashy in the ring, and I want to keep that image going. Shine in the ring; shine out of it. I want to stand out. Right now, I've got a lot of gold. But as the money comes in, you'll see platinum and the diamonds will be real."❑

In 2003, I wrote a column in which a dozen boxing luminaries reminisced about the first professional fight they saw. That led to a flood of memories from others in the boxing community.

FIRST FIGHT REVISITED

AL GAVIN

The first time I saw a professional fight, the memory that really stays with me, was watching Joe Louis on television through the window of a TV store on Fulton Street in Brooklyn. It was 1948. Louis was fighting Jersey Joe Walcott for the second time, and he knocked Walcott out in the second round. All my life, I'd heard about Joe Louis, and there he was. Not long after that, my uncle took me to see Jimmy Hering fight at Ridgewood Grove in Queens. Hering was a club fighter who lived in our neighborhood. He was pretty good but never made it to the bigtime. I was very excited that night. I remember, at the door to the arena, my uncle bought me a copy of *Ring Magazine*. Charlie Fusari was on the cover. It was the first time I'd ever seen *Ring Magazine*. Then we went inside and my uncle asked if I wanted peanuts. I told him, "What do I want peanuts for? I'm here to see fights." Anyway, Hering fought Aldo Minelli and lost a decision, but I had a great time.

JAMES TONEY

I was fourteen years old. Greg Owens took me. He was my first amateur coach and like a surrogate father to me. I'd been boxing with him for about six months. The fights were at The Olympia in Detroit. Willie Edwards and Alvin Hayes [two Kronk fighters] were on the card. There were a lot of knockouts and it was incredible. The whole place smelled of boxing, blood, and guts. I loved it.

STEVE SMOGER

I remember it well because it was one of the most exciting nights of my life. My dad took me to see Jersey Joe Walcott defend his title against Rocky Marciano. I was seven years old. We lived in New Jersey, and I was rooting for Walcott because of his name. We lived in the same state. Early in the fight, Walcott put Marciano down with a gorgeous shot, and I was in heaven. But Rocky wore him down and took him out in the thirteenth. That was it; the fight was over. We started to leave and I said to my dad, "I want to touch Jersey Joe." That didn't make sense to him. Walcott had lost. But he took me through the crowd to the tunnel that led to the dressing rooms from the arena. It was a mob scene. Walcott whizzed by. My dad was holding my hand. And I reached out and touched Walcott's robe. Thirty years later, Walcott was chairman of the New Jersey State Boxing Commission. He hired me as an inspector, which was my entry into professional boxing. And my first day on the job, I told him that story.

TOMMY HEARNS

It was Muhammad Ali's second fight against Jerry Quarry in Las Vegas [on June 27, 1972]. I had just started as an amateur. I was fourteen years old, and one of the coaches took me. All my life, I'd idolized Ali. I'd seen most of his fights on TV. He stopped Quarry [in the seventh round], and I felt like I was moved to a higher ground, like something wonderful was happening to me.

AL BERNSTEIN

It was club fights; a local card in Chicago in the mid-1970s. I don't remember who was in the main event. I went because Muhammad Ali was sparring a few rounds as part of the show to do a favor for Ernie Terrell who was somehow involved with the promotion. I'd loved boxing as a kid and watched fights on television with my dad all the time. When I finally got to one live, I remember being aware of a huge difference between Ali clowning around and the real fights and also being surprised by the intensity with which people reacted to the real fights. That's when I understood that going to a fight is very different from watching one on television. As an announcer, I give viewers the best television experience I can, but there's no way I can bring them into the arena with me.

STEVE FARHOOD

I was fourteen years old, living in Manhattan, and I never missed an Ali fight. To be honest, I was anti-Ali. I was a Joe Frazier man. I rooted against Ali every time. Ali was fighting Jimmy Ellis in the Astrodome and they had live fights at Madison Square Garden, so I went. Emile Griffith won a decision over Nessim Cohen, which I saw live. Then they lowered the big screen and Ali knocked out Jimmy Ellis in the twelfth round. I'd been to the Garden before for closed-circuit fights, but this was different. You know how you walk into Yankee Stadium as a child for the first time and you see the grass and it's something you've never seen before. Well, seeing the ring and the bright lights and the haze of smoke was just as magical. I wasn't close to the action. From where I sat, the fighters looked like little stick figures throwing their arms at one another. It was hard to tell who was winning the fights, but I knew I wanted to come back again.

VERNON FORREST

It was Meldrick Taylor against Terry Norris in Las Vegas [on May 9, 1992]. I grew up in Augusta and they didn't have pro fights there, so I'd never had the opportunity to go to a professional fight before. I'd just finished the Olympics. I was training in Las Vegas and Roger Mayweather brought me. I was surprised at how easily Norris won. He knocked Meldrick out [in the fourth round]. Otherwise, things were pretty much what I expected, except I realized that the atmosphere in the amateurs is more friendly than in the pros. In the amateurs, it's friendly competition and the people in the stands are relaxed. In the pros, there's more money on the line and you can feel the violence in the stands. As a fan, I like the pro atmosphere better. There's more tension and excitement.

JUDD BURSTEIN

At Bob Arum's request, I had just gotten an injunction on behalf of Terry Norris against Don King, and Bob invited me to see Oscar De La Hoya against Ike Quartey at the Thomas and Mack Center in Las Vegas. Norris was on the undercard and I was under the misimpression that, because I'd won this great legal victory, I'd have good seats. Needless to say, I was sadly mistaken and I hadn't brought my binoculars. But I found the level of excitement extraordinarily compelling. There's nothing that compares to the anticipation and energy in the arena before a big fight. It's the ultimate sports experience, and I've become a junkie for the excitement of it all.

TIM SMITH

I was a young reporter for the *Atlanta Journal-Constitution*, and they gave me the assignment of following Evander Holyfield around for a whole week before his first fight against Dwight Muhammad Qawi [in 1986]. Evander was working at a job then; something like pumping gas into planes at a small airport. But he wasn't working that week because he was in final preparation for the fight. I remember thinking he was a great guy. I was used to dealing with bigtime college athletes, who aren't always the nicest guys in the world. But Evander was friendly, laid back, down to earth. I met his wife and Evander Jr., who was a baby then. And I remember that, whenever we went into a restaurant, he'd order this concoction of ice tea and Coca Cola. The fight was at The Omni. I'd seen lots of fights on television before, but this was totally different. It wasn't antiseptic like television. I was excited and nervous because, during the week, I'd developed a real attachment for Evander. And it was one of the most grueling fights imaginable: fifteen rounds of brutal non-stop action. I remember sitting there, asking myself, "Are all fights like this live?" And I remember thinking that Evander was going to break at some point but he didn't. That fight was when people began to realize that Evander is something special. And it was also when I realized what a brutal sport boxing is. Before that afternoon, I'd thought boxing was just another sport. But when the day was done, I realized that you can go into a fight and not come out whole.

JIM THOMAS

My friend Joe Corley was the local site promoter for Evander's first fight against Dwight Muhammad Qawi. I'd worked with Joe on PKA fights for ten years, and he invited me. I'd fought previously in a number of amateur karate bouts and one professional full-contact kick-boxing contest, so I was used to seeing rings in arenas. I remember looking at Evander and being impressed with how chiseled he was. I had the feeling that, if I hit him in the head, it would hurt my hand. I was rooting for Evander because he was from Atlanta. It was a great fight. Evander won but, when it was over, he went to the hospital for observation. I thought then that it was the greatest fight I'd ever seen in any form and I still feel that way, although Evander's first fight against Riddick Bowe comes close.

JOE CORTEZ

It was at the old Madison Square Garden on Eighth Avenue and 49th Street. Gaspar Ortega was my hero. I lived in Spanish Harlem, and Gasper moved into my neighborhood when I was twelve years old. He was from Mexico and didn't speak English, so his manager hired me as an interpreter. Every time I interpreted for Gaspar before or after a fight, his manager gave me five dollars. Then, when I was fifteen, I started fighting myself and won the sub-novice 112-pound division championship in the New York Golden Gloves. Right after that, Gaspar gave me a ticket for my first pro fight. I went with his wife. It was one of the old Gillette Friday Night fights. Gaspar was in the main event and lost a ten-round decision. I'm not sure who he fought, but I remember walking into the Garden and being very impressed. Everyone was dressed up in suits and ties and hats; not like it is now. And later that year, in the same ring that I saw Gaspar fight in, I won the 118-pound Eastern Golden Gloves championship.❏

Boxing is a never-ending source of anecdotes and humor.

FISTIC NUGGETS

Muhammad Ali is well known for having employed a "rope-a-dope" defense in his 1974 championship victory over George Foreman. What's less well known is how the "rope-a-dope" got its name. Shortly before his death, John Condon (an Ali friend and former president of Madison Square Garden Boxing) described the origin of the phrase.

"The 'rope-a-dope' got its name in 1975," Condon explained. "Ali, [MSG pubicist] Patti Dreifus, and I were in an ice-cream shop at the Tropicana Hotel in Las Vegas right before Ali fought Ron Lyle; so we're talking about a point in time six months after he won the title from George Foreman. I kept telling Ali, 'You know, this stuff you're doing on the ropes; you've got to give it a name. You've done it against Foreman; you've done it against Wepner; you're gonna keep doing it. Give it a name.' So we're sitting there, and we come up with 'On the ropes . . . . If someone tries to hit you when you're on the ropes, he's a dope.' And then we came up with 'rope-a-dope.' Ali's eyes lit up, and he said, 'That's good.'"

Legend has it that boxing promoter Bob Arum was once driving along a highway with fellow promoter Cedric Kushner as his passenger when they saw Don King walking ahead along the side of the road. No other cars or pedestrians were in sight, and an evil thought entered Arum's mind. He pointed the car in King's direction, increased his speed, and . . . at the last minute, Honest Bob was overcome by a wave of conscience and swerved to the left to avoid his target. Thus, he was mortified to see King careening through the air into a ditch.

"Oh, my God!" Arum moaned. "I thought I missed him."

"You did," Cedric responded. "But I got him with the car door."

And speaking of Cedric—

Last April, Dr. Frank Borao performed gastric bypass surgery on

Kushner. Since then, Cedric has lost 141 pounds. He now weighs 244 and expects to reach 235 shortly.

"Something wonderful happened to me today," Kushner recently reported. "I dropped my pen under my desk."

And?

"A year ago, I would have had to call someone into my office to crawl under the desk and get it for me. But today, I simply said 'Oh, fuck,' bent over, and picked it up myself."

● ● ●

Another true story—

On March 15, 2002, a night of "black tie boxing" was televised by ESPN from Cipriani 42nd Street in New York. There was a lot of sexual energy in the room, due in part to the fact that a number of elegantly dressed women from the VIP Club (a local adult establishment) were sprinkled throughout the crowd.

At one point, a prosperous-looking man in his sixties was nuzzling a sensuously-styled young lady who was seated next to him. The man's cell phone rang. He answered it, turned ashen, and after a brief conversation, closed up the phone. Then he reported to those sitting around him, "That was my wife. She just saw me on television, and she is very unhappy."

● ● ●

Manager and boxing expert Bill Cayton once had a meeting with a Russian expatriate who was living in the United States and managing fighters. The man was quite proud of his fight expertise, and told Cayton that his favorite fight was "when Joe Louis knocked out that Jewish boy, Billy Conn." Then, later in the conversation, he repeated the statement that Conn was Jewish.

"Surely, you're joking," Cayton said. "Billy Conn was Irish."

That earned Cayton a look of utter disdain and the rejoinder, "Mr. Cayton, I assure you, Kahn is a Jewish name."

● ● ●

Deanna Piatelli Dempsey (Jack Dempsey's widow) was a successful businesswoman in her own right. Mrs. Dempsey met her future husband in 1956 in a jewelry shop that she owned in the Manhattan Hotel in New York. Dempsey asked her for a date, but she refused on grounds that they hadn't been properly introduced. During the ensuing week, several equally unsuccessful approaches followed. Finally, Dempsey stopped a passer-by in Ms. Piatelli's presence and asked, "Would you kindly introduce me to this lady."

"Madam," the stranger responded, "this is none other than the champ himself, Jack Dempsey."

They were married the same year and stayed married until Dempsey's death in 1983. The success of their union was no small feat given the fact that Dempsey previously had been divorced three times. In his 1977 autobiography, he took note of that fact in the dedication, which read, "To Deanna . . . Number Four should have been Number One. Thanks, honey."

● ● ●

Promoter Lou DiBella is building his future around a group of young fighters headed by Jermaine Taylor. One of those fighters is welter-weight Paulie Malignaggi.

"Paulie has had a rough life," DiBella notes. "His parents are divorced. His father moved back to Italy. Paulie lives alone in an apartment in Bensonhurst. He's a loveable kid, very genuine. What you see is what you get with Paulie, but there aren't a lot of people there for him. I like Paulie, and I think he likes me. I'm trying to teach him about managing money, living frugally, how not to get a girl pregnant. It's important for Paulie to know that I'm always there for him and that he can bring any of his problems to me."

And how does Malignaggi feel about his recently acquired mentor?

"Actually," says Paulie, "I like to solve my own problems. But it makes Lou feel good to know that he's there for me."

● ● ●

No one admires Muhammad Ali more than writer Jerry Izenberg. But as Izenberg points out, "Muhammad's grasp of geopolitics is limited." And as proof of that statement, he cites an incident that occurred in England several decades ago.

"Muhammad was in London," Izenberg remembers, "to cut the ribbon at the opening of a supermarket. And of course, everyone there loved him. There were hugs and kisses and cheers, the usual adulation. Muhammad was quite moved by it all and he said to me, 'These people in England are so nice. I'll bet, in their whole history, they never had a war.'"

● ● ●

Boxing promoter Robert Waterman and his partner Jim Evans are meeting with considerable success in England. Recently, Waterman recalled a breakthrough moment—his first televised show ever.

"It was a 2002 World Boxing Federation cruiserweight championship bout on EuroSport between John Buster Keeton and Butch Lesley," Waterman reminisced. "I was standing in the ring before the fight, feeling quite pleased with myself, when my cell phone rang. The fighters weren't in the ring yet, so I answered it. And the first thing I heard was my mother's voice saying, 'Tuck your shirt in. You look like a slob.'"

● ● ●

Yuri Foreman had a dilemma. The unbeaten junior-middleweight was at home readying to attend the final pre-fight press conference for his April 15th bout against Calvin Shakir. And there was no one to help him tie his tie.

"I always had help before," Foreman acknowledged upon arriving at Gallagher's Steak House wearing a perfectly knotted tie. "My boss at work, my wife. Someone was always there, but this time there was no one."

The solution?

"I went to Google," Yuri explained. "Then I found a site with pictures and instructions and here I am."

● ● ●

Back to Paulie Malignaggi—

To say that he's highly styled is an understatement. Malignaggi is a walking poster boy for hair gel, fancy clothes, and bling-bling. Arriving twenty minutes late for the press conference to announce his April 22, 2004, fight against Rocky Martinez, Paulie told the assembled media, "I apologize for being late. I was doing my hair."

● ● ●

The day before the second fight between Roy Jones and Antonio Tarver, promoter Don King was told about a gunnery sergeant named Nick Popaditch, who had just returned to the United States after losing an eye in Iraq. Cynics would say that King knows a good

PR opportunity when he sees one. DK's defenders would point to the reservoir of humanity and love in the man. Either way, minutes later, the phone in Sgt. Popaditch's home rang.

"Nick Popaditch," a voice boomed. "This is Don King. I'm just calling to tell you that you are America personified. I love you, man. God bless you."

"It crossed my mind," Popaditch said later, "that someone was pulling my leg. But no one is as over the top as Don King. His voice just sounds different from anyone else."

King invited Popaditch to the fight. Thus it was that, on fight night, Gunnery Sergeant Nick Popaditch stood in the ring with Don King just prior to the fight as the national anthem was played.

● ● ●

A bit of trivia—
Pete Rose had two amateur fights and lost both of them by decision.

● ● ●

And one for the road—
A priest, a rabbi, and an Islamic cleric decided to sit down with Mike Tyson and see if they could do something to improve his behavior. They got together in a small room, and the priest began the conversation on a philosophical note.

"Mike, I want to ask you something. Where is God?"

Iron Mike just sat there and didn't say a word, so the rabbi figured he'd give it a try.

"Mike, this is important. Where is God?"

There was still no answer, which made the Islamic cleric a bit angry. "Mike," he demanded, "Answer us. Where is God?"

At that point, Tyson stood up, walked out of the room, picked up his cell phone, called Shelly Finkel, and moaned, "Shelly, I'm in trouble again. God is missing, and everyone thinks I did it." ❑

Whenever I'm covering a big fight, I make a point of getting to the arena early. You never know what you might stumble upon.

A MOMENT IN TIME

Madison Square Garden was a lonely place on October 2nd at 1:30 p.m. In ten hours, Felix Trinidad and Ricardo Mayorga would enter the ring to do battle before 17,406 frenzied fans. But for the moment, the main arena was deserted except for a handful of technicians hooking up electrical cables and some maintenance workers mopping floors.

And there were ghosts.

Muhammad Ali . . . Joe Frazier . . . Joe Louis . . . Rocky Marciano . . . Jack Dempsey . . . Sugar Ray Robinson . . .

A solitary figure entered the arena. He was a black man in his mid-twenties; stocky, 5-feet-7-inches tall, wearing blue-jeans without a shirt. His torso was heavily-tattooed and there was an IBF world championship belt around his waist.

The man was alone. He walked down the aisle, climbed the stairs to the ring, stepped between the ropes, and began to shadow-box.

Jab . . . Jab . . . Straight right hand . . . Hook to the body . . . Another hook.

The assault continued until, finally, the man looked down at an imaginary foe lying on the canvas and raised his arm in triumph. Then he embraced an imaginary cornerman, waited for the announcement of his victory, raised his arm a second time, consoled his imaginary opponent, and left the ring.

Walking in the opposite direction along the path he'd traveled minutes before, he exchanged high-fives with imaginary fans and stopped to sign an imaginary autograph. Finally, he disappeared through the exit that leads to the dressing rooms beneath the stands.

Kelvin Davis is the International Boxing Federation cruiserweight champion of the world. His record stands at 21 victories, 2 losses, and 1 draw. He won the title on an eighth-round knockout of Ezra Sellers in Miami earlier this year.

Davis has fought in New York once, at Radio City Music Hall on the undercard of Roy Jones versus David Telesco three years ago.

What was the pantomime all about?

"Someday, I want to do my thing right here," Davis explained. "Madison Square Garden is history."❏

Bob Arum was not happy with this article.

THE TALE OF THE TAPE

In the early 1950s, there was a sign posted over the telephone in Stillman's Gym in New York. "Watch it, fellows," the sign read. "The cops may be listening."

Some people in boxing never learned that lesson. Thus the question, "What's on the tapes that the FBI reportedly gathered after wiretapping the telephones at Top Rank during the course of a two-year investigation?"

Wonder no more. A brief interlude in the life of Bob Arum follows:

The intercom on Bob Arum's desk buzzes.

Bob Arum: Yes?

Secretary: It's Don King on line one.

Bob Arum: Hello.

Don King: Hey!!! How's my main man?

Bob Arum: Business is good; the wife and kids are fine. And you?

Don King: The press is on me all the time. Sometimes it's feels like there are ten Internet sites with the domain name www.bashdk.com. And every time I turn around, I'm in court again.

Bob Arum: I heard about the Terry Norris settlement. It's a shame, what Judd Burstein did to you.

Don King: True. And the horrible allegations that Mike Tyson has made are weighing heavily upon my spirit, to say nothing of my bank account. I treated Mike like a son. And the ingratitude . . . If this case goes to trial, I wish there were a way I could show jurors the real Mike Tyson.

Bob Arum: Pay Robin Givens ten thousand dollars a day to sit next to you in court and hold your hand. My guess is that the jurors will see the real Mike Tyson pretty fast.

Don King: What if she won't do it?

Bob Arum: Then offer her fifteen thousand. Whatever it costs, it will be cost effective. And if you want the jurors to have an even better idea of how Mike reacts in certain situations, bring Ruth Roper and Mitch Green too.

Don King: Any more ideas?

Arum: Hire Greg Garrison and Vince Fuller as legal consultants. Mike will love seeing them in court again. It will bring back all sorts of memories.

Don King: That's what I like about you, Bob. Lots of people in boxing shove an umbrella up their enemy's butt. But you shove the umbrella up, and then you open it.

Buzz

Bob Arum: What is it?

Secretary: Jose Sulaiman on line two. He wants to create a Jewish youth title for Dmitriy Salita.

Bob Arum: Tell him I'll call back.

Click

Bob Arum: Where were we?

Don King: Umbrellas.

Bob Arum: Anyway, I've been fortunate that, unlike your experience with Tyson, Oscar has always been loyal to me. There was that miniscule period of time when he tried to break his contract and won a victory in court and made that offhanded remark about beating a big Jew out of Harvard, when I might have been a trifle miffed. But Oscar is very dear to me. He's my favorite Hispanic fighter, although I love all of them.

Buzz

Bob Arum: What now?

Secretary: Harry Reid on line two.

Click

Bob Arum: Don; I've gotta run.

Don King: Love you.

Bob Arum: Love you, too.

Click

Bob Arum: Senator; I'm glad you called.

Harry Reid: Bob, I just wanted to thank you for your generous campaign contribution.

Bob Arum: My pleasure. I appreciate the good work you're doing in Congress, protecting states rights and the rights of promoters against John McCain and those rapacious television networks.

Harry Reid: We're on the same page; rest assured.

Bob Arum: Be good.

Harry Reid: Will do.

Buzz

Secretary: Bob, there's a thirteen-year-old girl here. She wants to know if you'll buy some Girl Scout cookies.

Bob Arum: Absolutely. When I think of all the money I've spent on world sanctioning bodies, the least I can do is support a fine organization like the Girl Scouts of America. Tell her I'll take a hundred dollars worth.

Buzz

Secretary: Bob, she wants to know, would you like chocolate mint, caramel delight, shortbread, or peanut butter patties?

Bob Arum: Gee; they all sound so good. How about twenty-five dollars worth of each. And buy another hundred dollars worth of cookies as gifts.

Buzz

Secretary: Bob, she wants to know, who should she send the gift cookies to.

Bob Arum: That's a tough one.

Secretary: Cedric Kushner?

Bob Arum: Not anymore. Tell you what, put 'em in the press room before the next fight on Telefutura.

Secretary: Yes, sir.

Bob Arum: By the way, I saw Cedric the other day. Boy, he looks great. Now that he's down from 385 pounds to 244. I wonder who will take his place in the public mind as the boxing personality who most needs to go on a diet.

Secretary: Hold on, sir; the phone is ringing again.

Buzz

Secretary: It's you-know-who regarding the Nevada State Athletic Commission.

Unidentified voice: Bob, I've looked into that medical issue for you and I'm not sure there's anything I can do about it.

Arum: Look! Margaret Goodman is driving me crazy with burdensome medical requirements like MRIs for fighters. The woman is a neurologist; she's supposed to relieve pain. And she's giving me a massive headache.

Unidentified Voice: I know, but they won't terminate her. Maybe you could get her in the bag.

Arum: Only if it's Prada.

Buzz

Bob Arum: What is it?

Secretary: Charles Jay from TotalAction.com.

Bob Arum: Tell him I'm busy.

Click

Bob Arum: You were saying about Margaret Goodman . . .

Buzz

Bob Arum: What now?

Secretary: I told Charles you're busy, but he says it's important.

Bob Arum: [Expletive deleted].

Click

Bob Arum: What is it, Charles?

Charles Jay: Quick question. I keep getting confused about that famous quote of yours. Is it, "Yesterday, I was telling the truth; today, I'm lying," or the other way around?

Bob Arum: The other way around. I always tell the truth in the present tense.

Charles Jay: Thanks.

Bob Arum: Listen, as long as you're on the line, let me ask you something. You're into investigative reporting. Is there any truth to those rumors that the feds are looking into how dates have been given out for *ESPN2 Friday Night Fights*?

Charles Jay: What makes you ask?

Bob Arum: Just curious. Not that there's anything wrong with the way boxing is run in Bristol. But in this business, you hear things from time to time. Just the other day, someone told me that there are matchmakers who actually fix fights. It's horrible to think that sort of thing might be going on in boxing.

Buzz

Bob Arum: Hold on a second, Charles.

Click

Bob Arum: What now?

Secretary: Bob; someone from the FBI is at reception.

Bob Arum: Tell him I'm busy. I don't have time right now for those clowns from New Jersey.

Secretary: No Bob, not the IBF; the FBI. He says he wants to talk with you about phony medicals for fighters, fixed fights, tax evasion, and cocaine distribution. There's an allegation out there that someone at Top Rank told an F-I-B.❏

This was an article that I wrote for the MSG Network website.

FROM AND ABOUT GREAT FIGHTERS

Over the ages, great fighters have been a never-ending source of wisdom and humor. Given Madison Square Garden's status as the Mecca of Boxing, it seemed appropriate to fashion my inaugural column for the MSG Network website from the thoughts of great fighters and those who knew them.

John L. Sullivan: "Training is the worst thing going. A fellow would rather fight twelve dozen times than train once, but it has to be done."

Bob Fitzsimmons [responding to a threat by James Corbett that, if Fitzsimmons didn't give him a rematch, he'd lick Fitzsimmons every time they met on the street]: "Jim; if you ever hit me, I'll shoot you."

James J. Jeffries: "My father used to say, 'If an enemy smite thee, turn the other cheek.' I thought that was all right. But if he hit the other cheek too, whatever followed was his own fault."

Jack Dempsey: "You always think you're going to win. That's one thing a fighter must have. Otherwise, there isn't any use fighting."

Jack Dempsey [on his 75th birthday]: "I can still fight right now, punch with either hand. I couldn't go very long, but I can still fight."

Gene Tunney: "A good boxer can always lick a good fighter."

Tommy Loughran: "Boxers can't afford to lose our temper. If we do, we pay for it immediately. We get our heads knocked off."

John Schulian [on the death of Joe Louis]: "It is a strange business, this deciding who's to bless and who's to blame, who's a story and who's history. But with Joe Louis, there was never a question. He was a champion for all time."

Billy Conn: "I tried to be a real good fighter. I didn't want to be a bum. When you're good, you know all the fine points of the game. And the main thing is, they're not supposed to hit you."

Sugar Ray Robinson [on winning his first world title]: "The ring announcer was holding a microphone and blaring 'The new world welterweight champion . . .' And I could hardly hear him; my ears were almost bursting with the noise. Unless you've been in that ring when the noise is for you, there's no way you'll ever know what it's like."

Fritzie Zivic: "I boxed Sugar Ray Robinson a couple of times. Real tough; and everything I done, he done better."

Rocky Graziano [on his historic second fight against Tony Zale]: "I wanted to knock this guy dead. I was very mad at the guy. I really wanted to bust his goddamn head. And then, after the fight, as soon as I won, I was very nice to him. That's the way fighters are. One guy wins and the other guy loses, and you go over there and you kiss the guy and you like the guy. It's just a sport. It's a terrible sport, but it's a sport. Me and Tony made a lot of money together."

Tony Zale: "Boxing is the only sport that didn't go to college."

Rocky Marciano: "Why waltz with a guy for ten rounds if you can knock him out in one?"

Archie Moore: "Rocky Marciano didn't know enough boxing to know what a feint was. He never tried to outguess you. He just kept trying to knock your brains out. If he missed you with one punch, he just threw another."

Rocky Marciano [to a reporter who asked if he thought he'd win his upcoming fight against Joe Louis]: "That was a fucking dumb question. If I didn't think I was gonna win, why the hell would I be fighting?"

Rocky Marciano [explaining why he wouldn't come out of retirement for a big payday against heavyweight champion Ingemar Johansson]: "I don't want to be remembered as a beaten champion."

Gene Fullmer [on his 1963 loss to Dick Tiger]: "He beat me bad. My mother and father could have been judge and referee and I still wouldn't have won a round."

Alfredo Evangelista [on his 1977 fight against Muhammad Ali]: "Some people said the fight was boring. It certainly wasn't boring to me."

Muhammad Ali [on his braggadocious nature]: "You've got to be sure of youself or you don't belong in boxing."

Joe Frazier: "I loved fighting. I never backed down and I never backed off. Being a fighter gave me the opportunity to prove myself; to stand up and say, 'I'm the best; I matter; I am.'"

Sugar Ray Leonard [on his come-from-behind knockout of Thomas Hearns]: "I knew I was behind. I knew I had to keep the pressure on. There wasn't anything I could do but find out what was inside me."

Ray Arcel: "I was working with Roberto Duran when I got a phone call and this voice says to me, 'I'm sorry to tell you that Duran cannot fight on Friday night. He has a heart condition.' I said, 'How can Duran have a heart condition? He doesn't have a heart.'"

Evander Holyfield: "A champion shows who he is by what he does when he's tested."

Hugh McIlvanney [on George Foreman's knockout of Michael Moorer to capture the heavyweight title at age 46]: "George Foreman has captured the imagination of the multitude who dream of seeing a middle-aged fat man make nonsense of the natural laws of physical decline."

Mike Tyson: "I wouldn't have been very good in the military. I don't like to follow orders."

Roy Jones Jr: "I'm something else. I can fight at any weight from 170 pounds to infinity."

Shane Mosley: "The glory is the issue to me. Money comes and goes, but a legacy stays forever."❑

Don Elbaum is sui generis.

BORDELLO BOXING

Okay, gang. Listen up. This is a good one. It has long been said that boxing is the red-light district of professional sports, but this takes things to a new level.

If one were to make a list of great statesmen of the past century, it would most likely be headed by Franklin Roosevelt, Winston Churchill, Mahatma Gandhi, and Nelson Mandela. Any compilation of great minds would include Albert Einstein and Bertrand Russell. Sports figures of note would feature Babe Ruth and Muhammad Ali. Towering above them all is Don Elbaum.

Elbaum was born in the late 1930s and grew up in Erie, Pennsylvania. When he was nine, his uncle took him to see Willie Pep fight. "I was mesmerized by it," Elbaum recalls. "Ever since then, all I've wanted out of life is to be in boxing."

Elbaum started boxing at age thirteen and compiled an amateur record of 40 wins against 10 losses. "I had a great chin," he reports. "And I was a good boxer, but I couldn't break an egg. In fifty fights, I scored three knockouts. The first, when my opponent threw up between rounds and couldn't continue. The second, when an opponent who was pounding the crap out of me broke his hand on my head and couldn't continue. And the third, when I cut a guy and they stopped the fight."

Meanwhile, Elbaum's father was taking him to professional fights on a regular basis. At age fifteen, he was matchmaking for established promoters. Three years later, he promoted his first bout. One year after that, he got married.

"I was nineteen," Elbaum recalls. "She was twenty-nine, Irish and English, a great dancer, on her way to Paris when she met me. And then she made the biggest mistake of her life. She married me."

The marriage lasted on paper for fourteen years.

Meanwhile, over the decades, Elbaum has been the matchmaker for at least ten thousand fights. As a sideline, between 1960 and 1971, he had ten pro bouts of his own, compiling a record of 6 wins, 3 losses, and 1 draw with no knockouts either way.

Don Elbaum is the traveling salesman who sells magic potions from town to town. He's a poet at heart and adds a touch of romance to the sweet science. Like many in boxing, he is both sinner and saint.

Elbaum has been described by critics as a low-life, a hustler, pond scum, and a character. "Don't call me a character," he says. "I hate that word."

Don Elbaum is the man who introduced Don King to boxing.

Once, when Elbaum was confronted with the fact that a fighter he'd advertised as being seven-feet-one-inch tall was really only six-seven, he explained, "He's short for his height."

While serving time in prison for tax evasion, Elbaum observed, "It's not bad in here. I'm running into a lot of old friends."

It's also worth noting that there was a time when Elbaum promoted fights in Steubensville, Ohio. "It was a wild town with some of the best-run whorehouses in the country," he remembers. "The guys who ran them gave me professional hookers to use as round card girls for free. From my point of view, it was great. I didn't have to pay the girls, and I sold extra tickets because the people who ran the whorehouses bought seats for their customers in order to display their wares."

That brings us to the matter at hand.

Earlier this year, Elbaum decided it would be profitable to promote a series of fight cards in a bordello. Prostitution is legal in Nevada. So boxing's greatest personality [remember, use of the word "character" is forbidden] did some on-site research.

"It was fascinating," Elbaum reports. "The place is called Sherry's Ranch. It's the number-one bordello in Nevada; a real class operation, not like some of those places that are just trailer-trucks lined up on the road. They're located about seventy miles from Las Vegas. They've got a limousine that runs back and forth from Vegas and a helicopter that flies people in from Los Angeles. The place is like a resort. It has twenty-five rooms and about three hundred girls that rotate in and out. I met some of the girls. A bunch of them are married. Others are working their way through college. The girls are independent contractors who pay thirty-five dollars a day for their room and split their earnings fifty-fifty with the house. There's a $250 minimum for whatever you do, but I don't think you can get much for that."

Those who want to know more should read on.

"They've got what they call a 'house menu' with 'house specialties' written down," Elbaum continues. "Straight lay. Half-and-half—that's when the girl gives you oral sex so you get an erection and then you penetrate. Two-girl shows. Two-girl parties. A lady massaging you with her big breasts. Two ladies massaging you with their big breasts. A bondage room. An S & M room. They were looking to make the fights a monthly show. They figured, if a fight card cost them $60,000, they'd get back $150,000 the same night. The problem they had was, you need advertising for fights; but under Nevada law, you can't advertise to induce people to come to a bordello. You can have an internet site, but you can't have billboards or newspaper or radio or television advertising. But they thought they could get around that by making this some kind of charity venture."

Alas! As Robert Burns once wrote, "The best laid schemes o' mice and men gang aft a-gey."

In late October, the powers-that-be in Nevada declared their unwillingness to relax the restrictions on advertising for Bordello Boxing.

"It's an image thing," explains Elbaum. "They don't want boxing tied up with prostitution."

Probably, they thought it would be bad for prostitution.❑

This article was the continuation of a tradition that began in 1999.

GEORGE FOREMAN ON SETTING AN EXAMPLE

This is the fifth year in a row that I've devoted a holiday column to some thoughts from George Foreman. George has been punched in the face by Muhammad Ali, Joe Frazier and Evander Holyfield. Yet right now, he has the most joyous smile in boxing. And George doesn't just put on a cheerful face for the holiday season. It's there every day of the year. Not long ago, George and I sat and talked, as we do annually for this column. Some of his thoughts follow:

I've done a lot of things in my life. I've been married five times, and I'm proud of the fact that I've been married now to the same woman for twenty years. I have ten children: five boys and five girls. I've been a preacher, heavyweight champion of the world, and a businessman. And after all that, I can tell you that what I want to do most for other people is set a good example.

All of us are examples in life. Parents are examples for their children. Ten-year-olds in school set an example that younger children follow. Sometimes, you're an example for someone else and you don't even know it. I really believe that, until people are thirty years old or so, they need examples. They want them too. And the choice of who you choose to follow as an example says a lot about who you are.

To be a good example, you have to be consistent. I try to be the same person every minute of every day.

To be a good example, you have to be honest with other people and honest with yourself. Truth is wisdom.

A good example is always respectful of other people's feelings and who other people are. I can't stand it when a person puts labels on someone else. The fat guy . . . the stupid person . . . the gay guy . . . the ugly girl . . . the whatever. Talk like that makes me angry and sad. People are people. We're all different, but we're all the same.

Everyone goes through hard times in life. But if you're a good example, you don't let your troubles define who you are. You smile and do the best you can. Sometimes, that means walking away from a situation without solving all of the problems. But for every door that closes in life, another door opens wide. It's like that saying, "Lord, grant me the serenity to accept the things I cannot change, the courage to change the things that I can, and the wisdom to know the difference."

And to be a good example, you can't spend too much time talking about the past and the good old days and how much better things were back then because, if you do, you'll be giving up on now.

You know, part of the joy of living is that there are so many doors to open in life; and until you open them, you don't know what lies behind them. I have a few more doors to open before my own journey is done. I hope I never stop growing and never stop improving as a person. And I hope the world becomes better too. It's already a wonderful world for me to live in, but I'd like to see more opportunity and more hope for people who haven't been as fortunate as I've been.

That's what I want for other people. For myself, it's not about big things. It's about simple pleasures that I don't have time to do right now, like fishing and walking in the woods. And sometimes I fantasize about things that I know won't happen. I don't daydream a lot, but I do fantasize sometimes about weighing 196 pounds again.❏

This was one of those articles that I particularly looked forward to writing.

A CHRISTMAS CAROL

Boxing was dead. There was no doubt about that. There was no official register of its burial. But the major media had long since ceased to cover the sport; television ratings were down; and pay-per-view buys were negligible.

Don King had known that the sweet science was dying. As an excellent man of business, he had presided over its death throes for years. And although he was not dreadfully saddened by its demise, he spoke fondly of the sport upon its passing.

King was a tight-fisted covetous man; hard as flint from which no steel had ever struck a generous fire. The cold within him froze his features. He carried his own low temperature with him. No wind that blew was more bitter than he.

On Christmas Eve, Don King sat in his office, busy at his desk. Outside, the weather was bleak and biting. His office staff had all gone home except for an aging employee who was sweeping the floors.

"I suppose you'll want tomorrow off," King said.

"If convenient, sir," the employee told him.

"It's neither convenient nor fair for a man to be paid a full day's wages for no work. Christmas is nothing but an excuse to pick a man's pocket every December 25th."

"But it's only once a year, sir."

"Very well, then. Be off with you. And make certain you're here early on the morning of the 26th."

"Thank you, sir. And Merry Christmas."

"Bah! Humbug! What reason have you to be merry? If I had my way, every man who goes about with 'Merry Christmas' on his lips would be boiled in oil and buried with a stake of holly through his heart."

That evening, King partook of a melancholy dinner at his usual melancholy tavern and went home for the night. He turned his key in the keyhole, entered the small gloomy room in which he lived, and lit a candle.

A small candle. Darkness was cheap, and King loved it. He disrobed, put on his stocking cap and pajamas, and climbed into bed.

Fog poured into the bed chamber through the keyhole and every chink in the walls. Then came a dull distant roar.

"Ali! Ali!"

The door flew open. Resplendent in a regal robe, the apparition of Muhammad Ali appeared, then vanished.

It had been him. King was certain. Still—

"I choose not to believe it," King told himself as he drifted off to sleep.

At midnight, the bells on the clock in the village square intruded upon King's slumber. A gust of wind swept through the room.

Then, translucent and bloated with a drooping walrus-like mustache, the ghost of Cedric Kushner entered the bed chamber.

"Spirit, why do you come?" King demanded.

"You stole Hasim Rahman from me," the apparition answered.

"But we were men of business."

"Mankind is our business. The common welfare of humanity is our business. Charity, mercy, and benevolence are our business. At this time of year, I suffer most," the apparition wailed. "I cannot rest for having walked among my fellow man with my eyes turned down, oblivious to the suffering I saw."

"Get out of my dream, motherfucker."

"A warning to you," the apparition cried. "Change your ways."

Then it, too, vanished.

King rose from his bed and examined the door through which he presumed the apparition to have entered and departed. It was double-locked from the inside, its bolts undisturbed.

"It was a bad dream," King told himself. "That's all. Nothing more than an undigested bit of beef, a seed of bad mustard, a sliver of rancid cheese."

And with that, King fell asleep again, only to be awakened by shrieks of anguish. He opened his eyes.

The room had been transformed into a chamber of horrors. Old rags, broken bottles, and bones littered the floor.

Bernard Hopkins stood before him, shrouded in a black robe that blended with the night and concealed everything but death-cold eyes staring at King through an executioner's mask.

Slowly, gravely, Hopkins whispered, "No peace; no rest."

A horrible moan sounded in the night. Mike Tyson appeared, wrapped in chains with ghostly eyes and tattoos all over his face and body.

The Tyson spirit let out a frightful cry and shook its chains with such fury that King trembled violently and shivered with horror.

"Dreadful apparitions," King cried, falling to his knees. "Why do you torture me so?"

"My wealth was of no use to me," the Tyson spirit answered. "I wear the chains I forged in my life. But if the course of one's life is departed from, the end too will change. That is my message to you."

And with that, King began to weep. "During my life," he wailed, "I have seen my nobler aspirations fall off one by one until only the passion for gold engrossed me. But I will no longer be the man you have known. I swear it. I will honor Christmas and keep brotherhood and love alive in my heart the entire year. But spare me this dream; I beg of you. I cannot bear it."

And then Don King was awake, his face wet with tears. It was Christmas morning. Bright sunlight streamed into the bed chamber.

King opened the shutters, leaned out the window, and shouted to a small boy on the street below.

"You there, small boy. What day is it?"

"Why, it's Christmas, of course, sir."

"Thank God! I haven't missed it."

Glowing with good intentions, King put on his finest clothes and rushed out onto the street. "Merry Christmas" he shouted joyfully to everyone who passed by. "Merry Christmas! Merry Christmas," he shouted again and again, punctuated by loud booming laughs.

And let it be said that Don King was true to his word. He became as good and honest and generous and kind a man as the world has ever seen. And under his wise leadership, boxing was reborn.

Some people snickered at the changes in King. But he heeded them not at all; for his heart was brimming with love and joy, and that was enough for him.❏